AFRICA AND THE DISCIPLINES

AFRICA ▉AND THE▉
DISCIPLINES

THE CONTRIBUTIONS OF RESEARCH IN AFRICA
TO THE SOCIAL SCIENCES AND HUMANITIES

EDITED BY

Robert H. Bates, V. Y. Mudimbe, and Jean O'Barr

The University of Chicago Press   *Chicago and London*

The University of Chicago Press gratefully acknowledges the assistance of the Ford Foundation and the Social Science Research Council in the publication of this book.

The University of Chicago Press, Chicago 60637
The University of Chicago Press, Ltd., London
© 1993 by The University of Chicago
All rights reserved. Published 1993
Printed in the United States of America
02 01 00 99 98 97 96 95 94   2 3 4 5

ISBN: 0-226-03900-5 (cloth)
        0-226-03901-3 (paper)

Library of Congress Cataloging-in-Publication Data

Africa and the disciplines : the contributions of research in Africa
    to the social sciences and humanities / edited by Robert H. Bates,
    V. Y. Mudimbe, and Jean O'Barr.
        p.   cm.
    Includes bibliographical references and index.
    1. Africa—Historiography.   2. Humanities.   3. Social Sciences.
I. Bates, Robert H.   II. Mudimbe, V. Y., 1941– .   III. O'Barr, Jean.
DT19.A3   1993
960'.072—dc20   93-3770
                                                                    CIP

To three dedicated Africanists

Margaret Rouse Bates
M. Elizabet Mudimbe-Boyi
William McAlston O'Barr

CONTENTS

ACKNOWLEDGMENTS

THIS PROJECT OWES MUCH to many people. Catharine Newbury and Tom Lodge helped to launch the project, encouraging its initiation and shaping its content. David Featherman of the Social Science Research Council and John Gerhart of the Ford Foundation generously marshaled the counsel of their colleagues and the financial resources of their institutions. Without their assistance, the project could not have succeeded. We wish to thank the African Studies Association and, in particular, Victor Le Vine, chair of its Program Committee, and Edna Bay, its executive secretary, for enabling us to present these papers at the 1991 Annual Meetings in St. Louis. Our thanks go to Sara Berry, Bogumil Jewsiewicki, and David Laitin for their criticisms, comments, and encouragement. And we wish to acknowledge the invaluable assistance received at each step of the way, from conception to completion, from Doris Carr Cross.

At the time this project was reaching conclusion, Robert H. Bates and Suzanne Preston Blier accepted appointments at Harvard University. They are listed here, however, at the universities with which they were affiliated while working on this volume.

Robert H. Bates
V. Y. Mudimbe
Jean O'Barr

Duke University
Durham, North Carolina

INTRODUCTION

Robert H. Bates, V. Y. Mudimbe, Jean O'Barr

THE PURPOSE OF THIS VOLUME can be portrayed in various forms. Most dramatically, it can be cast as an encounter.[1] Consider a scene in which a job candidate is being interviewed for a position in a leading university. The provost, dean, or departmental chair is interviewing the candidate, who has conducted the bulk of her research in Africa. For purposes of illustration, imagine that the candidate's area of expertise is economics. She is required to answer two questions: "Given that resources are scarce and that I am trying to build a top-ranked department of economics, why should I invest in someone who works in Africa?" and "What has been the contribution of research in Africa to this discipline?" Disciplines reside within departments; departments dominate universities. The administrator's questions thus cut to the core of the standing of African studies in the modern university.

One purpose of this volume is to trace the impact of the research in Africa on the core disciplines; we therefore asked prominent scholars to answer the challenge posed by these questions. Our contributors responded by looking back and showing how the study of Africa has shaped their fields. We also asked them to look forward to identify the central problems, themes, and questions in the disciplines and the contributions of African research to their agendas. We did so by posing two additional questions: "How does the study of Africa contribute to the cutting edges of your discipline?" and "How does it shape your field?"

To enter the highest ranks, a modern university must build strong departments in literature, philosophy, art, history, economics, anthropology, and political science. In the papers in this volume, we draw on leading figures from each of these fields. Had resources permitted, we could easily have added scholars from other disciplines. The contributions to this volume more than suffice, however, to make our case: that the study of Africa has shaped—and will shape—major fields of knowledge.

Our defense for the study of Africa differs strikingly from that advocated by others, most notably those engaged in debates over multiculturalism (see Gless and Herrnstein Smith 1992; *Partisan Review* 1991). Attacking the universalistic claims of those who subscribe to the values of a particular culture, insurgent scholars have sought equal access to the curriculum of the modern university. Members of the African diaspora have participated in this struggle, championing the study of African culture as a subject equally valid as the study of other cultures, most notably that of Europe. While raising many basic issues, in our view these debates miss a profoundly significant point: that while the curriculum may be controlled by the disciplines, the study of Africa has helped to define these very disciplines. We therefore abstain from claims for equality of access. For our major point is that, to a degree unacknowledged by either side in these debates, the study of Africa is already lodged in the core of the modern university.

Nor does our defense for the study of Africa parallel that offered by those who champion the cause of Africacentricity (see, for example, Jean 1991 and Asante 1990). While often failing to achieve universal knowledge, disciplines are distinguished by their commitment to that ideal. The analytic and methodological rigors that define them provide tools with which to winnow the shallow from the penetrating, the merely persuasive from the definitive, and the fallacious from the credible. When a discipline fails to achieve its own standards, its methods can be turned against itself. Fields can be—and have been—de-constructed. The result is not an abandonment of disciplinary knowledge, but rather self-correction. The disciplined effort to achieve deeper understandings continues.

Viewed through the lens of a discipline, then, knowledge from Africa is equally as significant and persuasive as knowledge from Europe, no less—and no more. And knowledge produced by an African is equally as significant as that produced by a European, no less and no more, if it has been generated, analyzed, and assessed in ways capable of withstanding the analytic and methodological rigors of the author's discipline. From this perspective, several of the arguments central to the debates over Africacentricity appear beside the point. Arguments are not privileged by their origins, geographic or cultural; arguments become knowledge when they have been refined by logic and method, and these defenses presently fall in the province of the academic disciplines. The fields of knowledge form the focal point of our attack. It is because the study of Africa has shaped them that we claim it to be central to the modern university.

Other Defenses for the Study of Africa

Conscious of the growing significance of international trade, the need for international "competitiveness," and the continuing dangers posed by misunderstandings and conflicts of interests among nations, academic leaders seek to "internationalize" the modern university. They encourage students to learn foreign languages, study in universities abroad, and steep themselves in the history and culture of other nations. In addition, they promote faculty exchanges, affiliations with foreign universities, and international programs. The study of Africa can be justified as part of these broader efforts to heighten the awareness of scholars, both students and faculty, of global realities and to foster the skills necessary to participate effectively and peacefully in a competitive international environment. In this sense, the study of Africa receives the same justification as do other forms of area studies.

Appeals to self-interest underlie this first justification. For many, however, appeals to broader human values prove more powerful. The academy should internationalize, they argue, not so as to enhance our capacity to compete but rather to enhance our capacity to nurture. The mark of a superior international order is not one in which *we* are better off but rather one in which humanity as a whole is better off and in which even the poorest and weakest share in the gains. For those who subscribe to this position, education implies the refinement of human sensibilities. Rather than promoting competition at the global level, universities should instead promote the capacity for human understanding and moral conduct. Given that the inhabitants of Africa number among the poorest and the least powerful members of human society, this alternative vision of "internationalization" thus also provides a justification for the study of Africa.

Domestic agendas also impinge on the modern university, and these too shape the study of Africa. Within nearly all the nations of the world, voices, once excluded for reasons of race, class, or gender, now register their claims. They seek full representation not only in the political order; they demand as well full participation in the modern university. Of no group has this been more true than the members of the African diaspora. Research into the experiences of persons of African descent in the modern world poses fundamental challenges to Western society's understanding of itself. No university can separate itself from its society; no great university would want to do so. These considerations too justify the study of Africa in the modern university.[2]

The justification offered in this volume lies embedded within these and other powerful arguments. It is both narrower—and perhaps more powerful. It aims not only at what universities share with the rest of society—their membership in a national or international community—but also at what differentiates universities from the rest of society: their specialized fields of knowledge. Fields of knowledge become disciplines in part because they aspire to universal truths; disciplines provide generalized understandings. To emphasize once again: we believe that the study of Africa belongs in the core of the modern university precisely because research in Africa has shaped the disciplines and thereby shaped our convictions as to what may universally be true.

Each essay in this volume recounts the robust dialogue between those who work in Africa and their colleagues in their discipline. In each, a leading scholar discusses the way in which research in Africa has shaped a field of knowledge. It should be noted and stressed that none of the essays attempt to survey all of the work done by those members of their discipline who have studied Africa. The focus here is on the disciplines, not on studies of Africa.[3] Nor do the essays single out the many contributions made by African scholars or by scholars of African descent. Given the orientation of this volume, such an emphasis would not be appropriate.

What, then, is our case? How have the contributors responded to the challenges set for them? What has been the contribution of research in Africa to the core disciplines?

The Social Sciences

In at least one instance, the case is straightforward. As revealed in the chapter by Sally Falk Moore, if a discipline could be said to possess a tap root, then research in Africa could be said to be a tap root of anthropology. It is virtually impossible to train as an anthropologist without having to take into account research conducted on the cultures of Africa.

As Moore notes, the intellectual core of anthropology was shaped by challenges raised in African research to the methodological dictates of Bronislaw Malinowski. Consolidated during the colonial era, early work in Africa shaped the conception of anthropology as an inductive search for cross cultural generalizations. The conception of the field subsequently broadened and fragmented, again, Moore argues, in large part because of work out of Africa. Studies of labor migration, urbanization, and urban life in Africa shifted attention away from the "traditional." With the end of colonialism, researchers were compelled to recognize a basic reality: that even the rural societies originally viewed as functionally integrated, culturally coherent, locally bounded entities, frozen in time, had in fact been open to outside influence, internally conflictual, and dynamic. For decades they had been parts of the colonial order and subject to intrusive forces unleashed by Western occupation. Indeed, the image of these societies as constructed by anthropologists had been shaped by the anthropologists' own participation in the colonial enterprise. The result of this realization was a fractionating of anthropology itself, as it, in a sense, turned inward to explore its own ways of knowing.

Historically, anthropology has confidently pursued "local knowledge"; it has sought to archive and to ponder the significance of different practices in different regions of the world. Fields such as economics, by contrast, have historically challenged the significance of particularities, insisting instead on the universal applicability of formal constructs. Cultural, national, or regional differences constitute, for most economists, merely idiosyncratic sources of error about more general regularities; they are either meaningless because random or controllable using standard methodologies. Given the prevalent mind-set of the discipline, then, the field of economics could be expected to be resistant to the impact of African studies.

Against this background, Paul Collier's chapter constitutes a major surprise. Not only have distinguished economists worked in Africa—in addition to those he notes, such as Joseph Stiglitz, James Tobin, Peter Diamond, and Angus Deaton, one could add others who began their careers there: E.A.G. Robinson and Phyllis Deane, the great economic historians, or Robert Baldwin, the trade theorist—but also, and more importantly, work done in Africa has entered the core of economics. Collier notes, for example, the significance of open economy and macromodels which explore the impact of external shocks and the domestic regulation of markets. He notes as well the significance of work at the microlevel: studies of capital markets, for example, and path-breaking studies of markets for labor, as well as research into the internal decision making of households. Africa, Collier stresses, can be expected to play an even greater role in the future of economics. Scholars are already taking advantage of country-specific and regional differences to test theories: differences between the Franc zone and Anglophone Africa enable tests of models of rule-governed versus discretionary macroeconomic policies, while differences between the educational policies of Kenya and Tanzania test of models of skill formation. Research in Africa, Collier argues, has, should, and will influence the work of economists.

Research in Africa has shaped political science as well. As Richard Sklar notes, the field of political development was launched by, among others, James S. Coleman, a noted Africanist (Almond and Coleman 1960). Political scientists studying Africa pioneered systematic research into the politics of modernization, ethnic conflict, and rational choice forms of political economy. To these contributions we can add others.

- Africanists contributed to the rise of dependency theory; the notion of neocolonialism was first featured in the writings of Kwame Nkrumah (1965).
- And Africanists helped to produce its downfall; indeed, Sklar's own work (1974 and 1979) did much to discredit this approach.
- Nowhere has ethnicity been so central to modern politics as in Af-

rica; those studying ethnicity in Eastern and central Europe would do well to consult some of the classic studies in Africa (Young 1976; the works reviewed in Rothchild and Olorunsula 1983).

- Research in Africa uncovered the revolutionary potential of the peasantry before studies in Vietnam (Weiss 1967).
- Political scientists working in Africa were among the first to investigate the weakening of the state structures brought on by the crises of the 1980s (Chazan 1983); the failure of socialist forms of development (Bates 1981); the politics of economic adjustment and policy reform (Calaghy 1990); and the renaissance of democracy (Sklar 1987 and Diamond, Linz, and Lipset 1988)—themes subsequently taken up by researchers in other parts of the world.

At each step in the development of modern political science, then, or at least of the subfield of development studies, the study of Africa has made major contributions.

As Sklar suggests, research in Africa will continue to shape this discipline. For political scientists in Africa, he argues, are uniquely positioned to investigate the role of "dual authority" in modern nation states. Within Africa, "modern" states dwell in the midst of "traditional" political systems. Political identities receive cultural confirmation. The result is an intricate balancing and blending of political claims and the development of sophisticated political strategies. As Sklar documents, these phenomena are difficult for outsiders, such as Western political scientists, to comprehend; but they are central to the political life of Africa. They thus pose new challenges for the discipline. The renewed outbreak of cultural subnationalisms in Eastern Europe, the disintegration of the Soviet empire, and the polarization of regional and ethnic identities in North America—all underscore the value of the lessons that can be learned by studying this feature of African politics.

In economics and political science, as in anthropology, research in Africa has thus strongly shaped the disciplines; and, as identified by Collier and Sklar, it offers further possibilities for doing so. And yet, as Sklar rightly stresses, while African research is acknowledged as central in anthropology, it receives far less recognition in other social science disciplines. Economics denigrates area knowledge. While far less dismissive of area studies, political science fails to accord the same recognition to the results of research in Africa as it accords, say, to the results of research in Europe or Latin America. Exploring possible reasons for the consistent undervaluation of African research, with the exception of anthropology, that has prevailed in the social sciences lies beyond the tasks we have set for ourselves. Rather, through this volume, we seek to mount a counterattack, highlighting the contributions that have and can be made.

Before turning to the papers that address the impact of African research on the humanities, a last comment is in order. Moore skillfully records the impact of African research on anthropology, but she omits a discussion of anthropology's impact on other disciplines. It is important to recognize that anthropology has crossed conventional boundaries, invaded other disciplines, and has shaped virtually all fields of knowledge. The impact of anthropology is evident in each of the papers in this volume. Steven Feierman stresses the ways in which anthropology's engagement with "the other," particularly in Africa, has decentered notions of space and time, thereby undermining the capacity to write universal history. Had he chosen, he could also have related the development of social history to the impact of anthropology, with its concern for the everyday practices of human life, in the widest possible diversity of settings. Suzanne Preston Blier, an art historian, virtually writes as an anthropologist. Each culture, she recognizes, makes universal claims; viewing her discipline as a culture, Blier analyzes the ways in which it makes universal claims for what constitutes "good art." While writing on philosophy, V. Y. Mudimbe and Kwame Anthony Appiah themselves turn to anthropology. Employing anthropological materials from Africa, they seek the evidence with which to identify the boundaries between kinds and forms of reason.

As in the humanities, so too in the social sciences: Sklar, in his review of the development of modern political science, stresses the impact of the functional school of anthropology. As noted by Moore, this branch of anthropology most likely reached its culmination in the study of Africa. More surprising, perhaps, is the impact of anthropology on economics. As noted by Collier, the study of the household as a unit of consumption and production occupies a central place in modern economics; and with it comes a blending of anthropological and economic perspectives on economic behavior.

As suggested by Christopher Miller, however, it is perhaps in literature that anthropology has most profoundly shaped ways of thought. Anthropological research, much of it in Africa, reveals how rules, once considered binding, in fact are negotiated (Van Velsen 1969); how past history is interpreted to secure present advantage (Cunnison 1951; Vansina 1985); how symbols are mobilized to create obligations, instill awe, elicit deference, or shape conceptions of what is appropriate and valid at a given place or time (Turner 1967, 1969). Africa, and other non-Western cultures, were once seen as tradition bound; given the work of anthropologists, tradition, we now recognize, is socially constructed (Colson 1974; Hobsbawm and Ranger 1983), including our own traditions—such as the canon: the texts to which we give pride of place in the academy and in our culture. Armed with these insights, as Miller shows, literary theorists investigated the process by which privilege is secured and tradition formed in our own culture and, in the process, began to undermine the unchallenged standing of revered texts.[4]

Anthropology has thus proven to be one of the most revolutionary disciplines. Built on a base resting firmly in Africa, it has taunted, challenged, and overturned received wisdoms everywhere in the academy. And through it, research in Africa has penetrated virtually all the fields that inhabit the core of the modern university.

The Humanities

When asked a question, philosophers, it has been noted, are given to responding with a question; they often call into question the possibility of the question itself. When asked about the contributions of African studies to their discipline, many of the authors, and particularly those in the humanities, themselves responded with queries that addressed the very foundations of their fields. The essays in this portion of the volume, therefore, offer an intriguing contrast to those written by the social scientists. For social scientists, Africa appears to pose a problem of incorporation; for the humanities, it appears to offer an avenue for reformulation.

As argued by Steven Feierman, for example, the study of Africa has compelled scholars to examine the assumptions that underlie the writing of history. In making this contention, Feierman is not just raising questions of method, such as how historical research should be conducted in the absence of written documents. Rather, he is addressing core assumptions that structure the writing of history. Feierman challenges the tradition of universal history, by which he means studies of the processes by which Western, capitalist states encircled the globe, politically, culturally, and economically, and brought other societies into one world history. Feierman reviews the way in which historians—such as Eric Hobsbawm, William McNeil, Eric Wolf, Fernand Braudel and others—have addressed this theme. Writing from the vantage point of an Africanist, he finds fault with their use of facts: hence his attack on diffusionist interpretations of state formation and material culture. More importantly, he finds fault with the assumptions on which universal history rests: they are assumptions about space—a center of high culture, a periphery laying about the core; about time—an ascending historical progression, leading to a culminating epoch; and about civilization—that the idea is meaningful and that its properties can readily be defined. Working with materials drawn from the Ibo, the Lemba healers, the Nuer, and others, Feierman explores the weaknesses of these assumptions. In doing so, he uses African materials to criticize his discipline. Feierman ends by posing questions about time and space and notions such as progress that shape the structure of historical narrative.

Suzanne Blier, an art historian, begins her essay on the same note: What is art, she asks, when artistic objects are used as implements in every day life? When they are made of clay instead of gold? Or when they are not made by artists but by ordinary members of the community? Blier then takes an additional step. She examines the language used by her discipline when discussing African art; then, exiting from the role of observer and entering that of the observed, she turns and applies that language to the discipline itself. Students of African art note the power of custom. Custom means one thing when applied to the study of art in Africa, Blier points out. When applied to the field of art history itself, it means all that and more: conventional ways of categorizing and thinking that privilege some forms of art while devaluing others. Fetish, too, is a term applied to African art by members of her discipline, who use it to refer to something whose meaning is artificially contrived and willfully constructed. But, Blier contends, art history also has its fetishes: the primacy placed on the past, the cult of the identity of the artist as a source of meaning and of value, and others. So, too, with the notion of magic, that is the dangerous quality of the other. In essence, seizing the power of the language of her field, Blier herself becomes a magician. She transforms what she sees, thereby making it susceptible to analysis and control. What once appeared normal now appears strange. And what had once appeared universal now appears arbitrary. Through her eyes, we see the discipline of art history as if for the first time and are better able to comprehend the way in which the field creates, organizes, and institutionalizes knowledge. Through the study of African art, then, Blier is able to analyze the habits of mind and social practices that define her discipline.

As noted by Feierman, studying Africa requires historians to call into question key assumptions. For Blier, studying Africa enables her to theorize about the discipline itself. A central question remains, however. Granting that the study of Africa has highlighted self awareness and sharpened our knowledge of how knowledge itself is created, has it enabled a core discipline to advance its understanding of central intellectual problems? On the basis of the article by Appiah and Mudimbe, the answer would have to be *yes*.

Mudimbe and Appiah briefly survey contemporary philosophy, focusing on the United States. Addressing the works of Lucien Lévy-Bruhl, Claude Lévi-Strauss, and others, they then turn to the field's encounter with materials out of Africa. They take as their challenge two central questions: What does it mean to be rational? and What distinguishes scientific knowledge from other forms of reason? Mudimbe and Appiah adopt a strategy of juxtaposing contemporary works on the philosophy of science with E. E. Evans-Pritchard's classic investigation of inferential reasoning in divination. This strategy enables them to illustrate the distinctive attributes of scientific reasoning. In instance after instance, they illustrate how supposed contrasts between scientific and religious thought fall aside; in important respects, both employ reason. Their discussion powerfully highlights the few differences that remain. As a consequence of their investigation, we gain a heightened awareness of the significance of skepticism as a habit of mind, of the role of method as a rule for reasoned discourse, and of the ways in which argument is structured in debate within scientific communities. Research on inference in Africa is thus used by Appiah and Mudimbe to investigate a central philosophic question: the distinctive features of scientific reason.

As noted by the last of the authors, Christopher Miller, the study of Africa has already led to a questioning of basic concepts in the field of literature. What, for example, is the meaning of literature in societies without writing? And what is the meaning of "African literature" when the texts themselves are written in European languages? As in the case of art history, the field of literature has not only been challenged but also transformed. Echoing the position of Blier, Miller stresses: "Since the dawn of 'Western' literature in Homer, the act of imagining Africa has helped . . . Western cultures to define themselves." Under the impact of comparative research, students of literature have been able to see how society confers value, privileging some voices above others, while shaping notions of what is universal and familiar, what peculiar and foreign. It has gained a deeper—and radical—understanding of the organization and construction of knowledge.

The encounter between Africa and the disciplines has thus been productive; how then, can it best be sustained? Not within departments, Miller argues. So long as departments are dominated by students of Western literature, the study of African voices will remain marginal. Similar dangers lie in teaching Africa texts within departments of African studies, Miller implies; thus he criticizes cultural nationalism which threatens merely to canonize a new set of texts. Rather, Miller seems to be arguing, what is needed is continued tension. The exposure of the received knowledge of the disciplines to materials out of Africa introduces doubt and compels revision. It unsettles and disorganizes and, in so doing, promotes intellectual growth.

Conclusion

Miller's contribution brings us back to the central purpose of the volume. The production of knowledge is related to the structure of power;

as Miller notes, only because this is true can an attack on literary canons become an attack on "the West." The purpose of these essays is to consider the disciplines that are lodged within the departments that number among the most powerful in any university. We seek to address the defining characteristics of those disciplines, naming for them the contributions of research on Africa to those fields. For those who hold power within a discipline and who have not considered the impact of African scholarship to their intellectual homes, these observations may be both new and unsettling. We seek to create such tension in order that the contribution of African scholarship be valued, recorded, and institutionalized.

We have found that some social sciences, most notably anthropology, rest solidly on foundations built in significant part of African materials. This is true to a lesser but still significant degree in political science; and, more surprisingly, it is increasingly true for economics as well. We have also found that the impact of African studies in the humanities may be even greater, albeit of a different kind. Rather than merely adding to knowledge, research in Africa—and in other cultures as well—has instead transformed understandings. It has forced a reinterpretation of basic themes, calling into question the very assumptions of the disciplines themselves. It has thereby increased our awareness of the way in which knowledge is produced and organized. In important ways, it has exposed the foundations of the disciplines.

In this book, we address two primary audiences: those who hold power in the academy and Africanists who, by and large, do not. Any chair, dean, or provost who doubts the significance of research from Africa will find in this book reason to change. Attitudes change slowly, however, particularly in institutions, and Africanists will no doubt be required—yet again—to defend their claims to full membership in the academy. By way of preparation, let Africanists turn to the essays in this volume and engage in conversation with their disciplines. All will find a feast and, we hope, an armory.

NOTES

1. Indeed, in the editors' written challenge to the authors, it was cast precisely in such a form.

2. For a probing discussion of these issues, see Gless and Herrnstein Smith (1992). Also see *Partisan Review* (1991).

3. Such surveys have been provided elsewhere. A classic is Lystad (1965). See as well the more recent *African Studies Review* (1981), which contains papers commissioned by the Joint Committee on African Studies of the American Council of Learned Societies and the Social Science Research Council.

4. See in particular Richard Shweder's provocative thoughts on the Nietzschean strain in modern anthropology (Shweder 1991).

REFERENCES

African Studies Review. "Social Science and Humanities Research in Africa: An Assessment." *African Studies Review* 43, nos. 2/3 (1981): 1–274.

Almond, Gabriel A., and Coleman, James S. *The Politics of the Developing Areas.* Princeton: Princeton University Press, 1960.

Asante, Molefi Kete. *Kemet, Afrocentricity, and Knowledge.* Trenton, N.J.: Africa World Press, 1990.

Bates, Robert H. *Markets and States in Tropical Africa.* Berkeley and Los Angeles: University of California Press, 1981.

Calaghy, Thomas. "Lost Between State and Market: The Politics of Economic Adjustment in Ghana, Zambia, and Nigeria." In *Economic Crisis and Policy Choice: The Politics of Adjustment in the Third World,* edited by Joan M. Nelson. Princeton, N.J.: Princeton University Press, 1990.

Chazan, Naomi. *An Anatomy of Ghanaian Politics: Managing Political Recession.* Boulder, Colo.: Westview Press, 1983.

Colson, Elizabeth. *Tradition and Contract.* Chicago: Aldine Publishing Company, 1974.

Cunnison, Ian. *History on the Luapula.* Rhodes-Livingstone paper no. 21. London: Oxford University Press for the Rhodes-Livingstone Institute, 1951.

Diamond, Larry; Linz, Juan J.; and Lipset, Seymour Martin, eds. *Democracy in Developing Countries: Africa.* Boulder, Colo.: Westview Press, 1988.

Gless, Darryl J., and Smith, Barbara Herrnstein, eds. *The Politics of Liberal Education.* Durham, N.C.: Duke University Press, 1992.

Hobsbawm, Eric, and Ranger, Terrence. *The Invention of Tradition.* Cambridge: Cambridge University Press, 1983.

Jean, Clinton M. *Behind the Eurocentric Veils.* Amherst: University of Massachusetts Press, 1991.

Lystad, Robert A., ed. *The African World: A Survey of Social Research.* New York: Frederick A. Praeger, 1965.

Nkrumah, Kwame. *Neo-Colonialism: The Highest Stage of Imperialism.* London: Heinemann, 1965.

Partisan Review. The Changing Culture of the University, ed. Edith Kurzwell. Special issue of *Partisan Review* 58, no. 2 (1991): 1–253.

Rothchild, Donald, and Olorunsula, Victor A., eds. *The State versus Ethnic Claims.* Boulder, Colo.: Westview Press, 1983.

Shweder, Richard A. *Thinking through Cultures: Expeditions in Cultural Psychology.* Cambridge, Mass.: Harvard University Press, 1991.

Sklar, Richard L. *Corporate Power in an African State*. Berkeley and Los Angeles: University of California Press, 1974.

———. "The Nature of Class Domination in Africa." *Journal of Modern African Studies* 17, no. 4 (1979): 531–52.

———. "Developmental Democracy." *Comparative Studies in Society and History* 29, no. 4 (1987): 686–714.

Turner, Victor. *The Forest of Symbols*. Ithaca, N.Y.: Cornell University Press, 1967.

———. *The Ritual Process*. Chicago: Aldine Publishing Company, 1969.

Vansina, Jan. *Oral Tradition as History*. Madison: University of Wisconsin Press, 1985.

Van Velsen, Jap. "Procedural Informality, Reconciliation, and False Comparisons." In *Ideas and Procedures in Customary Law*, edited by Max Gluckman. London: Oxford University Press, 1969.

Weiss, Herbert G. *Political Protest in the Congo*. Princeton, N.J.: Princeton University Press, 1967.

Young, Crawford. *The Politics of Cultural Pluralism*. Madison: University of Wisconsin Press, 1976.

PART ONE: THE SOCIAL SCIENCES

I

Changing Perspectives on a Changing Africa: The Work of Anthropology

SALLY FALK MOORE

Anthropology before 1960

Introduction

IN ITS HUNDRED YEARS OF EXISTENCE social anthropology has been re-thought and reconstituted many times. To say that African studies have played a central role in these theoretical and methodological transformations may understate the case. The large body of data that has already been accumulated on African society is bound to make Africa a continuing locale for anthropological research of major importance. The present focus of anthropology is more and more on understanding process over time, rather than on what were once imagined to be ancient and fixed "traditions" and "customs." African studies in anthropology are and will be central to the new processual studies, as well as to many other key projects in the discipline.

In the nineteenth century the dominant theoretical prism through which all non-European peoples were perceived was evolutionary. Non-European societies were seen as locked in ancient traditions, as living archeological specimens, surviving relics of the dim past of the then "modern" world. The process of shaking off this time-conception, of coming to see non-Western peoples as contemporaries, living in the same period of history, occupying a different part of the same world, has been the big story in the development of anthropological theory and practice in the past fifty years. Experience in Africa has had much to do with this transformation.

Social anthropology was once described by C. Daryll Forde as the study of communities small enough to be treated as closed systems (referred to in Lienhardt 1976, 179–85). The "closed" characterization would scarcely be appropriate today and has not been for decades. Moreover, the location of the "system," if any, is now continually in question. Today no anthropologist would do a local study in Africa without acknowledging the world beyond the community. The global political-economy is in sight, even from the food gardens of the most peripheral settlements. Intense local study is a method of investigation, not a definition of the anthropological problem. Today a local study may still be small-scale in geographical scope, but it must be large-scale in conception. A central challenge to the social sciences worldwide is to generate an ongoing understanding of the significance of localism in this time of violent ethnic, sectarian, and regional separatism. Localism can only be fully explored in the context of links with a wider world. There is no better place to address this matter than Africa.

For these and many other reasons, African studies have frequently served the discipline of anthropology as the central site of major innovations in theory and technique. The fact that Africa itself has changed profoundly has been an important element in this theoretical development. Africa, the object of the analysis, has changed the way of thinking of the analysis. Thus Africa has not only been the growing field for a bountiful harvest of non-European social and cultural studies, but it has been increasingly a locale for the study of dynamic transformation.

Anthropology did not come into existence as a formally recognized academic discipline until late in the nineteenth century. There were two initial preoccupations: to identify what was universal about all of humankind, and to trace the evolution of human society through its successive stages. The evolutionary account was conceived to culminate in the triumph of Western civilization, seen as the most advanced form of human society ever known.

The period at which this intellectual development emerged both preceded and coincided with the expanded Anglo-European colonization of Africa. For anthropology this political fact eventually meant that access to an enormous domain of ethnographic knowledge would open up, and that this access would be under conditions set by the colonial presence. Thus the exotic "others" who were the object of scholarly investigation in early anthropological work were simultaneously the object of the "civilizing efforts" and writings of missionaries and government administrations (Stocking 1987, 237). The most accessible examples for the Americans were the conquered Native American peoples; for the British and Europeans, the peoples of their colonies— hence Africans among others. German anthropological work in Africa flowered early and terminated early with the loss of Germany's colonies at the end of the First World War. France and Britain then dominated the Africanist ethnographic project for decades. The Americans, having no colonial connection with Africa, entered the scene much later on. For want of space, this review is principally concerned with the mainstream of French, British and American anthropological work in Africa, though there have been substantial contributions from anthropologists in other countries: Africans, Belgians, Dutch, Germans, Japanese (see Peek 1990, on Japan; see also Pan African Association for activities of present-day African anthropologists).

As new data about indigenous peoples began to accumulate, so did various schemes of classification. By 1930, one of the classifying frameworks that had appeared was an American innovation, the "culture area." This concept had emerged in American anthropology toward the end of the nineteenth century. It arose from the need to devise a mode of categorizing an almost bewildering number of Native American cultures (Kroeber 1931; Wissler 1917). The "culture area" was a geographical region in which there were a number of socially separate societies which nevertheless had certain features in common. The most fundamental of these common features, and the one on which most culture area classifications were founded, was the mode of food production. What is of interest for Africanists about this early framework of American anthropology is that in the 1920s, Melville Herskovits, who was to become the doyen of American Africanists, applied Clark Wissler's idea of the culture area to the map of Africa in his doctoral thesis (Herskovits 1926, 1930). Herskovits divided Africa into six areas but reduced these still further into two categories, the dominantly pastoral and the dominantly agricultural. However imperfect this attempt was to make order out of ethnographic chaos, it was a large step forward in the effort to separate evidence-based classification from any conjectural evolutionary schemes. The firm grounding which the culture area typology had in economy gave an integrated core of earning-a-living realism to the classification.

Applying the culture area classification to African societies was quite a different enterprise from applying it to Native American cultures. Native American peoples had been conquered, often decimated, and many moved from their lands and confined to reservations. By 1900, with a few exceptions, their way of life had been radically changed by their defeat and displacement. They were a tiny minority in a land overwhelmingly dominated by the descendants of Anglo-Europeans. The sorting out of the culture areas of native North America was an act of historical reconstruction, closely tied to museum work and archeology. But Africa was a place in which it was the Anglo-Europeans who were a tiny minority. Though the colonial period was one of domination and forced change of many kinds, Africans continued to have viable societies, which, though transformed by the advent of colonial rule, were not destroyed to the degree that most Native American societies had been. Many African rural economies continued long established agricultural and pastoral practices. Indigenous languages, and social and cultural frameworks, though profoundly affected by the colonial transformations, remained strikingly different from those of the Europeans. There was an African Africa that was a going concern. Ethnological fieldwork in Africa would thus take place in an entirely different kind of milieu from that which existed in much of native North America.

The years from 1920 to 1960 have been called the classic period of the growth of anthropology (Stocking 1987, 289). It was also the period in which ethnographic fieldwork came into its own. And for at least the last two of those decades, the fieldwork done in Africa was central to the formulation of the major theoretical perspectives of anthropology. This is particularly true of Anglophone anthropology. For the time that British social anthropologists dominated theory-building in social anthropology (roughly 1930 to 1960), that dominance was associated with paradigms built up out of the African experience. Models of African "systems" were a central showpiece. There was a preoccupation with the "tribal" and "traditional," and with classifying these as "types." By the 1960s, the applicability or inapplicability of these British models to other areas of the world, or indeed their utility for interpreting the African scene itself, had become the subject of lively criticism and the stimulus for new theoretical invention. What is implied in the choice of 1960 as the terminal date of the era of the dominance of structural/functional theory is that it was also the terminal date of the colonial period in many African countries. Postcolonial anthropology took new paths. To understand the special circumstances surrounding the outpouring of British studies in Africa during the late colonial period, it is useful to compare that flow with the much more limited work of the French and Americans in the same decades. The force of the subsequent reaction against British structural functional theory was proportionate to its earlier influence. African studies took a new turn, as did anthropology in general. Many of the eclectic theoretical frames now in use emerged from the postcolonial period of critical discourse. Thus in the past, African studies has twice been the locus of pivotal contributions to the direction and redirection of intellectual developments in anthropology. The thirty years before 1960 constituted one such period and the thirty years since constitute another. There is reason to believe that the present moment, politically marked by the end of the cold war, is another one of those thresholds in African history that will have profound effects on the social sciences.

Some American and French Anthropologists in Africa: 1920–1940

As indicated earlier, except for the work of a very few, virtually until the end of World War II, anthropology in the United States was principally concerned with the native peoples of the Americas. Some ethnographic work was also done in the Pacific. The one American anthropologist whose enthusiastic interest was centered on Africa has already been mentioned. It was Herskovits, and he was to become the teacher of most of the next generation of Americans who worked in Africa. It was largely through Herskovits' efforts that African Studies eventually came into its own in the U.S.[1] Herskovits' major influence was not so much through any achievements as a field worker as through his indefatigable lecturing, publishing, and teaching about Africa and the African diaspora and his considerable organizational skill in building at Northwestern University "the leading center of African Studies in the U.S." (Dike 1963, 2). But despite Herskovits' great energy, it was not until the 1950s that his interest was shared by enough scholars in a variety of disciplines to make possible the founding of the African Studies Association (in the U.S.) in 1957. Its first President was, of course, Herskovits, "not merely a pioneer, but a scholarly figure of exceptional force, a prolific writer and an indefatigable traveler" (Southall 1983, 64). A participation in the organized scholarly world of African studies had two marked effects on American anthropology. One was to commit anthropologists to ongoing interdisciplinary contact, and the other was to further internationalize the profession, since French and British anthropologists had long preceded most of the Americans into Africa.[2]

In France the pioneers were Maurice Delafosse and Marcel Griaule.[3] Delafosse had been a colonial officer with many years of service in West Africa who later undertook a second career—teaching at the Ecole Coloniale and the Institut d'Ethnologie. He trained many colonial officers in ethnographic method and became the first professor of Black African languages at the Ecole des Langues Orientales. He died in 1926. The principal French Africanist for twenty years thereafter was an anthropologist, Griaule. Griaule's major achievement and that of his "school" was an extraordinary set of works on the Dogon of (what is now) Mali. The early journeys Griaule led to West Africa were strongly oriented toward museum work. Many artifacts were assembled, photographs, maps and recordings made, and documents brought back to France. Later Griaule's ethnographic interests focused more and more on Dogon thought, on the meaning of ritual, myth, and symbol. His larger objective, beyond the Dagon, was to distill the essence of West African philosophies and religion. How much the product of this endeavor was actually an African vision and how much Griaule's remains in debate. Jean Copans says of Griaule's attempt to capture the core of West African thought, "the mind accounts for and is the basis of the social concept and African societies are worthy of interest because their spiritual forthcomings are quite the equal of 'ours' (of Christianity, obviously). To this idealism is added an ideological vision of the colonial phenomenon as a boon or blessing" (1977, 23). Griaule's field methods and preoccupations influenced a coterie in France but did not have much wider effects.

The Colonial Context and British Social Anthropology

The opposite was true of British fieldwork in Africa in the 1930s and 1940s which was to have deep methodological and theoretical effects on the whole profession of anthropology for many decades. There were three factors which together produced the dominant style of the British Africanists. One was the historical context, that is, the British colonial situation in Africa. The second was the professional commitment to lengthy, intensive periods of fieldwork with a focus on social and political relationships. And the third factor was the existence of a prevalent theoretical model, the functionalist or structural-functionalist approach. To compress it crudely, this analytic framework postulated that all of the contemporaneous cultural and social features of a stable society could be assumed to form part of a coherent and interdependent system. The task of the interpreter was to infer the connections.

The self-definition of British colonial policy in Africa was that it would operate by means of "Indirect Rule." Local government should, wherever possible, be carried on through indigenous political institutions. This assumed the existence of self-governing "tribes" as the underlying units of native political organization. The enunciation of this plan for African government is associated with Sir Frederick Lugard, the first Governor of British Nigeria (1914–19). Obviously, the process of ruling "through" African organizations deeply changed the nature of local structures and the conditions of their existence, even where indigenous forms appeared to be retained.

What were the implications for anthropology? The policy of formally delegating power to native authorities and native courts made knowledge of African political and legal institutions an important prerequisite of colonial administration. Anthropologists thought of themselves as useful and expert in the study of such societies. The government sometimes agreed and used anthropologists for the collection of information, or even occasionally in administrative roles. But in general there was a strong preference for using local political officers for these purposes whenever possible (Lackner quotes Lugard and another official report to this effect, 1973, 134, 136). For one thing, many administrative officers were needed, and there were very few trained anthropologists. For another, the official view was that it was usually easier and more efficient to teach a British political officer some anthropology rather than to put up with the peculiar ways of anthropologists whose interests were not always congruent with those of the administration.[4]

However, undeterred by these attitudes, anthropologists would have preferred to be seen as useful. Certainly the profession was sorely in need of more opportunities for, and sources of financial support for, research. In London, the profession tried intermittently to persuade the government that anthropology could indeed be helpful in the affairs of colonial rule. The Royal Anthropological Institute made representations to that effect from early on in the century (Lackner 1973, 138–42). By the mid-1920s the nature of the interface between scholarly and administrative interests in Africa had become clearer.[5]

The complex intertwinings between the needs of colonial administration and the interests of anthropologists and other scholars of Africa was epitomized in the affairs of the International Institute of African Languages and Cultures which was founded in 1926. The Institute was launched with funding from the Rockefeller Foundation, the Carnegie Foundation, and some colonial governments, and Lord Lugard was made the head of its Executive Council (Feuchtwang 1973, 83). The Institute's five-year plan for itself was modeled on an article the anthropologist Bronislaw Malinowski had published in Africa on "Practical Anthropology" (Malinowski 1929; Feuchtwang 1973, 83). The Institute had "the express aim of achieving a closer association between scientific knowledge and research and the interests of African peoples, colonial governments, and other European agencies in African territories" (Forde 1953, 847). The study of "culture contact" and social change was envisioned as a prominent part of its work from the beginning.[6]

These connections between anthropology and the colonial enterprise became the subject of considerable academic invective in the 1960s and 70s. Thus the "colonial connection" became a political issue among internal critics of anthropology just at the point at which such connections no longer had any practical relevance, that is, in a postcolonial reaction. Other attacks came from African academics who wanted to repossess the control of scholarship concerned with their own societies. This invective went on for decades (see Rabinow in Clifford and Marcus 1986, 252). Apart from the vituperation of the 1960s and 1970s, which often became as drearily conventionalized as the conceptual straw men it attacked, there was in addition considerable serious questioning of the models on which so much of anthropological theory had been founded. The ahistoricity and selective constructions of the structural-functional paradigm became strikingly clear. The "colonial period mentality" critique was only one dimension of the more general proposal that a new set of problematics be addressed. A full history of the many facets of the African studies controversies of the 1960s and 70s has yet to be written. The categorical terms within which the academic fights over these issues took place in that period were surely just as deeply entangled with the larger politics of the immediate postcolonial decades, as was the anthropology of the colonial period interwoven with the colonial situation. Both frameworks now look very much out of date.

British Social Anthropology from the 1920s through the 1950s

In 1927 Malinowski was appointed to the first chair in Anthropology at the London School of Economics where he had already taught on and off for several years. He was no Africanist, but he was to have many students who were and his influence on them was profound. The superb quality of his Melanesian fieldwork and the use he made of it in argument changed the course of professional anthropology.[7]

Malinowski's method redefined the anthropological project: it became the intensive, in-depth study of a small community "from the inside." On a theoretical plane, Malinowski constructed a "functionalist" rationale, an integrated systemic interpretation of the way of life of the Trobrianders. As he saw it, the small-scale society was not just the physical unit of study for practical reasons, it was the theoretically defined totality in which the functions of institutions and their integration within a cultural whole could be demonstrated.

Not only did a number of those who participated in Malinowski's seminar at the L.S.E. in the 1930s do their fieldwork in Africa but a particular male subgroup of these Africanists eventually came to dominate all the major departments of social anthropology in Britain, and a number of the women achieved academic prominence elsewhere.[8] Malinowski's own interest in Africa was considerable from early on in his teaching career at the L.S.E. and intensified in his association with the International African Institute and his connection with the many young Africanists who flocked to sit at his feet.[9] Despite his atemporal functionalist theorizing in some contexts, when it came to the African scene, Malinowski also had a strong interest in social change. Thus, the monographs written by participants in his seminar did not always confine themselves to analyses of the "traditional."[10]

In 1937 A. R. Radcliffe-Brown, another influential non-Africanist who was to have a major impact on African studies, moved from the University of Chicago to Oxford and soon replaced Malinowski as the central figure in British social anthropology (Kuper 1973, 65). Radcliffe-Brown's theoretical constructs, to which he devoted himself fully in his nine years at Oxford, were often recognizably built on Emile Durkheim's works and were concerned with cultural comparison. From *The Rules of Sociological Method* (Durkheim 1962 [1895]) Radcliffe-Brown derived the proposition that anthropology was a comparative sociology, which should be devoted to the discovery of social laws. The "laws" of cultural regularities would be like the laws of natural science. Such laws would be discovered through systematic comparison and classification. From *The Elementary Forms of the Religious Life* (Durkheim 1961 [1912]) he borrowed his emphasis on the importance of groups and of the way group solidarity was both constituted by and represented in a common stock of cultural norms. He stressed that all customs and rules were to be understood as a contribution to the social "life of the whole" (Radcliffe-Brown 1952, 181). Societies were presumed to be integrated social systems. The project for anthropologists was to identify and "explain" the systematic connections among seemingly disparate practices. The validity of these explanations could be demonstrated by showing that the same complexes of connected cultural features were recurrent in different societies. Radcliffe-Brown's form of structural functionalism was a framework that not only opened a theoretical place for new fieldwork findings, but invited comparisons.

What Radcliffe-Brown needed were well-described examples. The tremendous flow of ethnographic work in Africanist social anthropology being produced at the time supplied them. The fact that the Africanists at Oxford, Cambridge, London (and eventually at Manchester) all knew one another, and all worked within a general framework of common assumptions, gave a remarkable impetus to their creativity.[11] Comparisons made in the service of theory were the medium of intellectual contact and the rationale for constant intercommunication. The effect was synergistic. African studies surged and so did theory building in anthropology. Particular works of this period illustrate how the originality of individuals and the momentum of the group combined to produce a remarkable series of analyses.

In 1937 E. E. Evans-Pritchard published his path-breaking book about a people of the Sudan, *Witchcraft, Oracles and the Magic among the Azande*. The effect on all subsequent discussions of witchcraft and religion in Africa was so great as to be incalculable. What Evans-Pritchard achieved was to show the intellectual logic that lay behind Zande beliefs. He showed that these were not a miscellaneous scattering of disparate "superstitious" notions but rather a systematic set of logically reasoned ideas about the social causality of misfortune.[12] The explanatory territory conquered by Evans-Pritchard's Azande work has never been retaken. It stands as a major ethnographic and conceptual contribution to anthropological theories of knowledge.

Evans-Pritchard worked at Oxford under Radcliffe-Brown, and from 1939 to 1941 was joined there by Meyer Fortes. The three of them generated a number of major works in those years of intense contact. Thus, in 1940 Fortes and Evans-Pritchard edited a theoretically innovative comparative volume called *African Political Systems*. In the Radcliffe-Brownian mode, it sought to classify African systems into two types, those with centralized systems of rule and those without. Both Evans-Pritchard and Fortes had done ethnographic work among peoples with segmentary lineage systems, hence their preoccupation was to explain the ways in which politics functioned in societies without centralized government. This was a body of new data and a new analysis on which they also published major ethnographic monographs.[13] In Evans-Pritchard's famous ethnography of the Nuer (1940*a*) his interest in African modes of thought is as evident as it was in the work on the Azande. His style was either to take a Western concept, such as the concept of time, and to address the variety of ways in which Nuer thought of it, or to take a word from the Nuer vocabulary that had no direct translation into English, and to elucidate its various referents. These two themes in his work, the interest in political group organization and structure, and the interest in modes of thought, stimulated many others to work along these lines. A third theme in his work, the conviction that history is an essential part of anthropology, now has much currency in anthropology.[14]

Though Fortes had been a psychologist before becoming an anthropologist, and also had an interest in African ideas and religions, and though his monographs on the Tallensi were surely strongly stimulated by Radcliffe-Brown's theoretical interests, he constructed substantial theoretical frameworks of his own. Fortes was preoccupied with lineage structure, and he strongly stressed the norms of kinship among the Tallensi, the ties of relationship and the nature of obligation. But he did not neglect the political structuring of alliances and enmities among and between clans, to which he devoted one of his books (1945, 1949). Both Fortes and Evans-Pritchard were attentive to the large scale political structuring of noncentralized societies, not only to the domestic domain of kinship, and Fortes attempted to draw a clear theoretical boundary between the kinship domain and the politico-jural domain. The intellectual context of this work and its striving for generalization can be seen in the preoccupation with comparison in the collection of papers entitled *African Systems of Kinship and Marriage* (1950) edited by A. R. Radcliffe-Brown and Daryll Forde.

Fortes' friend and sometime teacher from South African days, Isaac Schapera, also contributed to this explosion of Africanist ethnography with a pair of monographs on the Tswana of Bechuanaland, a *Handbook of Tswana Law and Custom* (1938) and *Married Life in an African Tribe* (1940; see also Schapera 1928, 1956). Schapera was a skeptical and fact-minded critic in the arena of British anthropology. He had some antipathy for the theoretical ambitions of his colleagues, and a strong interest in practical questions, in administration, and in social change in a period when that topic was not yet the center of theoretical discourse. His work among the Tswana has been heavily relied upon by all subsequent ethnographers of the area, and for many years in his role as professor at the London School of Economics, his voice was an important one among the growing number of Africanists.[15]

Another major figure to emerge in anthropology in these decades was C. Daryll Forde.[16] His fieldwork in Southern Nigeria provided unsettling evidence of the great importance of secret societies and other non–kinship-based associations (1956, 1964). This complicated the picture of African social organization. The heavy emphasis that Radcliffe-Brown, Fortes, and Evans-Pritchard had put on lineage frameworks was clearly only one aspect of a much more complex galaxy of variant organizational forms. Anthropology had to enlarge its conceptual tool-kit.

Forde's interests were very wide-ranging and he published on everything from African thought to applied anthropology, from African history to colonial government (1939, 1946, 1953, 1954, 1967). His was a pivotal position in the development of African studies in anthropology. As director of the International Africa Institute, as editor of *Africa,* and also as editor of the *Ethnographic Survey of Africa* and professor at University College, London, his importance in furthering the field can scarcely be sufficiently emphasized.[17]

The work of this whole first generation of post-Malinowskian Africanists falls into two main genres. One was the closed description of the way of life of particular African peoples, a kind of timeless abstraction of "the way it probably was" before the colonial period, as if native life could be conceived as a self-contained system uncontaminated by outside contacts. The second mode of description was entirely different and was concerned with the historical moment at which the fieldwork was done, and provided data on everything from labor migration to the impact of colonial institutions. Not only were monographs turned out in the timeless typological mode, but work in the second, contemporary-historical mode was produced virtually from the beginning of the florescence of Africanist fieldwork. However, only the first fitted into Radcliffe-Brown's comparative project, and, consequently,

only the first was treated as theoretically worthy and potentially productive of social laws and theoretical inference.[18] Yet the anthropolo-
gists-as-ethnographers were well aware of the living Africa that was not
the "traditional" one of the comparative models, and many of them
wrote about that living Africa. This was to become more and more the
case, and a great push in that direction was given by the research done
at the Rhodes-Livingston Institute in Northern Rhodesia.[19]

In the African situation, whenever analytic attention was focused
on rural-urban relations, or on the movement of persons from one domain to the other (or to other labor centers such as plantations and
mines), it was obvious that the "tribes" from which those people came
could no longer be imagined as closed autonomous entities. It was all
too obvious that the African countryside was imbedded in a much
larger set of political and economic relations. Rural contacts with the
agents and agencies of the colonial administration, with missionaries
and with settlers, with cash cropping and tax paying, let alone the membership of Africans in a migratory labor force made that plain.

The changes wrought by these circumstances were prominent in
many of the writings of anthropologists from the late 1930s on (for
example, see Hunter (later M. Wilson) 1936; Mair; 1938; Richards
1939, 1940; G. Wilson 1941–42). The rural areas fed the towns and
cities and supplied them (and the plantations and mines) with labor. In
turn, the cities ruled the countryside, taxed it and regulated it. It is no
wonder that the setting of several early studies of town life and of labor
migration should have been in South Afraica where all these phenomena were firmly established at a relatively early date (see Hellman
1935, 1937, 1948, 1949, and Schapera 1947).

The urban work shows that even at the very moment of the dominance of the structural-functional paradigm, there were studies being
done of change, of migration, of cities, and of local history that did not
easily fit the traditional "tribal" model. It is no wonder, then, that the
study of African life in urban environments generated some profound
disagreements about what questions to ask, and how to understand
what was going on. Those disagreements reveal otherwise hidden aspects of the political imagination of the time. On one side were the
anthropologists preoccupied with the question how much of the rural
"tribal" system the African migrants imported into town. How "tribal"
did they continue to be? Or, to a similar effect, how many of their
"tribal" values and ideas were being shattered by the experiences in
town. This preoccupation with "tribalism" saw Africans as emerging
from stable social systems into a state of disruption and anomie, as

neither fully African nor fully Europeanized. In this version of what was happening, African culture was "breaking down" (see Wilson and Wilson 1945). The process of breakdown was called "detribalization," a term that came to have other political meanings in the postcolonial nation-building period. Later versions of this general "tribalist" perspective on urban life seemed to imply that the maintenance of tribal custom in urban settings was an unfortunate form of resistance to assimilation, a way of refusing progress (see Mayer and Mayer 1961).

The more labor-minded group of anthropologists at the Rhodes-Livingston Institute rejected these perspectives out of hand. William Watson argued that, "the concept of "detribalization" implies that an African must choose between two systems of social relations and values. . . . But a man can participate in two different spheres of social relations . . . the spheres exist conjointly" (1958, 6). In Clyde Mitchell's work the treatment of the urban versions of tribal membership was a new form of ethnicity rather than an old form of cultural "conservatism" (1956, 1969). This was a significant advance. Not only was it a completely new take on the "tribal," but it addressed the concept of identity which has come to have a central place in recent work. As Max Gluckman put it in a frequently quoted passage, "An African townsman is a townsman, an African miner is a miner" (Gluckman 1961, 61). The research team that he led saw African urban systems as variants of industrial urbanization elsewhere, not as an entirely different phenomenon. (For some useful bibliographies, books, and articles on African labor migration and African cities by anthropologists, see n. 18.)

Gluckman, who had joined the Rhodes-Livingston Institute in 1939 and had started fieldwork on the Lozi kingdom in rural Barotseland, became director of the R.L.I. in 1942. While Gluckman implemented many of the plans for research of his predecessor, Godfrey Wilson, he went far beyond them, since he had his own approach to the transformations, urban and rural, that were taking place in British Central Africa. Gluckman was deeply interested in conflict. The outcome of conflict, as he saw it, was sociologically most interesting when it produced one of two results: when the end of a dispute reaffirmed previous social relationships and cultural norms, or when it produced radical change. He interpreted the resolution of disputes between individuals largely as normatively reaffirming, but saw political conflict and group conflict as potentially transformative and revolutionary. His vision of African society was that it was inherently "conservative," that one chief might rebel against and assassinate another, or one ruling lineage replace another, but that once in office the new incumbent would tend to perpetuate the political structure. He distinguished between rebellion and revolution in this way. Rebellion merely produced a replacement of personnel in key positions of power, but revolution actually altered the structure of the political economy. Gluckman considered himself something of a Marxist, hence the analytic emphasis on revolution and its absence in African indigenous society. This polar model of change suited both a structural-functional vision of precolonial African political systems and also accounted for the durability of the native-colonial relationship. Gluckman's was clearly a radically subversive view of the colonial situation, but a rather static conception of precolonial African society.[20]

Thus it is not at all as a theorist of change that Gluckman made his most remarkable contributions to anthropological thought, but rather it is as a dogged and insistent investigator of conflict and competition in many settings: his methodological use of the "case method" in ethnography; his approach to African law which went beyond the "rules and norms" style of his predecessors to study litigation; his insistence on the legitimacy of doing unconventional, nontribal ethnography in modern Africa; and as an organizer, encourager, goad and critic of the research of others, first at the Rhodes-Livingston Institute and later at Manchester (1940, 1941, 1942, 1943a, 1943b, 1949, 1955, 1965, 1975).

Just as the L.S.E. and later the Oxford school had been a nucleus for the development of new ideas, and the number of Africanists involved formed a critical mass of persons with common interests that gave the analytic enterprise tremendous impetus, so did the Rhodes-Livingston Institute become a hothouse for new subject matter, new research methods, and new theoretical constructs.[21] The influence of the new approaches and of the "Manchester School" spread far beyond Northern England.

The innovative use of three techniques (some of them entirely new to ethnography) by the R.L.I.-"Manchester" group was so successful that these methods soon became staples of the fieldwork enterprise. These were: the collection of statistical data, the collection of extended case histories, and the study of social networks (see Epstein 1967; see in particular the work of Kapferer 1972, 1976; and that of Mitchell 1966, 1969). All three methods were to figure significantly in urban studies. It was evident from the start that urban areas could not be studied effectively in what had been the conventional Oxford way of addressing rural society, in the mould of total "tribal systems," with a focus on the norms of kinship organization and collective ritual. Case histories were bound to follow the adventures of strategizing individuals. An actor-centered anthropology was beginning to take its place alongside the study of societal "systems." Moreover in Central Africa, the "total system" had to include the colonial presence, industrial enterprise, and migrant labor. (See the volume edited by Epstein 1967 on *The Craft of Social Anthropology* as well as Werbner's 1984 paper on "The Manchester School.")[22]

Victor Turner's *Schism and Continuity in an African Society: A Study of Ndembu Village Life* (1957) is an example of the way members of the Rhodes-Livingston and Manchester groups not only used but went considerably beyond the problematic set by Gluckman and built new wings on the house of the Oxbridge social structuralists even when doing ethnography in rural areas. First of all, like many of the Rhodes-Livingston products, Turner's book was about village life not about "the tribe" writ large. Second, it concerned itself with structure not as an integrated harmonious whole as Radcliffe-Brown might have conceived it but as an entity thoroughly riddled with conflict. Strains were built into its very normative core. Third, Turner's research methods included an innovative use of a detailed extended case about particular persons in a particularly long, drawn-out dispute about the succession to a headmanship. Turner called his long case histories "social dramas," and he presented disputes over succession and inheritance and their management as ultimately group affirming. He made a similar interpretation of the use of ritual in situations of conflict. But despite this Gluckmanesque commitment to the paradox that group cohesion can be an important social product of conflict, the technique by which this was demonstrated was much more than a normative structural-functional statement about groups. It was about struggles and confrontations and about the process of group maintenance under divisive circumstances. Turner's social drama described the way things came about over a particular period of time. His account was temporally situated, and quite specifically so. And though Turner generalized in classical normative terms about Ndembu rules of residence and marriage and the like, he also enlarged this information with statistical surveys of a number of villages in which he showed the incidence of conformity and nonconformity. These surveys were temporally and geographically situated. They were made in a particular year about particular places and persons. Through these practices, though it was not consciously rejected, the ahistorical normative structural-functional mold was in fact being broken. The emphasis on competition and conflict, on the specific extended case history, and on the statistical survey were to become hallmarks of Rhodes-Livingston research and of what subsequently came to be known as the "Manchester School." The temporal and situational specificity of the data collected and the fact that it involved real individuals, not just an account of "traditions," marked an emerging change of ethnographic technique that was to have profound theoretical consequences.

By 1960, social anthropology was moving along new paths. What had spelled the death knell of the structural-functional model? A number of factors coincided. One was the post–World War II momentum toward the decolonization of Africa, with all of its nontribal, nontraditional implications. A second circumstance was that with the passage of time it had become more and more apparent that Radcliffe-Brown's "scientific" goal of discovering social laws through ethnographic comparisons was a promise that would never be realized. When, in 1946, Evans-Pritchard succeeded Radcliffe-Brown as professor at Oxford, a new generation had come to control the British university scene. The earlier era gradually came to a close. The third element was surely the expanding influence of the kind of present-oriented, actor-focused, ethnographic work of which the studies produced at the Rhodes-Livingston Institute were probably the most important initiating experimental example.

Decolonization and the Africanist Anthropology of the 1960–1990 Period

Introduction

Beginning before the period of independence and continuing afterwards, in addition to the ever accumulating number of monographs, there were several attempts by anthropologists to sum up the total anthropological knowledge of "indigenous Africa." Enthusiasm for this kind of reference work inevitably waned as the theoretical interest in tribal system-comparisons itself faded.[23]

One ambitious (and failed) attempt to compress everything into a single reference book was George Murdock's *Africa: Its Peoples and Their Culture History* (1959). Both the classifications and the interpretations in Murdock's volume must be approached with caution since they are by no means uniformly reliable.[24] By far the most respected and extensive collection of summary descriptions was the multivolume *Ethnographic Survey of Africa* started in 1950 under the aegis of Forde and the International African Institute and continued for some years after decolonization; it remains a useful bibliographical resource, but a very dated one. For the now conventional critique of its "tribal" approach, see Tonkin 1990.

As has been made clear, the monographic and compendious works of the colonial period were preoccupied with identifying and comparing what were treated as the distinct "ethnic" or "tribal" groups of Africa often conceived in terms of a precolonial way of life. See, for example, Gulliver's review of anthropology to 1965 where he says, "The 'natural' unit of study for the anthropologist in Africa has been the tribe." Yet, by 1960, the meaning of the "tribal" in Africa had become a complex political fact. Detribalization was part of the nationalist discourse of many African leaders. For them, any political emphasis on ethnic difference was thought to be potentially divisive and to detract from the program of nation-building. For anthropologists, the existence and form of the precolonial tribe and its colonial reconstruction had come to be seen as a subject for historical inquiry and questioning, not as an unchanged and taken-for-granted institution amenable to ethnographic observation.

Even during earlier periods of study, in the 1930–60 period, it had long been evident that no single monograph could encompass all the details of a whole "way of life" or "mode of thought" of a particular language group or political unit, nor were those ever as homogeneous and unitary as had once been assumed. In the post-1960 period when "new nations" were being built, when the interdigitation of language groups in African towns and cities was obvious, when the question to what extent tribes were categories of colonial administration rather than sociologically definable units of analysis had been posed, the problem of identifying meaningful boundaries of social fields when all social fields were penetrable was a serious one. The "tribe" was not an adequate answer to such questions. The idea of the "tribe" was (and is) firmly fixed in the consciousness of Africans and outsiders. But it was far from a "natural" unit of analysis. It was patently not natural, and for many issues was not the most meaningful unit of study. By the postcolonial period, "change" became the dominant preoccupation that "custom" had once been. Much that had been seen as tradition was reinterpreted as an artifact of a particular historical period, perhaps locally legitimated by being connected with past practice but not necessarily having great historical depth in its current form.

Thus, the postcolonial wave of ethnography, even in its monographic form, has gone far beyond an earlier de-historicized interest in Africa, into intellectual territory in which the history of the colonial and postcolonial experience of any people, and its contacts with central governments, with other peoples in Africa's generally plural societies, and with a transforming political economy, weigh in heavily. Elements of local cultural distinctiveness remain of interest but only as these fit into a more complex and historically specific series of sequential pictures. As I hope I have made clear, this shift of focus in anthropology was not a sudden one. The groundwork was laid down during the colonial period in the many studies that were not simply confined to folk traditions.[25] What changed in the postcolonial period was that in Anglophone Africanist studies at least, one of what had been two parallel tracks of earlier monographic production, the "traditions of" and the "current situation of" particular populations, simply gradually became one track in the new literature. The exclusively "traditions of" monograph was over as a major anthropological art form (Hart 1985, 249–50; Werbner 1984).

This general shift of intellectual focus owed much of its impetus to the changes in Africa. But other contemporaneous circumstances in academe surely enhanced further transformations. By the 1960s the discipline was populated with very many more professional anthropologists than there had ever been before World War II. The new entrants into the field could build on existing general ethnographic studies and could identify more specialized themes for detailed study. Anthropology diversified and divided itself into many subspecialties: economic anthropology, political anthropology, the anthropology of religion, urban anthropology, legal anthropology, historical anthropology, and so on. This process of internal fission and subspecialization, as well as its progressive intensification, has continued and is clearly visible in the Africanist anthropology of the present day.

Balandier and the French Marxists

Except for the long Dogon project of the Griaule School in France, and the occasional Herskovits student in the United States, the almost exclusive dominance of British social anthropology in Africanist studies lasted well into the 1950s. In that decade more French and American anthropologists began to appear on the scene. In France there is no doubt that the turning point was the influence of Georges Balandier, himself well acquainted with, and profoundly influenced by, his British predecessors and contemporaries. "Most French Africanists today owe their careers to him, even those who now work in different schools of thought" (Meillassoux 1984, vii, viii, ix). Balandier's institution-building activities were of great importance in going beyond the earlier, Griaule-inspired, French tradition of study which had been preoccupied with indigenous African thought and philosophy.[26] Balandier's 1950s books *Sociologie des Brazzavilles Noires* (1955), *Sociologie Actuelle de l'Afrique Noire* (1955), and *Afrique Ambigue* (1957) marked a major change in perspective. They directly addressed the varieties of communities in a modern Africa and how these had come into being. The Brazzavilles book was about urban life, the first such study by an anthropologist in Francophone Africa. This innovative urban research was produced at roughly the same time as the various Rhodes-Livingston

"Manchester School" studies of the towns of the Copper Belt in what was then Northern Rhodesia (Epstein 1958; Mitchell 1956b).

In these mid-century books, the history as well as the economic and demographic transformations which African societies had undergone were central topics. New religious movements were interpreted as political reactions to colonial power. Balandier also raised questions about the then current attitudes of the decolonizing period. In *Sociologie Actuelle,* he specifically compares the histories of the Fang and the Ba-Kongo and their reactions to the colonial situation. This was not fieldwork in the manner of Malinowski nor of the British School. He did not write detailed descriptions of day to day life, nor of the interactions of individuals. Though Balandier had interviewed many persons, had been in the field and gave substantial attention to the structures of kinship, the material he presented was organized as a historical and sociological overview. This relied heavily on reinterpreting administrative records, censuses, and other archival materials as well as on statistical data produced through the use of surveys and questionnaires. The thrust of the historical argument was to carry forward (to the [then] present) a documented description of the effects of imposed changes on particular African peoples and their reaction to the shocks of the colonial period. For the French, in particular, this was a major change in direction. It was an ambitious attempt to "elucider la relation entre phenomenes sociaux totaux et dynamique social totale" (Balandier, 1963 ed. of *Sociologie Actuelle,* 503). The changes in temporal and analytic perspective initiated by Balandier were infused with a high degree of political awareness. Indeed, Balandier's short, general, textlike essay, *Political Anthropology,* became a minor classic (1970).

What followed in France from the 1960s on was a substantial recasting and harnessing of the Balandier models by his students to the purposes of a Marxist anthropology. As Copans has put it, Balandier's approach was close enough to Marxism for the transition from "a dynamic to a Marxist explanation to be made by filiation and not by rupture" (1977, 25). Of Balandier's students, Claude Meillassoux stands as an early and influential example of what became of the Marxist themes when applied to the history of particular African peoples. Meillassoux's study of the Gouro (1964a) follows the Balandier pattern but explicitly injects a new preoccupation, the theoretical question whether Marxist models could be effectively applied to the societies and cultures of so-called "precapitalist" societies. By implication, the further question posed was whether Marxist models themselves could be revised and refined in the light of such an application. In the Gouro project Meillassoux combined intermittent periods of fieldwork in the Ivory Coast with investigations of the archives to reconstruct a picture of a precolonial system and its subsequent transformation. The ethnography he eventually produced gives little sense of that immediacy of contact with Africans and the lively and specific instances of strategies used in managing a mundane daily life, that are regularly found in accounts produced in the British School. The temporal choices made by Meillassoux may have made that impossible. After all, his fieldwork was not contemporaneous with either of the historical periods with which he was theoretically most concerned, the precolonial and the early and middle colonial. The seminal idea which Meillassoux generated from the Gouro material and wanted to extend to other social types was an abstract model of a self-sustaining precapitalist society (1960, 1964a, 1964b, 1968, 1984). Meillassoux's work, and that of other French Marxists, often combined two quite different interests—an evolutionist's fascination with timeless self-reproducing primitive "types" and a passionate political preoccupation with the transformations worked by colonial domination and capitalist penetration.

The French Marxists were by no means in agreement with one another, neither on all points of anthropological theory nor on matters of French and African politics (for a very useful summary of the issues and personalities of the period see Kahn and Llobera 1980; see also Bloch 1984). Though they could all be characterized as major participants in the Marxist discourse from the 1960s to the present, Emmanuel Terray, Georges Dupré, Pierre Philippe Rey, Jean Copans, and Marc Augé have all approached African studies and anthropology itself from quite different perspectives. Terray's thesis fieldwork was among the Dida of the Ivory Coast, and his book about the Dida was produced within Balandier's conceptual framework (1969a). However, Terray's theoretical work took another turn. His *Le Marxisme devant les sociétés primitives* (1969b, translated in 1972) was an attempt to apply the formulations of Louis Althusser to a rereading of Lewis Henry Morgan and to serve as the basis for yet another reconstruction of Gouro society. He then turned his hand to a further reconstruction, this time that of the history of the Abron Kingdom of Guyaman (1974). These works had much more to do with the then ongoing Marxist professional dialogue in Paris than they did with the contemporary realities of life in Africa. On an entirely different track are Rey's books which are concerned with colonialism, neocolonialism, the development of capitalism, and class formation particularly in Congo-Brazzaville (1971, 1973). He, too, had participated in the purely theoretical arguments of the late 1960s. In that heady period, very much influenced by Althusser, Rey and Dupré collaborated to produce an influential article proposing a theory of exchange (Dupré and Rey 1969). After C. Coquery Vidrovitch's attempt to identify a specifically "African mode of production" (1969), Rey also published on "the lineage mode of production," a concept which has been perceptively criticized by Guyer (Rey 1969, 1975; Guyer 1981). Of this group of Balandier's Marxist students, perhaps the most durably and currently influential has been Augé. His Africanist work has followed a very different route, being much more concerned with symbol, thought, and ideology (1969, 1975, 1977). Augé's purely theoretical book *Symbole, Fonction, Histoire* provides a glimpse of the extent to which he considers works of the British School to be fundamental to a general definition of the anthropological project (1979, translated in 1982). The influence of Balandier is unmistakable.

Economy, Kinship, and Gender

Many publications of the post-1960s period focused on local economies. They built on earlier studies.[27] The emphasis of the new writing (and of some older monographs as well) was on transformations, variations, and economic differentiation. Through the foundational work on kinship, the way had been prepared for the domestic domain and its economy to come into the limelight as a distinct field of study. An argument not unlike that of A. V. Chayanov (which was not widely known to English speakers until years later, when it was translated in 1966) had been incorporated into anthropological thought in 1958 with the publication of *The Developmental Cycle in Domestic Groups* (J. Goody, ed.). The fact that the labor available to a household expands and contracts at various points in the history of a family and that the number of economically unproductive dependents is also variable over time destroyed once and for all the notion that "the family" could be thought of as having a single form in any society. Variability was not only normal, but inevitable, and had distinct economic consequences. This amending of the classic structural model of kinship shifted the center of theoretical discussion from norms to practices, from culture to demography, from standardization to variation, from structure to process.

That Jack Goody's interest in kinship had a distinctly property-oriented cast from the beginning is also evident in his monograph, *Death, Property and the Ancestors* (1962). This preoccupation with the relationship between kinship organization and the control of property later reemerged in his large-scale comparison between Africa and Europe, *Production and Reproduction: A Comparative Study of the Domestic Domain* (1976). That was a statistically grounded effort to identify related clusters of variables surrounding radically different family systems. Goody built his argument on the difference between marriage and inheritance in societies in which class was a major structural feature (Europe and Asia) and societies in which it was not (Africa).[28]

Study of the domestic economy leads quickly to the gender-marked division of labor in Africa and, indeed, to the whole question of the construction of gender and the control of marriage in African society.[29] There now is a growing literature on the subject of the gendered division of labor and on other aspects of the situation of African women.[30] This topic is one on which the last word has surely not been spoken. For an excellent introduction to the literature on households, see Jane Guyer 1981, and Guyer's own fieldwork (1980, 1984a). In one comparative paper Guyer has attacked the assertion that root crops are "women's crops" because they are "naturally" better fitted to women's domestic duties (1984b). Conventional thought on the subject was that root crops fitted in better with women's schedules because there is considerable choice about the timing of root crop harvesting (which can even be done piecemeal) and much less leeway about grains, which often must be harvested at one particular moment (1984b). Guyer answers by shifting to a different question. She shows instead the relevance and importance of the social capacity to mobilize collective labor for the harvesting of grain crops, a mobilizing capacity which women are regularly denied in many African societies. Three important questions about the situation of women will surely continue to be addressed in the African context as they are elsewhere. Who has control over women's lives? What kind of return do women get for their labor? What sorts of choices are open to women as they negotiate their positions in the world? In Africa today these issues are being raised with great urgency since the situation of many African women is worsening, yet their role in a faltering system of production remains critical.

A major work of the 1960s drew the attention of economic anthropologists in a very different direction. It was the Polanyi-inspired collection of papers on African markets edited by Paul Bohannan and George Dalton (1962; see also Meillassoux 1971). This was followed a few years later by Laura and Paul Bohannan's *Tiv Economy* (1968) which built on their earlier general ethnography (1953). In 1969 the perception of marketing issues was considerably expanded by Abner Cohen's excellent study of Hausa traders in Ibadan. Trading diasporas had long been central to the regional economy of West Africa, but as long as anthropologists confined themselves to studying "tribes" and small local communities as isolates, the cultural implications of these networks of long-distance exchange were not given adequate attention. Cohen's was not only a major contribution to an understanding of the extensive geographical reach of ethnic trading monopolies in West Africa, but it showed the links among ethnicity, religion, and economy. His book addressed the idea of "tribal" identity as a construct, noting the existence of a politically cogent "re-tribalization," the building and hardening of new versions of ethnic boundaries. The passage of time was an important part of Cohen's analysis. He showed that the evolution of new Islamic religious practices and, consequently, of new forms of ethnic distinctiveness had both political and economic consequences for the Hausa. The analytic boundaries between conventionally conceived institutional systems—economy, religion, politics—were once again being broken down by attention to a new cluster of ethnographic facts.

Polly Hill's book on migrant cocoa farmers in Ghana broke further new ground in describing lively African entrepreneurial activity and its social concomitants (1963). Her later work in Northern Nigeria sketched a historical sequence of economic transformation among the Hausa (1977). And by the mid-1980s Hill was ready for an all-out attack on development economics (1986). This sequence in her work represents a widespread set of attitudes in Africanist economic anthropology in the decades after independence. There was a fascination with ongoing African economic activity and the social relations surrounding it, a growing preoccupation with economic history in Africa, and dismay over many of the development policies of governments and international agencies.

The questions addressed were broadened. On a historical theme which also had vast regional implications, several anthropologists edited books on the history of slavery (Meillassoux 1975; Miers and Kopytoff 1977). Anthropology was expanding its problematic. Keith Hart wrote an overview of the rise of commercial farming in West Africa and its impact on the communities of the area (1982). Colin Murray's book on the disrupting effects of migrant labor on family life in southern Africa set a very high standard of evidentiary documentation and empathy (1981). D. Cruise O'Brien depicted the close connections among colonial policy, the rise of the Islamic Mourides brotherhoods in Senegal, and the related spread and development of peanut farming (1975). In East Africa, David Parkin addressed the socially transformative consequences of the expansion of the palm wine business in a succinct and persuasive account (1972). The theme of transformation came to dominate the literature (Colson 1971; Colson and Scudder 1975; Karp 1978; Vincent 1982; Parkin 1987; Colson and Scudder 1988; Pottier 1988; Jules-Rosette 1981; Linares 1992). There seems little doubt, too, that rural studies were in this respect affected by anthropological inquiries into the patterns of growing inequality and ethnic separatism in the urban areas.[31]

A recent highly varied set of writings illustrate the current degree of specialized attention to urgent practical issues in anthropological approaches to African economic life. See, for example, Johan Pottier's edited volume on *Food Systems in Central and Southern Africa* (1985) and Parker Shipton's bibliographical survey of the literature on African famines (1990).[32] The far-reaching consequences of chronic food shortage are plainly very much a part of the present in Africa. Drawn together, the story is one of suffering, of ingenuity, and sometimes of heroic courage. The continent-wide comparative survey Shipton has provided of life-saving strategies in the face of famine adds a generalizing dimension to the classical preoccupation with localized community study in ethnography. Along similar methodological lines, A. F. Robertson has made a comparative survey of share contracts all over Africa, showing how widespread and how much of a creative resource this strategy of production can be and how remarkably varied in its local details (1987). In a gloomier work, the social and political factors surrounding land tenure in eleven localities are addressed. A collection edited by R. E. Downs and S. P. Reyna (1988) emphasizes restrictions on access, growing insecurity of tenure, increasing economic differentiation, and the failure of many policies of land tenure reform. Demonstrating that land reform measures in Kenya have increased, not decreased, rural inequality, Bernard Riley and David Brokensha, a geographer and an anthropologist, add their voices to an increasing number of skeptical assessments of development policies (1988).[33] The Marxist tradition continues in new forms (for example, see Donham 1990). These recent products of the decades of postcolonial economic anthropology show how anthropology itself has been affected by the changing economic circumstances of rural and urban Africans. A strong "social problem" component is visible, but prescriptions and solutions are in short supply. While these works on economy are all concerned with the way particular Africans make a living and strategize about doing so, they are also in varying degrees given to setting those activities within large-scale social, political, and historical frameworks. Simultaneously they ask questions about the subjects' conceptions, intentions, and ideologies. The location of "culture" in these discussions is variable and by implication raises the question whether "culture" is any longer the all-purpose analytical concept it once seemed to be.

French Structuralism and Other Approaches to Modes of Thought, Religion, and the Symbolic Order

Social anthropology in the post-1960s decades also experienced a renaissance of interest in religion, ritual, and other symbolic forms. On the eve of this period John Middleton's study of Lugbara religion presented a detailed case study of the political struggles imbedded in the ritual life of one village of that Northern Uganda people (1960). The book rapidly became a classic, fitting as it did within the tendency of the British School to see ritual as an expression of social relations. Turner had linked ritual and small scale politics in the playing out of an ongoing "social drama" (1957), while Middleton developed the topic considerably further but with a less harmonious interpretation. Fortes and Germaine Dieterlen gave further momentum to the study of religion and cosmological ideas by together editing an influential book on *African Systems of Thought* (1965). At around the same time, the structuralism of Claude Lévi-Strauss crossed the channel and became a prominent theme in some British symbolic interpretations though it never enjoyed the same dominance it had in French writings. The British School never suspended its interest in politics and economy.[34] For a very useful general survey of writings on African ideology and belief, that is, not only anthropological, and not only structuralist, and including indigenous systems as well as Islam and Christianity, see MacGaffey 1981 (see also Fernandez 1978, 1979).

For structuralists, the Lévi-Straussian method revealed a hidden or submerged grammarlike order in symbolic systems. Antistructuralists saw the method itself as producing, rather than uncovering, the orderliness it "discovered" (Goody 1961, 1972, 1977). And others "explained" African religions or symbolic systems with other rationales, as modes of reasoning that could be likened to Western scientific speculation (Horton 1967), or as comprehensible in terms of the unconscious meanings they expressed which, it was argued, could be recovered through psychoanalytic interpretation (Beidelman 1966), or as organizing metaphors (Fernandez 1974), or as modes of protest (Bourdillon 1971; Jean Comaroff 1985). Others join the debate about meaning from other points of entry.[35] Medical anthropology, for one, offers quite a different and very important locus for the discussion of symbolic constructs, an approach that is broadened and illuminated by its practical and "applied" context (Augé and Herzlich 1984; Mullings 1984; Buckley 1985; Sargent 1989). Histories of African medicine often draw on anthropological perspectives. Thus, a very recent set of essays in the tradition of Michel Foucault addresses the European colonial discourse on African illness (Vaughan 1991). It uses archival materials on the symbols and practices of biomedicine as an access route to the colonial imagination.

As one might expect, quite a different vision of the significance of symbol and ritual is found in the various Marxist interpretations. Thus one version put forward by the politically minded emphasizes that ritual communication furthers and concerns the interests of dominant groups (Bloch 1984). To a different effect is an interpretation of religion as the expression of a particular mode of production (Rigby 1981; Augé

1975). Outside the Marxist tradition there also are others who contend that ritual and symbol at the very least serve "to inculcate respect for tradition and hierarchy" as Wyatt MacGaffey characterizes J. S. La-Fontaine's position (MacGaffey 1981, 253; LaFontaine 1977, 1985; see also Kopytoff on ancestors and elders 1971, 1981; and Parkin 1991 on spatial images that reflect history).

Within another stream of research, some works of recent decades have addressed the nature of Islamic and Christian influences in Africa and the local variation of experience, practice, and thought (Comaroff and Comaroff 1991; Holy 1991). The first volume of Jean and John Comaroff's history concerns itself with early missionary contacts, with, as they put it, "the colonization of consciousness and the consciousness of colonization." Ladislav Holy addresses the intertwining of Islam and local "custom" in a gendered form. He argues that among the Berti, Islamic practice is primarily conceived of as male, while local, non-Islamic practices are very much in the female domain. The preoccupation of the Comaroffs and of Holy with the nature of consciousness, with the contents of the imagination, is in keeping with significant present currents in anthropological thought.

The process of acceptance or rejection of the proselytizing world religions has become part of the interest in multilevel analysis. A rich literature has grown up around local cults and the alternative versions of world religions devised by Africans. Significant works include studies of missionizing, of conversion, of the political significance of regional cults, and, perhaps most important of all, of the characteristics of the indigenized churches, of ethnic and class religious practice, and the self-conscious symbolic intent of some of the new religions of Africa.[36]

Politics, Pluralism, and Law

Most topics in Africanist anthropology necessarily have political dimensions. Much political observation appears as a kind of substratum in ethnographic studies whose explicit focus is on economy, kinship, ethnicity, religion, and the like. In such work the tendency is to describe local micropolitics. There are far fewer works that have much to say about the large, national scale, how its existence is experienced locally, let alone how the political level of supranational activity penetrates local life. One anthropological approach much in favor at the moment is to ask the question, How are individual and collective identity constructed and used? This way of putting the matter necessarily implies attending to both local and large scale issues. The reframing of questions about cultural politics in terms of "identity" has been responsive both to the intensive politicization of ethnic difference in many parts of the world today and to a growing interest in individual experience.

The emerging "identity framework" represents a substantial departure from the preoccupations of the "classical period" of African political anthropology. Much of the mid-century political anthropology in African studies and even later work was concerned with elaborating the two types set out earlier by Fortes and Evans-Pritchard, when they contrasted acephalous systems with centralized systems (1940), and with a third type, the segmentary state, introduced by Aidan Southall (1954, 1988).[37]

Of course, with very few exceptions, the actual fieldwork observation of African politics and government during the preindependence period involved studying African hierarchies operating under the aegis of colonial authorities. To the extent that some anthropologists conceived their task as confined to the analysis of the "purely" African side of the equation, such approaches were often insufficiently attentive to the effects of the larger political environment. However, by no means was all ethnographic work limited in this way (see, for example, Forde 1939; Gluckman 1940, 1943b, 1949). With the end of colonial rule and, in many countries (though not all), the rejection of African rulers perceived as colonial agents, a new era opened and another set of questions was posed. As early as 1966 Peter Lloyd was editing a volume on *The New Elites of Tropical Africa* (on elites also see Cohen 1981).

In the first flush of independence and new nationhood, there were some anthropological attempts to address the potential character of the new African states. Internal diversity was the issue. One perspective considered the central process of incorporating local systems into national ones (as in Cohen and Middleton 1970). Another, more pessimistic view was to examine the extent to which cultural pluralism in Africa had been hardened and officialized into a structurally "corporate" form (Mitchell 1960; Kuper and Smith 1969). The example of South Africa was very much in the minds of these theorists of African pluralism. In short, in postcolonial anthropology the analysis of the politics of cultural difference became part of the discipline as never before. Culture lost whatever political innocence it ever had.

The importance, moreover, of interethnic contacts, polyethnic communities, cults that stretch over multiethnic regions, and political, economic and other interethnic interdependencies came to have increasing attention in anthropology (see Parkin 1990, commenting to this effect on the East African literature, as pioneering works, citing Southall 1954, 1970; Rigby 1969; Spencer 1973). Urban studies undoubtedly fed back into rural ones some of the emphases on complex multiethnic relationships (namely, Parkin 1975). There has been a growing tendency to rethink many Africa situations in this way, and to question the utility of relying on the supposed ethnic isolate as the premise of analysis. The political importance of ethnic boundaries is clearly a circumstantial creation, not a "natural" accompaniment of cultural difference. And, on the other side of the puzzle, polyethnic connections are by no means of only one type. The increasingly sophisticated intertwining of politics, cultural issues, administrative policy and individual strategies in analysis is manifest not only in the theoretical work on pluralism but in many politically oriented studies of particular peoples.[38]

After the first postindependence wave of optimism, for the most part postcolonial anthropologists were silent on the subject of African national regimes. No doubt this was for practical professional considerations as well as for reasons imbedded in the discipline's localist methods. Presumably a silence about the national level was in part motivated by the wish of the anthropologist to be permitted to return to the country being studied. Anthropologists cannot diplomatically analyze topics that would lead them to criticize directly the very governments whose permission they need to carry forward their research projects. Also, on methodological grounds, the long tradition of local, small-scale studies to which anthropology has made such a signal contribution seems to conveniently justify silence about the large scale. Both of these circumstances have no doubt contributed to anthropological reticence about national politics. Of course, no such inhibitions pertain to the colonial period since it is over. Consequently the colonial era has been an inviting field for retrospective analysis. This is particularly so for certain topics on which there are ample records. Thus, for example, both Francis Snyder and Sally Falk Moore have written ethnographic monographs which trace century-long transformations of local forms of African law (Snyder 1981; Moore 1986). Both books follow the deep economic changes that underlay apparent manifestations of cultural continuity, Snyder in a Marxist mode, Moore in an eclectic vein. The idea of "customary law" would never be the same again nor, indeed, the idea of "custom" itself (see also the work of Chanock 1985 and the historical volume edited by Mann and Roberts (1991).[39]

There is much ferment in anthropology today on the topic of African politics what with the transformations now under way from South Africa to North Africa, and the way the pervasive issue of cultural differences and commonalities plays into those changes. The next few years will surely see a new anthropology of new African political situations (for a recent general overview of the history of political anthropology by an Africanist, see Vincent 1990). But for present purposes two works will illustrate the kinds of strong topical shifts that may be expected. One is the book by David Lan, *Guns and Rain* (1985). It is a monograph about the cultural aspects of an instance of modern guerrilla warfare, the fighting that was waged with the blessing (and practical help) of local spirit mediums in what is now northeastern Zimbabwe. The northeastern Shona, about whom Lan writes, live on both sides of the Mozambique-Zimbabwe border and crossed back and forth in the many-years war to liberate Southern Rhodesia. The spirit mediums and chiefdoms of the area had been studied in an earlier period by G. K. Garbett (1966, 1969, 1977) and by M. F. Bourdillon (1979, 1981, 1982). Lan drew on their material and added new data. The central feature of Lan's fieldwork was a set of interviews with veterans of the fighting and with the spirit mediums who helped them. Lan is able to show the extraordinary symbiosis, commonality of purpose, and syncretism of belief that developed between the mediums and the fighters during the war, and to identify some of the local political background that fed into the construction of that extraordinary relationship.

The other book which illustrates the changing focus in political anthropology is James Ferguson's recent *The Anti-Politics Machine* (1990), a work that describes in considerable detail the case history of a "failed" development project in Lesotho, and the way the project nevertheless strengthened the hand of central government. The book is about how all those involved conceived of the project of "development," not simply about what happened, though it describes that as well. The problematic interlock between the simultaneous acknowledgment and denial of "the political" is the theoretical center of this extended case history. While the impoverished Lesotho villagers were economically dependent on sending men to South Africa as migrant laborers, the international funding agencies involved in their "development" chose to ignore this dimension of their economy and defined their "problem" solely as a need to improve local agricultural and stock-raising practices. Quite understandably, these agencies did not address the wages and circumstances of labor migration over which they had neither jurisdiction nor control. However, to deliberately ignore the central staple of the economy as they did gave their policy pronouncements about the place of stock and agriculture a peculiar unreality. They also systematically ignored local views about other matters. Fieldwork among villagers demonstrated that their supposedly "traditional" interest in cattle was actually a strategic use of "tradition" and, in fact, was a strongly present-oriented attitude. Fieldwork among officials (and analysis of their documentary products) showed their quite different construction of indigenous thought and social environment in which the officials were working. Like Lan's book this one draws on multisite study, on multiple interpretations of "reality" held by different people with different perspectives who manage to interact with each other without understanding each other. Both of these books are action centered, one on a revolution from below, the other on an attempted transformation worked from above. Both deal with intentional transformation and its unintended consequences.

The recent legal and political books mentioned here (and this is far from a comprehensive list) are studies conducted among particular "peoples" of Africa. Distinctive local cultural practices are part of the story. But these books are not primarily about culture but rather about a particular moment in history and what happened at the time. These are action studies in which "tradition" figures as one feature of the scene but not dominantly as the determinative one. And perhaps most important of all, this is not an agentless anthropology of forces, cultural, economic, or whatever. Reports are being made about specific persons, specific occurrences, and the intentions and justifications expressed during those events.

Past and Future: A Concluding Note

Anthropology has been witness to many deep changes in Africa, from the decades of colonial rule to the brief elation of political independence. And from that giddy period of high expectation and noble intention, Africa has been seen to arrive at a less optimistic moment of self-questioning and reconstruction. Meanwhile the continent is beset by innumerable misfortunes of both human and natural origin. It is no wonder that anthropology itself has moved from a period of studying supposedly archaic and static social types to a time of observing dynamic struggles and cultural inventions. The interaction between discipline and subject matter is patent. What has been seen has changed the way the beholder sees. For ethnographers today, what happens in Africa is African whatever its cultural origin. The old overvaluation of the authentically indigenous and exotic has largely passed. The reconstructed indigenous forms, ostensibly purified of external influence and free of changing circumstance, are now left for the elegant coffee table books of others. Anthropologists ply a different trade.

Despite the ever increasing diversity of subspecialties in recent social anthropology, one can identify a few key intellectual issues that cut across them all. For obvious reasons, in Africanist anthropology the overarching preoccupation for the past thirty years has been with process over time, with the active construction of culture and the nature of social change. The beginnings of that interest were already visible in some of the studies produced in the late 1940s and in the 1950s, particularly those concerned with urban populations, with labor migration, with rural cash cropping, and with the interventions of state agencies and church missions.

However, present perspectives, even on the same phenomena, have changed considerably. The general framework of historical awareness in anthropology has recently undergone substantial metamorphoses. Anthropologists who study African lives at first hand have become caught up in the broad stream of interpretive, reflexive, and critical thought that has pervaded the social sciences and the humanities. No longer conceiving of themselves as simply producing "literary" and "descriptive" accounts of "others," anthropologists see themselves as implicated and self-aware interlocutors whose work, whatever its specialized content, engages two focal themes: power and meaning.

Questions flowing from those two ideas wind in and out of virtually all the specialized anthropological monographs written today, sometimes implicitly, more often explicitly. Deceptively simple in appearance, power and meaning are culturally intertwined in exceedingly complex ways. Power constitutes meanings, and meanings, power. Discourse is attended both for what it says and what it does not say. Whether the topic is a local form of economy, kinship or gender, a matter of religion, medicine, law or politics, or an account of historical sequences or current practices, aspects of those master themes are bound to appear in the heart of almost any contemporary ethnographic work. Who is in control of what and of whom? And who is defining the situation? How are the terms of the cultural discourse being formed? What is the distribution of social knowledge? The contestability and incontestability of various versions of reality are now assumed to be part of every ethnographic scene even as they are part of the arena of professional commentary.

The new Africa that is just now emerging—the post–Cold War Africa, that is—as always, a mix of the heroic, the tragic, and the mundane, presents anthropology with new challenges, applied, practical, and theoretical. Anthropology may be poised for yet another phase of theoretical and methodological revision. And what will be the involvement of African scholars? During the colonial period and soon thereafter a handful of Africans became anthropologists. Some published classical ethnographic monographs on their own peoples, others on other concerns, such as migration. See, for example, Jomo Kenyatta (1938), K. A. Busia (1951), J. B. Danquah (1968), F. M. Deng (1971, 1972), A. B. Diop (1965, 1979). These men were all trained in a British or European tradition and wrote very much in the intellectual style of the departments from which they received their degrees. The postindependence era did not bring an increased surge of interest in anthropology on the part of Africans. Quite the contrary. In many places anthropology fell into political disfavor. The subject was banished from certain African universities. The discipline was regarded with suspicion because of its association with the colonial period.

Not surprisingly, the group of Africans trained as anthropologists has remained small, but it is growing. The numbers are now sufficient so that a Pan African Association of Anthropologists has recently been launched in Africa. There seems every likelihood that the shadow of the colonial past will no longer be allowed to interfere with the continued development of what could become an important and lively international intellectual exchange.

In fact, given that intellectual explorations in the social sciences are not independent of the milieu they study, the direction of the new anthropology will surely be affected by the paths taken by the new Africa, its scholars, and its other citizens. Even now local fieldwork studies are becoming more and more engaged with questions about the large politico-economic frames within which local communities are embedded. Power and meaning are not merely local affairs. The world economy, world politics, worldwide systems of communication, and the World Bank play tunes to which many sectors of Africa must dance. Hence, not only in Africa but wherever in the world anthropologists pitch their intellectual tents, they now arrive with a very broad picture of the larger social environment in their minds. By indirection this raises complex problems of causality, of scale, and of history for anyone doing local ethnographic work. Fin de siècle anthropology in Africa, as elsewhere, will thus begin the twenty-first century as a self-conscious analytic form of current history—before it becomes something else.

NOTES

1. Herskovits and his wife spent five months in Abomey in Dahomey in the 1930s and in 1938 published a two volume study, *Dahomey, an Ancient African Kingdom* (Herskovits 1938). But Herskovits was not only occupied with Africa's past. He had a strong sense of the importance of studying change in Africa. Thus on the eve of independence, together with W. R. Bascom, he edited an influential book entitled *Continuity and Change in African Cultures* (1959).

2. A. R. Radcliffe-Brown, whose theoretical work was later to dominate British social anthropology for nearly two decades, also contributed to this internalization of young American scholars. He taught at the University of Chicago for several years beginning in 1931. Through him several Americans interested in Africa were introduced to British anthropologists. So, for example, Lloyd Fallers were sent to A. I. Richards, by then the Director of the East African Institute of Social Research, and she provided him with assistance in making contacts for his fieldwork. Other Americans who received training

in Britain and did fieldwork in Africa in the early years were Hortense Pow-dermaker, Paul and Laura Bohannan, and the Harrises (McCall 1967, 28).

3. For a description and appreciative critique of their work see Clifford 1988, 55–99.

4. Some administrative officers were interested in anthropology and were given special opportunities to make extensive ethnographic investigations. Several (Talbot 1915, 1923, 1926; Rattray 1923, 1929; Meek, 1925, 1931, 1937) were seconded for various periods as "government anthropologists" (Forde 1953).

5. But until after the Second World War, "Although the resources in men and funds devoted to anthropological study and teaching . . . were exiguous in the extreme and such studies did not receive any significant support from colonial administrations, the influence of academic anthropology did to some extent filter throughout the administrative services through contacts with the universities and with the Royal Anthropological Institute, of which many of the more scholarly administrators became Fellows" (Forde 1953, 843, 844, cites a long list of these and notes some of their many publications).

Very often, however, "the very existence of social anthropology in the colonial period constituted a source of potential radical criticism of the colonial order itself" (James 1973, 42). And, of course, the expression of that criticism had to be indirect and tactful.

6. The I.A.I. journal, *Africa,* published articles by anthropologists, administrators and colonial educationists "concerning both the broader aspects and particular instances of social change in relation to governmental action" (Forde 1953, 848).

7. Before Malinowski came along, to the extent that there were any detailed ethnographies of African peoples, these had been written by missionaries. As for example, Henry A. Junod's *The Life of a South African Tribe* (1912), or E. W. Smith and A. Dale's *The Ila-speaking Peoples of Northern Rhodesia* (1920), or Bruno Gutmann's *Das Recht der Dschagga* (1926). These were remarkable works, but strongly skewed by the proselytizing interests, special roles, and related preconceptions of their authors. There were also a few monographs commissioned by colonial governments. See, for example, those by Northcote Thomas on the Ibo and then on the Timne (1913, 1916), Rattray on the Ashanti (1923, 1929) and Meek in Nigeria (1937). But as Evans-Pritchard commented about them, "It must be said . . . that even at their best the writings of these administrator-anthropologists seldom satisfy the professional scholar" (1962, 111).

Seligman's African study in this early mode was the "compendious" *A Survey of the Pagan Tribes of the Nilotic Sudan* (with B. Z. Seligman 1932; for a brief comment on Seligman see Lienhardt, 1976, 182).

8. At various stages, Africanist participants in the Malinowski seminar included E. E. Evans-Pritchard, Audrey Richards, Hilda Kuper (then Beemer), Isaac Schapera, Phyllis Kaberry, Hortense Powdermaker, Meyer Fortes, S. F. Nadel, Gordon Brown, Max Gluckman, Ellen Hellman, Godfrey Wilson, and Monica Hunter (later Wilson) (A. Kuper, 1973, 90–92, 154–57; Brown 1973, 187).

9. Malinowski conceived of anthropologists as able to supply administrators with information about African ways of life which would prevent colonial governments from making serious errors of policy out of ignorance of indigenous culture (Malinowski 1929, 1930).

10. On the one hand, Malinowski wrote the introduction to Jomo Kenyatta's "traditionalist" ethnography of the Kikuyu, *Facing Mount Kenya* (1938). On the other, he gave much encouragement to his student Monica Hunter whose *Reaction to Conquest* (1936) was "a study of the Pondo not only in their 'tribal' setting, but also as labourers on European farms and in the towns of South Africa, has been singled out as a notable example of a diachronic or historically-dimensioned study at a time when ahistorical and static studies are said to have dominated the field" (Brown 1973, 187).

The most ambitious attempt to formally reconcile the Malinowskian functional model with the study of social transformation in Africa was to be embodied later in Godfrey and Monica Wilson's *The Analysis of Social Change* (1945).

11. Not only were they all active in each other's seminars, and in the International African Institute in London, but they were in close communication with colleagues in the research institutes in Africa. Particularly important were the East African Institute of Social Research in Uganda, first headed by Audrey Richards and later by Lloyd Fallers and Aidan Southall, and the Rhodes-Livingstone Institute in Northern Rhodesia first led by Godfrey Wilson and later by Max Gluckman and eventually by Elizabeth Colson and Clyde Mitchell. Indeed, some of them did research under these auspices.

12. On the basis of much less adequate, much earlier ethnographic reports, previous interpretations, such as those of the French philosopher Lucien Levy Bruhl, had used witchcraft ideas to argue that there were two quite different forms of thought, the "prelogical mentality" of primitives and the "logical mentality" of moderns (*Les fonctions mentales* 1910). Instead, Evans-Pritchard demonstrated in great detail that if one showed the premises with which the Zande operated and the use that they made of their mystical beliefs in their ordinary lives, the consistency and logic of the system would emerge and that it was not different from the logic used in practical affairs anywhere.

Evans-Pritchard's contentions were consciously and intentionally directed as a counterargument to the two modes-of-thought views of Levy Bruhl (Evans-Pritchard 1934; see also Douglas 1981, 27–31). The debate about the nature of rationality, and about the simultaneous existence in any society of multiple realities and a multiplicity of modes of thought continues to simmer (see, for example, Tambiah 1990).

13. Thus in the same year (1940) Evans-Pritchard published two more monographs on peoples of the Anglo-Egyptian Sudan, *The Nuer* (1940*a*) and *The Political System of the Anuak* (1940*b*), and Fortes was hard at work on his two major monographs on the Tallensi of Ghana, which were published just after World War II, *The Dynamics of Clanship among the Tallensi* (1945) and *The Web of Kinship among the Tallensi* (1949).

14. That theme was evident at mid-century in Evans-Pritchard's publication of a historical book on the Sanusi order (1949).

15. The forties and fifties was a rich period in African ethnography. Audrey Richards published her *Land Labour and Diet in Northern Rhodesia* (1939) on the Bemba (see also Richards 1955, 1959). M. Green published *Land Tenure in an Ibo Village* in 1941 (see also Green 1947). S. F. Nadel wrote a remarkably "modern" and complex monograph on the Nupe kingdom as a totality, addressing its political structure, its villages and towns, its economy in the colonial period, and its general history, *A Black Byzantium* (1942, see also Nadel 1954). Later in his life Nadel published one of the clearest statements of the theoretical paradigm of the Radcliffe-Brown school (1967). In 1947 Hilda Kuper published *An African Aristocracy: Rank among the Swazi*. This was a sketch of an African kingdom's constitutive structure. Like Nadel's it addressed a unit much larger and more complex than a village, lineage, or clan. Phyllis Kaberry did a pathbreaking study of women in the Bamenda Grassfields, Cameroon (1952). Monica Wilson soon began publishing what were to become a long series of monographs on the Nyakyusa (1952, 1957, 1959, 1982). Aidan Southall proposed a new political paradigm in his analysis of Alur society, the "segmentary state," an innovative concept he subsequently developed further and which has proved to be analytically durable and useful (1954, 1988). These are only some of the products of this very active period of monographic writing, since it defies summary description.

16. His first impact on the field came in 1934 with the publication of his classic comparative work on ecology and culture, *Habitat, Economy and Society*. He had experienced a period of study in the United States that had brought him into contact with the culture area tradition and its ecological orientation. The latter was strongly manifest in his 1934 book.

17. Though his was not as strong a voice in the production of theoretical models as those of Evans-Pritchard and Fortes, and the University of London was not considered to have the prestige of Oxbridge, his conception of the breadth of the discipline, his own ethnographic and historical contributions, and his tireless organizational labors to further African studies left an enduring legacy. African studies would never have developed as it did without his remarkable presence.

18. Thus, not only did Monica Hunter (later Wilson) write *Reaction to Conquest* in 1936, but Fortes wrote "Culture Contact as a Dynamic Process," in 1936, and Max Gluckman wrote a famous paper on the ceremonial opening of a bridge in which the British and Zulus participated in 1940, as well as a small monograph in 1941 on "The Economy of the Central Barotse Plain." Godfrey Wilson wrote on "The Economics of Detribalization in Northern Rhodesia" in 1942. Schapera published *Migrant Labor and Tribal Life* in 1947. For some useful bibliographies, books, and articles on African labor migration and on African cities by anthropologists see Balandier 1955; Diop 1965; Meillassoux 1968; Banton 1957; Gugler and Flanagan 1978; Gulliver 1955; Mitchell 1956, 1966; Epstein 1958; Parkin 1969, 1975, 1978; Forde 1956; Southall 1961, 1973; Kapferer 1972; Lloyd 1974; Kuper 1965; Little 1970, 1973; Gutkind and Wallerstein 1985; MacGaffey 1987; Miner 1967; Morrison and Gutkind 1982; Southall and Gutkind 1957. (See also additional references in notes 25 and 27 herein.)

19. Its first director was Godfrey Wilson, a man who was preoccupied with a changing Africa. His plans for the Institute were that research should be undertaken among urban Africans and in the townships of the mining areas, not only in the rural countryside (see Brown 1973, and the chapter by Kapferer in that volume).

20. The theoretical framework that appears in much of his earlier writing was this oppositional one, the contrast between social reproduction and radical transformation. Werbner has represented his perspective as "a dialectical view," and, in part, it was (1984, 163).

21. The Institute was financed by colonial governments and by the copper companies but remained "a surprisingly independent centre of learning" and "was . . . the servant of neither" the colonial authorities nor the copper companies (Brown 1973, 197). Under Gluckman's direction, and under its subsequent leaders, Elizabeth Colson and Clyde Mitchell, the Rhodes-Livingston Institute was a locus of enormous anthropological productivity. It funded fieldwork. Colson's remarkable series of articles and monographs on the Tonga which started in a classical British social anthropological mode of reconstruction and gradually diverged into contemporary commentary are striking examples of the kind of work associated with the Institute, as is Mitchell's book on the Yao together with his subsequent innovative excursions into urban work and network analysis (Colson 1948, 1953, 1958, 1960, 1962, 1971; Colson and Gluckman 1951; Colson and Scudder 1975; Mitchell 1956a, 1956b, 1966, 1969). But as important as its sponsorship of fieldwork, the Institute provided a center for the presentation of work in progress and for a critical discussion of the issues involved.

22. Despite what now seems Gluckman's own rather old-fashioned personal ethnographic agenda in the Barotse work, to reconstruct as best he could a no longer existing "tribal political system," Gluckman's fieldwork among the Lozi nevertheless broke important new ground. He was the first ethnographer to spend substantial time listening to legal cases in an African court (Gluckman 1955; Moore on Gluckman 1978).

23. Among the early works which are now seldom consulted are Herskovits' pioneering "culture areas" papers (1930) and Seligman's *Races of Africa* (3d ed., 1957). Gulliver cites critically a German version of the culture area approach which was published by Bauman in 1943 (Gulliver 1965, 79).

24. Murdock's work on Africa was an offshoot of the Human Relations Area Files, an enormous compendium of world cultural information that aspired to put in one huge accessible file with a common index all that existed in hundreds of ethnographic works. Murdock was no Africanist but rather an industrious compiler and classifier.

25. Even during the colonial period, many writings went far to include what was visibly and notably changing in Africa (see, for example, some of Gluckman's early work, 1940, 1941, 1942, 1943a, 1943b, 1949; G. and M. Wilson 1945; Read 1938; Fortes 1936; Firth 1947; Forde 1937, 1939; Hunter 1936; Richards 1955; Schapera 1947; Gulliver 1955b, 1958).

26. In 1954 Balandier organized a program of study, "Sociologie de l'Afri-

que Noire," in Section VI of the Ecole des Hautes Etudes of the Sorbonne to which other programs were later added. These programs of teaching and research constituted the nucleus of the Centre d'Etudes Africaines established in 1957. Balandier also founded and became Director of the African Studies Section of the Foundation des Sciences Politiques (Paris) in 1959 to undertake the study of African political parties, doctrines, and ideologies (Balandier 1960). He also served as the Director of the International Research Office on Social Implications of Technological Change and was a member of the Executive Council of the International African Institute.

27. Such as those of Richards on land, labor, and diet, (1939), Forde and Scott on the native economies of Nigeria (1946), and Paul Bohannan on farming, exchange, investment, and the impact of money (1954, 1955, 1959), those of Gulliver on the property of pastoralists, on labor migration, and on land tenure (1955a,, 1955b, 1958), and of M. G. Smith on Hausa economy (1955).

28. See also Goody and Tambiah (eds.), *Bridewealth and Dowry*, 1973. Interest in the bridewealth question has continued as witness John Comaroff's edited volume on *The Meaning of Marriage Payments* (1980) and Adam Kuper's *Wives for Cattle* (1982).

29. It is no accident that two of Meillassoux's major books were preoccupied with the relationships among marriage, kinship, and property in precapitalist and capitalist circumstances. In the Gouro book he made a striking interpretation of the relationship between economic production and reproduction, the manner in which male elders once controlled the labor of juniors through the manipulation of bridewealth payments and the timing of marriage (1964a, 1964b). The theoretical argument is restated in much more general terms, particularly in relation to modern labor migration in his *Maidens, Meal and Money* (1975, translated in 1984).

30. A few examples are Paulme 1960; Obbo 1975; Wilson 1957; Bledsoe 1980; Etienne and Leacock 1980; Oppong 1981, 1983; Swantz 1985; Little 1973; LeVine 1979; Bay 1982.

31. Little 1973; Lloyd 1974; Parkin 1978; see also Coquery Vidrovitch 1991 for an extensive discussion of urban studies.

32. See also Shipton's essay on good and evil money (1989).

33. See also Horowitz and Painter 1986; and Shipton 1988.

34. In its "pure" form the Lévi-Straussian focus on the order in symbolic systems and the regularities of combination, opposition, and parallelism to be found among the symbolic elements was emphatically nonsociological, noneconomic, nonpolitical. However, there were many Africanists, even among those who did not see his approach as the only acceptable one, who found and continued to find in the question of symbolic classification and semiotics an illuminating approach to African cosmologies, rituals, myths, and other symbolic inventions (DeHeusch 1958, 1972, 1985; Douglas 1966; Willis 1974; Bourdieu 1977; Barley 1983).

35. For example, emphasizing the differences in perspective between insider and outsider, and dealing with religion as a performative presentation

(Harris 1978), or, as Sperber does, attacking the idea that there are "underlying" meanings in symbols which can be discerned by semiologists and anthropologists, arguing instead that these frequently are insertions of the observer's views (Sperber 1974; for a diverse range of interpretation of African thought and symbol see also Richards 1967; J. Beattie and J. Middleton 1969; I. Karp and C. S. Bird 1980; Thornton 1980; Beidelman 1966, 1968, 1986; James 1988).

36. Fernandez 1978, 1979, 1982; J. Beattie and J. Middleton 1969; Horton 1971, 1975; Beidelman 1974, 1982, 1986; Lewis 1966; Jules-Rosette 1975; Cohen 1969, 1981; J. Comaroff 1985; Peel 1968, 1977; MacGaffey 1981, 1983; Werbner 1977; Daneel 1971, 1974; Murphee 1969.

37. This typologizing led to two major streams of work. One focused on acephalous organization and its varieties, with some "intermediate" and "mixed" types also noted (Gulliver 1955a; Smith 1956; Middleton and Tait 1958; Lewis 1961; Spencer 1965; Dyson-Hudson 1966; Stewart 1977; Baxter and Almagor 1978). The other concentrated on African rulers and on African bureaucracy (Nadel 1942; Gluckman 1943a, 1943b; Kuper 1947; Colson and Gluckman 1951; Southall 1954, 1988; Fallers 1956, 1964; Schapera 1956; Mitchell 1956a; Richards 1959; Smith 1960; Southwold 1960; Mair 1962; Buxton 1963; Middleton 1965; Ruel 1969; Beattie 1971). Weak kings and strong kings, princes and chiefs, village headmen, lineage leaders, hierarchy and equality, social order with and without rulers, these were the structural preoccupations of political anthropology. And then there also were monographs like Turner's (1957) and Middleton's (1960) that depicted the machinations of ambitious men at the micropolitical level, showing their strategies of competition. For an excellent review of the ethnographic literature exposing a full range of these issues in the Sudan and Ethiopia, see Wendy James 1990.

38. Colson 1971, 1976; Parkin 1975; Bond 1976; Karp 1978; Burnham 1980; Colson and Scudder 1988; Van Binsbergen and Geschière 1985.

39. The anthropological study of African law went through a series of additive and revisionist phases that led up to this recent processual, historico-ethnographic approach. First there was a stream of attempts to set down "customary law" in the form of a set of rules which could guide judges (Schapera 1938; Holleman 1952; and, for a later example, Allott 1969). Gluckman's ethnography introduced the quite different strategy of listening to litigation in a Lozi court and giving accounts of the facts of specific cases and such legal rules and principles as were enunciated in the decision-making process (1955). Bohannan followed with a short book on Tiv hearings in and out of the formal court system emphasizing indigenous key concepts as the path to understanding legal thought (1957). Subsequently Gluckman (no doubt affected by the discussions generated by the Bohannan work) wrote a concepts book of his own, about the guiding "ideas" and "principles" in Barotse law distilled from his earlier field experience (1965). In the same period, Philip Gulliver's analysis of social control among a group of agricultural Masai (the Arusha) introduced a new angle (1963). He deemphasized "customary rules" and "concepts" as

determinative of case outcomes and contended instead that in certain systems outcomes depended more on the political power of the winning litigant than on normative propositions. Comaroff and Roberts responded to this controversy over "rule orders" versus "power" by developing a complex picture of practice (1981). They showed the contenders' perspective in great detail. Snyder and Moore's two studies (1981, 1986) differed from the others in that though they analyzed instances of litigation, they were analytically centered on the historical context within which disputes between individuals took place, rather than concentrating exclusively on the disputing process.

REFERENCES

Allott, A. N. "The Restatement of African Law Project of the School of Oriental and African Studies." A general report on the period 1959–1969. Mimeographed. London, 1969.

Augé, Marc. *Le Rivage Alladian*. Paris: Orstom, 1969.

———. *Theorie des Pouvoirs et Ideologie*. Paris: Hermann, 1975.

———. *Pouvoirs de Vie, Pouvoirs de Mort*. Paris: Flammarion, 1977.

———. *Symbole, Fonction, Histoire*. Paris: Hachette, 1979.

———. *The Anthropological Circle, Symbol, Function, History*. Cambridge: Cambridge University Press, 1982.

Augé, Marc, and Herzlich, Claudine. *Le sens du mal: anthropologie, histoire, sociologie de la maladie*. Montreux: Editions des Archives Contemporaires, 1985.

Balandier, Georges. *Sociologie des brazzavilles noires*. Paris: A. Colin, 1955.

———. *Afrique ambigue*. Paris: Plon, 1957.

———. "The French Tradition of African Research." *Human Organization* 19, no. 3 (1960): 108–11.

———, ed. *Sociologie actuelle de l'Afrique noire*. Paris: Presses Universitaires de France, 1963 (orig. 1955).

———. *Political Anthropology*. New York: Vintage Books. Random House, 1970.

Banton, Michael. *West African City*. London: Oxford University Press, 1957.

Barley, Nigel. *Symbolic Structures: An Exploration of the Culture of the Dowayos*. Cambridge: Cambridge University Press, 1983.

Bascom, W. R., and Herskovits, M. *Continuity and Change in African Cultures*. Chicago: Chicago University Press, 1959.

Baxter, P., and Almagor Uri, eds. *Age, Generation and Time: Some Features of East African Age Organization*. New York: St. Martin's Press, 1978.

Bay, Edna G. *Women and Work in Africa*. Boulder, Colo.: Westview Press, 1982.

Beattie, J. H. M. *The Nyoro State*. London: Oxford University Press, 1971.

Beattie, J. H. M., and Middleton, J., eds. *Spirit Mediumship and Society in Africa*. New York: Africana, 1969.

Beidelman, T. O. "The Ox and Nuer Sacrifice: Some Freudian Hypotheses about Nuer Symbolism." *Man* 1, no. 4 (1966): 453–67.

———. "Some Nuer Notions of Nakedness, Nudity and Sexuality." *Africa* 38, no. 2 (1968): 113–32.

———. "Social Theory and the Study of Christian Missions." *Africa* 44 (1974): 235–49.

———. *Colonial Evangelism*. Bloomington: Indiana University Press, 1982.

———. *Moral Imagination in Kaguru Modes of Thought*. Bloomington: Indiana University Press, 1986.

Bledsoe, C. M. *Women and Marriage in Kpelle Society*. Stanford: Stanford University Press, 1980.

Bloch, Maurice, ed. *Marxist Analyses and Social Anthropology*. London and New York: Tavistoch Publications, 1984 (orig. 1975).

Bohannan, Paul. *The Tiv of Central Nigeria*. London: International African Institute, 1953.

———. *Tiv Farm and Settlement*. London: H. M. Stationary Office, 1954.

———. "Some Principles of Exchange and Investment among the Tiv." *American Anthropologist* 57 (1955): 60–70.

———. *Justice and Judgment among the Tiv*. London: Oxford University Press, 1957.

———. "The Impact of Money on an African Subsistence Economy." *Journal of Economic History* 19 (1959): 491–503.

Bohannan, Paul, and Bohannan, Laura. *Tiv Economy*. Evanston, Ill.: Northwestern University Press, 1968.

Bohannan, Paul, and Dalton, George. *Markets in Africa*. Evanston, Ill.: Northwestern University Press, 1962.

Bond, G. C. *The Politics of Change in a Zambian Community*. Chicago: University of Chicago Press, 1976.

Bourdieu, Pierre. *Outline of a Theory of Practice*. New York: Cambridge University Press, 1977.

Bourdillon, M. F. "Some Aspects of the Religion of the Eastern Korekore." Ph.D. diss., University of Oxford, 1971.

———. "The Cults of Dzivaguru and Karuva amongst the North-East Shona Peoples." In *Guardians of the Land: Essays on Central African Territorial Cults,* edited by J. M. Schoffeleers. Zimbabwe: Mambo Press, 1979.

———. "Suggestions of Bureaucracy in Korekore Religion: Putting the Ethnography Straight." *Zambezia* 10 (1981): 119–36.

———. "Freedom and Constraint among Shona Spirit Mediums." In *Religious Organization and Religious Experience,* edited by J. Davis, pp. 181–94. ASA Monograph. London: Academic Press, 1982.

Brown, Richard. "Godfrey Wilson and the Rhodes-Livingston Institute." In

Anthropology and the Colonial Encounter, edited by Talal Asad. London: Ithaca Press, 1973.

Buckley, Anthony D. *Yoruba Medicine.* Oxford: Clarendon Press, 1985.

Burnham, Philip. *Opportunity and Constraint in a Savanna Society: The Gbaya of Cameroon.* London: Academic Press, 1980.

Busia, K. A. *The Position of the Chief in the Modern Political System of the Ashanti.* London: Oxford University Press for the International African Institute, 1951.

Buxton, J. *Chiefs and Strangers.* Oxford: Clarendon Press, 1963.

Chanock, Martin. *Law, Custom and Social Order.* Cambridge: Cambridge University Press, 1985.

Chayanov, A. V. *The Theory of Peasant Economy.* Homewood, Ill.: Richard D. Irwin for the American Economic Association, 1966.

Clifford, James. *The Predicament of Culture.* Cambridge, Mass.: Harvard University Press, 1988.

Cohen, Abner. *Custom and Politics in Urban Africa.* London: Routledge and Kegan Paul, 1969.

———. *The Politics of Elite Culture.* Berkeley and Los Angeles: University of California Press, 1981.

Cohen, Ronald, and Middleton, John, eds. *From Tribe to Nation in Africa.* Scranton, Penn.: Chandler Publishing Co., 1970.

Colson, Elizabeth. "Rain Shrines of the Plateau Tonga of Northern Rhodesia." *Africa* 18 (1948): 272–83.

———. "Social Control and Vengeance in Plateau Tonga Society." *Africa* 23 (1953): 199–212.

———. *Marriage and Family among the Plateau Tonga of Northern Rhodesia.* Manchester: Manchester University Press, 1958.

———. *Social Organisation of the Gwembe Tonga.* Manchester: Manchester University Press. 1960.

———. *The Plateau Tonga of Northern Rhodesia: Social and Religious Studies.* Manchester: Manchester University Press, 1962.

———. *The Social Consequences of Resettlement.* Manchester: Manchester University Press for the Institute of African Studies, University of Zambia, 1971.

———. "From Chief's Court to Local Court: The Evolution of Local Courts in Zambia." *Political Anthropology* 1 (1976): 15–29.

Colson, Elizabeth, and Gluckman, Max, eds. *Seven Tribes of British Central Africa.* Oxford: Oxford University Press for the Rhodes Livingston Institute, 1951.

Colson, Elizabeth, and Scudder, Thayer. "New Economic Relationships between the Gwembe Valley and the Line of Rail." In *Town and Country in East and Central Africa,* edited by David Parkin, pp. 190–210. London: International African Institute, 1975.

————. *For Prayer and Profit: The Ritual, Economic and Social Importance of Beer in Gwenbe District, Zambia, 1950–1982.* Stanford: Stanford University Press, 1988.

Camaroff, J. J., ed. *The Meaning of Marriage Payments.* New York: Academic Press, 1980.

Comaroff, J. J., and Roberts, Simon. *Rules and Processes: The Cultural Logic of Dispute in an African Context.* Chicago and London: University of Chicago Press, 1981.

Comaroff, Jean. *Body of Power, Spirit and Resistance.* Chicago: University of Chicago Press, 1985.

Comaroff, Jean and John. *Of Revelation and Revolution: Christianity, Colonialism and Consciousness in South Africa.* Chicago: University of Chicago Press, 1991.

Copans, Jean. "African Studies: A Periodization." In *African Social Studies,* edited by Peter C. W. Gutkind and Peter Waterman, pp. 11–31. New York and London: Monthly Review Press, 1977.

Coquery Vidrovitch, C. "Recherches sur un mode de production Africain." *La Pensée* 144 (1969): 61–78.

————. "The Process of Urbanization in Africa." *African Studies Review* 34, no. 1 (1991): 1–98.

Cruise O'Brien, D. *Saints and Politicians: Essays in the Organization of a Senegalese Peasant Society.* Cambridge: Cambridge University Press, 1975.

Daneel, M. L. *Old and New in Shona Independent Churches.* Vols. 1 and 2. The Hague: Mouton for Afrika-Studiecentrum, 1971, 1974.

Danquah, J. B. *The Akan Doctrine of God.* London: Cass, 1968.

DeHeusch, Luc. *Essais sur le symbolisme de l'inceste royal en Afrique.* Brussels: Institut de Sociologie Solvay, 1958.

————. *Le Roi Ivre.* Paris: Gallimard, 1972.

————. *Sacrifice in Africa.* Manchester: Manchester University Press, 1985.

Deng, F. M. *Tradition and Modernization: A Challenge for Law among the Dinka of the Sudan.* New Haven, Conn.: Yale University Press, 1971.

————. *The Dinka of the Sudan.* New York: Holt, Rinehart and Winston, 1972.

Dike, K. Onwuka. "In Memoriam: Melville Jean Herskovits." *African Studies Bulletin* 6, no. 1 (March 1963).

Diop, A. B. *Societe toucouleur et migration.* Initiations Africaines 18. Dakar: Institut Francais d' Afrique Noire, 1965.

————. *La Societe Wolof: Tradition et changement.* 2 vols. Mimeographed. University of Paris, 1979.

Donham, Donald. *History, Power, Ideology.* Cambridge: Cambridge University Press, 1990.

Douglas, Mary. *Purity and Danger.* New York: Praeger, 1966.

————. *Edward Evans-Pritchard.* Harmondsworth, Middlesex, England: Penguin Books, 1981.

Downs, R. E., and Reyna, S. P., eds. *Land and Society in Contemporary Africa.* Hanover and London: University Press of New England, 1988.

Dupré, Georges, and Rey, P. P. "Reflexions sur la pertinence d'une théorie des echanges." *Cahiers Internationaux de Sociologie* 46 (1969): 133–62.

Durkheim, Emile. *The Elementary Forms of the Religious Life.* New York: Collier Books, 1961 (orig. 1912).

———. *The Rules of Sociological Method* New York: The Free Press of Glencoe, 1962 (orig. 1895).

Dyson-Hudson, N. *Karimojong Politics.* Oxford: Clarendon Press, 1966.

Epstein, A. L. *Politics in an Urban African Community.* Manchester: Manchester University Press, 1958.

———. *The Craft of Social Anthropology.* London: Tavistock, 1967.

Etienne, Mona, and Leacock, E., eds. *Women and Colonization: Anthropological Perspectives.* New York: Praeger, 1980.

Evans-Pritchard, E. E. "Levy-Bruhl's Theory of Primitive Mentality." *Bulletin, Faculty of Arts.* Vol. 2, Part 2, pp. 1–36, Cairo, Egypt: Farouk University, 1934.

———. *Witchcraft, Oracles and Magic among the Azande.* Oxford: Clarendon Press, 1937.

———. *The Nuer.* Oxford: Clarendon Press, 1940*a*.

———. *The Political System of the Anuak of the Anglo-Egyptian Sudan.* London: Percy Lund Humphries and Co., 1940*b*.

———. *The Sanusi of Cyrenaica.* Oxford: Clarendon Press, 1949.

———. *Social Anthropology and Other Essays.* New York: Free Press of Glencoe, 1962.

Fallers, Lloyd. *Bantu Bureaucracy.* Cambridge: Heffer for the East African Institute of Social Research, 1956.

———. *The King's Men.* London: Oxford University Press, 1964.

Ferguson, James. *The Anti-Politics Machine.* Cambridge: Cambridge University Press, 1990.

Fernandez, J. W. "The Mission of Metaphor in Expressive Culture." *Current Anthropology* 15 (1974): 119–45.

———. "African religious movements." *Annual Review of Anthropology* 7 (1978): 195–234.

———. "Africanization, Europeanization, Christianization." *History of Religions* 18, no. 3 (1979): 284–92.

———. *Bwiti: An Ethnography of the Religious Imagination in Africa.* Princeton, N.J.: Princeton University Press, 1982.

Feuchtwang, Stephen. "The Discipline and Its Sponsors." In *Anthropology and the Colonial Encounter,* edited by T. Asad, pp. 71–100. London: Ithaca Press, 1973.

Firth, Raymond. "Social Problems and Research in British West Africa." *Africa* 17 (1947): 77–91, 170–79.

Forde, C. D. *Habitat, Economy and Society.* London: Methuen, 1934.

———. "Social Change in a Cross River Village Community." *Man* 37 (1937): Act. 5, 10–12.

———. "Government in Umor: A Study of Social Change and Problems of Indirect Rule in a Nigerian Village Community." *Africa* 12 (1939): 129–62.

———. "Applied Anthropology in Government: British Africa." *Anthropology Today,* edited by A. L. Kroeber, pp. 841–65. Chicago: University of Chicago Press, 1953.

———, ed. *African Worlds.* London: Oxford University Press, 1954.

———. *Efik Traders of Old Calabar.* London: Oxford University Press, 1956*a*.

———. "Social Aspects of Urbanization and Industrialization in Africa: A General Review." In *Social Implications of Industrialization and Urbanization in Africa South of the Sahara,* UNESCO. Paris: International African Institute, 1956*b*.

———. *Yako Studies.* London: Oxford University Press, 1964.

Forde, C. Daryll, and Scott, R. *The Native Economies of Nigeria.* London: HMSO, 1946.

Forde, C. Daryll, and Kaberry, P., eds. *West African Kingdoms of the Nineteenth Century.* Cambridge: Cambridge University Press, 1967.

Fortes, Meyer. "Culture Contact as a Dynamic Process." *Africa* 9 (1936): 24–55.

———. *The Dynamics of Clanship among the Tallensi.* London: Oxford University Press, 1945.

———. *The Web of Kinship among the Tallensi.* London: Oxford University Press, 1949.

Fortes, Meyer, and Dieterlen, Germaine, eds. *African Systems of Thought.* London: Oxford University Press, 1965.

Fortes, Meyer, and Evans-Pritchard, E. E., eds. *African Political Systems.* London: Oxford University Press, 1940.

Garbett, G. K. "Religious Aspects of Political Succession among the Valley Korekore." In *The Zambesian Past: Studies in Central African History,* edited by E. Stokes and R. Brown, pp. 137–70. Manchester: Manchester University Press, 1966.

———. "Spirit Mediums as Mediators in Valley Korekore Society." In *Spirit Mediumship in Africa,* edited by J. Beattie and J. Middleton. 1969.

———. "Disparate Regional Cults and Unitary Field in Zimbabwe." In *Regional Cults,* edited by R. Werbner. ASA Monograph 16. London: Academic Press, 1977.

Gluckman, Max. "Analysis of a Social Situation in Modern Zululand." *Bantu Studies* 14 (1940): 1–30, 147–74. Reprint. Rhodes-Livingston Papers, No. 28. Livingstone, Northern Rhodesia: Rhodes-Livingstone Institute, 1958.

———. *Essays on Lozi Land and Royal Property,* Rhodes-Livingston Papers, No. 10. Livingstone, Northern Rhodesia: Rhodes-Livingstone Institute, 1943*a*.

———. *Administrative Organization of the Barotse Native Authorities.* Rhodes-Livingston Institute Communications, No. 10. Livingstone, Northern Rhodesia: Rhodes-Livingstone Institute, 1943*b*.

———. "The Village Headman in British Central Africa." *Africa* 19 (1949): 89–101.

———. *The Judicial Process among the Barotse of Northern Rhodesia* (Zambia). Manchester: Manchester University Press, 1955.

———. "Foreword." In *Tribal Cohesion in a Money Economy,* by William Watson. Manchester: Manchester University Press, 1958*a*.

———. "Some Processes of Social Change, Illustrated with Zululand Data." *African Studies* 1 (1942): 243–60. Reprint. Rhodes-Livingston Papers, No. 28. Livingstone, Northern Rhodesia: Rhodes-Livingstone Institute, 1958*b*.

———. "Anthropological Problems Arising from the African Industrial Revolution" in *Social Change in Modern Africa* edited by A. Southall. London, Oxford University Press for the International African Institute, 1961.

———. *The Ideas in Barotse Jurisprudence.* New Haven: Yale University Press, 1965.

———. *Economy of the Central Barotse Plain.* 1941. Reprint. Rhodes-Livingston Papers, No. 7. Livingstone, Northern Rhodesia: Rhodes-Livingstone Institute, 1968.

———. "Anthropology and Apartheid: The Work of South African Anthropologists." In *Studies in African Social Anthropology,* edited by M. Fortes and S. Patterson, pp. 21–40. London: Academic Press, 1975.

Goody, Jack, ed. *The Developmental Cycle in Domestic Groups.* Cambridge: Cambridge University Press, 1958.

———. "Religion and Ritual: The Definitional Problem." *British Journal of Sociology* 12 (1961): 142–64.

———. *Death, Property and the Ancestors: A Study of the Mortuary Customs of the Lodagaa of West Africa.* London: Tavistock, 1962.

———. *The Myth of the Bagre.* London: Oxford University Press, 1972.

———. *Production and Reproduction: A Comparative Study of the Domestic Domain.* Cambridge: Cambridge University Press, 1976.

———. *The Domestication of the Savage Mind.* Cambridge: Cambridge University Press, 1977.

Goody, Jack, and Tambiah, S. J., eds. *Bridewealth and Dowry.* Cambridge: Cambridge University Press, 1973.

Green, M. *Land Tenure in an Ibo Village.* Monographs on Social Anthropology, No. 6. London: London School of Economics, 1941.

———. *Ibo Village Affairs.* London: Sidgwick and Jackson; New York: Praeger, 1947.

Gugler, Josef, and Flanagan, William G. *Urbanization and Social Change in West Africa.* Cambridge: Cambridge University Press, 1978.

Gulliver, Philip. *The Family Herds.* London: Routledge and Kegan Paul, 1955*a.*

———. *Labour Migration in a Rural Economy.* E. A. Studies, No. 6. Kampala, Uganda: East African Institute of Social Research, 1955*b.*

———. *Land Tenure and Social Change among the Nyakyasa.* E. A. Studies, No. 11. Kampala, Uganda: East African Institute of Social Research, 1958.

———. *Social Control in an African Society.* London: Routledge and Kegan Paul, 1963.

———. "Anthropology." In *The African World, a Survey of Social Research,* edited by Robert A. Lystad, pp. 57–105. New York: Frederick A. Praeger, 1965.

Gutkind, Peter C. W., and Wallerstein, Immanuel, eds. *Political Economy of Contemporary Africa.* Beverly Hills, Calif.: Sage Publications, 1985.

Gutmann, Bruno. *Das Recht der Dschagga.* Arbeiten zur Entwicklungs psychologie, edited by Felix Krueger, vol. 7 Munich: 1926.

Guyer, Jane. "Food, Cocoa and the Division of Labor by Sex in Two West African Societies." *Comparative Studies in Society and History* 22 (1980): 355–73.

———. "Household and Community in African Studies." *African Studies Review* 24, nos. 2, 3 (1981): 87–137.

———. *Family and Farm in Southern Cameroon.* Boston: African Studies Center, 1984*a.*

———. "Naturalism in Models of African Production." *Man,* n.s. 19 (1984*b*): 371–88.

Harris, Grace G. *Casting Out Anger.* Cambridge: Cambridge University Press, 1978.

Hart, Keith. *The Political Economy of West African Agriculture.* Cambridge: Cambridge University Press, 1982.

———. "Social Anthropology of West Africa." *Annual Review of Anthropology* 14 (1985): 243–72.

Hellman, Ellen. "Methods of Urban Fieldwork." *Bantu Studies* 9:3 (1935).

———. "The Native in the Towns." In *The Bantu Speaking Tribes of South Africa,* edited by I. Schapera. London: Routledge, 1937.

———. *Rooiyard: A Sociological Survey of an Urban Native Slum Yard.* Rhodes Livingstone Papers, No. 13. Cape Town: Oxford University Press, 1948.

———. "Urban Areas." In *Handbook of Race Relations in South Africa.* London: Oxford University Press, 1949.

Herskovits, Melville. "The Cattle-Complex in East Africa." *American Anthropologist* 28 (1926): 230–72, 362–80, 949, 528, 633–64.

———. "The Culture Areas of Africa." *Africa* 3 (1930): 59–77.

————. *Dahomey, an Ancient African Kingdom*. 2 vols. New York: J. J. Augustin, 1938.

Hill, Polly. *The Migrant Cocoa Farmers of Southern Ghana: A Study in Rural Capitalism*. Cambridge: Cambridge University Press, 1963.

————. *Population, Prosperity, and Poverty: Rural Kano, 1900–1970*. Cambridge: Cambridge University Press, 1977.

————. *Development Economics on Trial: The Anthropological Case for a Prosecution*. Cambridge: Cambridge University Press, 1986.

Holleman, J. F. *Shona Customary Law*. Cape Town: Oxford University Press, 1952.

Holy, Ladislav. *Religion and Custom in a Muslim Society: The Berti of Sudan*. Cambridge: Cambridge University Press, 1991.

Horowitz, Michael M., and Painter, Thomas, eds. *Anthropology and Rural Development in West Africa*. London: Westview Press, Aldershot, 1986.

Horton, Robin. "African Traditional Thought and Western Science." *Africa* 37, nos. 1 and 2 (1967).

————. "African Conversion." *Africa* 41, no. 2 (1971): 85–108.

————. "On the Rationality of Conversion." *Africa* 45, nos. 3 and 4 (1975): 219–35, 373–99.

Hunter (later Wilson, which see), Monica. *Reaction to Conquest*. London: Oxford University Press, 1936.

James, Wendy. "The Anthropologist as Reluctant Imperialist." In *Anthropology and the Colonial Encounter,* edited by T. Asad, pp. 41–69. London: Ithaca Press, 1973.

————. *The Listening Ebony: Moral Knowledge, Religion and Power among the Uduk of Sudan*. Oxford: Clarendon Press, 1988.

————. "Kings, Commoners and the Ethnographic Imagination in Sudan and Ethiopia." In *Localizing Strategies,* edited by R. Fardon, pp. 96–136. Edinburgh and Washington: Scottish Academic Press and Smithsonian Institution, 1990.

Jules-Rosette, B. *African Apostles*. Ithaca: Cornell University Press, 1975.

————. *Symbols of Change: Urban Transition in a Zambian Community*. Norwood, N.J.: Ablex, 1981.

Junod, Henry A. *The Life of a South African Tribe*. Neuchatel, Switzerland, 1912.

Kaberry, Phyllis. *Women of the Grassfields: A Study of the Economic Position of Women in Bamenda, British Cameroons*. Res. Pub. No. 14. London: Colonial Office, 1952.

Kahn, Joel S., and Llobera, Josep R. "Towards a New Marxism or a New Anthropology." In *The Anthropology of Pre-Capitalist Societies,* 263–329. London: Macmillan, 1981.

Kapferer, Bruce. *Strategy and Transaction in an African Society*. Manchester: Manchester University Press, 1972.

————. "Introduction." In *Transaction and Meaning: Directions in the Anthropology of Exchange and Symbolic Behavior,* edited by Kapferer, 1–24. ASA Essays 1. Philadelphia: ISHI, 1976.

Karp. I. *Fields of Change.* London: Routledge and Kegan Paul, 1978.

Karp, I., and Bird, C. S., eds. *Explorations in African Systems of Thought.* Bloomington: Indiana University Press, 1980.

Kenyatta, Jomo. *Facing Mount Kenya.* London: Secker and Warburg, 1938.

Kopytoff, Igor. "Ancestors as Elders in Africa." *Africa* 41, no. 2 (1971): 129–42.

————. "The Authority of Ancestors." *Man* 16 (1981): 135–37.

Kroeber, A. "The Culture-Area and Age-Area Concepts of Clark Wissler." In *Methods in Social Science,* edited by S. Rice pp. 248–65. Chicago: University of Chicago Press, 1931.

Kuper, Adam. *Anthropologists and Anthropology: The British School 1922–1972.* New York: Pica Press, 1973.

————. *Wives for Cattle.* London: Routledge and Kegan Paul, 1982.

Kuper, Hilda. *An African Aristocracy: Rank among the Swazi.* London: Oxford University Press, 1947.

————, ed. *Urbanization and Migration in West Africa.* Berkeley and Los Angeles: University of California Press, 1965.

Kuper, Leo, and Smith, M. G. *Pluralism in Africa.* Berkeley and Los Angeles: University of California Press, 1969.

Lackner, Helen. "Colonial Administration and Social Anthropology: Eastern Nigeria, 1920–1940." In *Anthropology and the Colonial Encounter,* edited by Talal Asad. London: Ithaca Press, 1973.

LaFontaine, J. S. "The Power of Rights." *Man* 12 (1977): 421–37.

————. *Initiation: Ritual Drama and Secret Knowledge across the World.* Manchester: Manchester University Press, 1985.

Lan, David. *Guns and Rain: Guerrillas and Spirit Mediums in Zimbabwe.* London: James Currey; Berkeley and Los Angeles: University of California Press, 1985.

LeVine, Sarah. *Mothers and Wives.* Chicago and London: University of Chicago Press, 1979.

Levy Bruhl, L. *Les fonctions mentales dans les sociétés inférieures.* Paris: Alcan, 1910.

Lewis, I. M. *A Pastoral Democracy.* London: Oxford University Press, 1961.

————, ed. *Islam in Tropical Africa,* (1966). Reprint. Bloomington and London: Indiana University Press, 1980.

Lienhardt, Godfrey. "Social Anthropology of Africa." In *African Studies since 1945: A Tribute to Basil Davidson,* edited by Christopher Fyfe, pp. 179–85. London: Longman, 1976.

Linares, Olga. *Power, Prayer and Production: The Jola of Casamance, Senegal.* Cambridge: Cambridge University Press, 1992.

Little, K. *West African Urbanization.* Cambridge: Cambridge University Press, 1970.

———. *African Women in Towns: An Aspect of Africa's Social Revolution.* Cambridge: Cambridge University Press, 1973.

Lloyd, Peter C., ed. *The New Elites of Tropical Africa.* London: Oxford University Press for the International African Institute, 1966.

———. *Power and Independence: Urban Africans' Perceptions of Social Inequality.* London: Routledge and Kegan Paul, 1974.

MacGaffey, Janet. *Entrepreneurs and Parasites: The Struggle for Indigenous Capitalism in Zaire.* Cambridge: Cambridge University Press, 1987.

MacGaffey, Wyatt. "African Ideology and Belief." *African Studies Review* 24 nos. 2/3 (1981): 227–74.

———. *Modern Kongo Prophets: Religion in a Plural Society.* Bloomington: Indiana University Press, 1983.

Mair, Lucy. *Primitive Government.* Bloomington: Indiana University Press, 1962.

———. (ed.) *Methods of Study of Culture Contact in Africa.* International African Institute, memorandum 15, 1938.

Malinowski, Bronislaw. "Practical Anthropology." *Africa* 2 (1929): 1.

———. "The Rationalisation of Anthropology and Administration." *Africa* 3 (1930): 4.

Mann, Kristin, and Roberts, Richard, eds. *Law in Colonial Africa.* Portsmouth, N.H.: Heinemann Educational Books, 1991.

Mayer, Philip and Iona. *Townsmen or Tribesmen: Conservatism and the Process of Urbanization in a South African City.* 2d ed. London: Oxford University Press, 1971 (1961).

McCall, Daniel F. "American Anthropology and Africa." *African Studies Bulletin* 10, no. 2 (Sept. 1967).

Meek, C. K. *The Northern Tribes of Nigeria.* London: Oxford University Press, 1925.

———. *A Sudanese Kingdom.* London: K. Paul, Trench, Trubner, 1931.

———. *Law and Authority in a Nigerian Tribe.* London: Oxford University Press, 1937.

Meillassoux, Claude. "Essaid d'interprétation du phénomène économique dans les sociétés traditionelles d'autosubsistance." *Cahiers d'Etudes Africaines* 1 (1960): 38–47.

———. *Anthropologie Economique des Gouro de Côte d'Ivoire.* Paris: Mouton, 1964*a*.

———. "Project de recherche sur les systèmes économiques Africaines." *Journal de la Société des Africanistes* 34 (1964*b*): 292–98.

———. "Elaboration d'un modèle socio-économique éthnologie." *Epistémologie Sociologique* 1–5 (1968*a*): 283–307.

———. *Urbanization of an African Community: Voluntary Associations in*

Bamako. American Ethnological Society Monograph 45. Seattle: University of Washington Press, 1968*b*.

———, ed. *The Development of Indigenous Trade and Markets in West Africa.* London: Oxford University Press, 1971.

———. *Maidens, Meal and Money.* Cambridge: Cambridge University Press, 1984. (Orig. publ. in French, 1975).

Middleton, John. *Lugbara Religion.* London: Oxford University Press, 1960.

———. *Zanzibar: Its Society and Its Politics.* London: Oxford University Press for the Institute for Race Relations, 1965.

Middleton, John, and Tait, D. *Tribes without Rulers.* New York: Humanities Press; London: Routledge and Kegan Paul, 1958.

Miers, Suzanne, and Kopytoff, Igor. *Slavery in Africa.* Madison: University of Wisconsin Press, 1977.

Miner, Horace, ed. *The City in Modern Africa.* New York: Praeger, 1967.

Mitchell, Clyde. *The Yao Village.* Manchester: Manchester University Press, 1956*a*.

———. "The Kalela Dance." *Rhodes-Livingston Institute Papers*, No. 27. Livingstone, Northern Rhodesia: Rhodes-Livingstone Institute, 1956*b*.

———. *Tribalism and the Plural Society.* London: Oxford University Press, 1960.

———. "Theoretical Orientations in African Urban Studies." In *The Social Anthropology of Complex Societies*, edited by M. Banton, pp. 37–68. ASA Monograph 4. London: Tavistock, 1966.

———, ed. *Social Networks in Urban Situations.* Manchester: Manchester University Press for the Institute of Social Research, University of Zambia, 1969.

Moore, Sally Falk. "Archaic Law and Modern Times on the Zambezi." In *Cross-Examinations: Essays in Memory of Max Gluckman*, edited by Philip Gulliver. Leiden: E. J. Brill, 1978.

———. *Social Facts and Fabrications: "Customary Law" on Kilimanjaro 1880–1980.* Cambridge: Cambridge University Press, 1986.

Morrison, Minion K. C., and Gutkind, Peter C. W., eds. *Housing the Urban Poor in Africa.* Foreign and Comparative Studies/African Series 37. Syracuse: Syracuse University, 1982.

Mullings, Leith. *Therapy, Ideology and Social Change: Mental Healing in Urban Ghana.* Berkeley and London: University of California Press, 1984.

Murdock, George P. *Africa, Its Peoples and Their Culture History.* New York: McGraw Hill, 1959.

Murphee, M. W. *Christianity and the Shona.* London: Athlone, 1969.

Murray, Colin. *Families Divided: The Impact of Migrant Labor in Lesotho.* Cambridge: Cambridge University Press, 1981.

Nadel, S. F. *A Black Byzantium.* London: Oxford University Press, 1942.

———. *Nupe Religion.* London: Routledge, 1954.

––––––. *The Theory of Social Structure.* London: Oxford University Press, 1967.

Obbo, Christine. "Women's Careers in Low Income Areas as Indicators of Country and Town Dynamics." In *Town and Country in Central and Eastern Africa,* edited by D. Parkin. London: International African Institute, 1975.

Oppong, Christine. *Middle Class African Marriage.* London: George Allen and Unwin, 1981.

––––––, ed. *Female and Male in West Africa.* London: Allen and Unwin, 1983.

Pan African Association of Anthropologists, B.P. 1862, Yaounde, Cameroun.

Parkin, David. *Palms, Wine and Witnesses.* San Francisco: Chandler, 1972.

––––––. *Neighbors and Nationals in an African City Ward.* London: Routledge and Kegan Paul, 1969.

––––––, ed. *Town and Country in East and Central Africa.* London: International African Institute, 1975.

––––––. *The Cultural Definition of Political Response.* London: Academic Press, 1978.

––––––. "Eastern Africa: The View from the Office and the Voice from the Field." In *Localizing Strategies,* edited by Richard Fardon, pp. 182–203. Edinburgh: Scottish Academic Press; Washington: Smithsonian Institution Press, 1990.

––––––. *Sacred Void: Spatial Images of Work and Ritual among the Giriama of Kenya.* Cambridge: Cambridge University Press, 1991.

Parkin, David, and Nyamwaya, David, eds. *Transformations of African Marriage.* Manchester: Manchester University Press for the International African Institute, 1987.

Paulme, Denise. *Women of Tropical Africa.* Berkeley and Los Angeles: University of California Press, 1960.

Peek, Philip M. "Japanese Anthropological Research on Africa." *African Studies Review* 33, no. 1 (April 1990): 93–131.

Peel, J.D.Y. *Aladura: A Religious Movement among the Yoruba.* London: Oxford University Press, 1968.

––––––. "Conversion and Tradition in Two African Societies: Ijebu and Buganda." *Past and Present* 77 (1977): 108–41.

Pottier, Johan, ed. *Food Systems in Central and Southern Africa.* London: School of Oriental and African Studies, 1985.

––––––. *Migrants No More: Settlement and Survival in Mambwe Villages, Zambia.* Manchester: Manchester University Press for the International African Institute, 1988.

Rabinow, Paul. "Representations Are Social Facts: Modernity and Post-Modernity in Anthropology." In *Writing Culture,* edited by James Clifford and George Marcus, pp. 234–61. Berkeley and Los Angeles: University of California Press, 1986.

Radcliffe-Brown, A. R. *Structure and Function in Primitive Society.* London: Cohen and West, 1952.

Radcliffe-Brown, A. R., and Forde, Daryll, eds. *African Systems of Kinship and Marriage.* London: International African Institute, Oxford University Press, 1950.

Rattray, R. S. *Ashanti.* Oxford: Clarendon Press, 1923.

———. *Ashanti Law and Constitution.* Oxford: Clarendon Press, 1929.

Read, M. *Native Standards of Living and African Culture Change, (Ngoni, Nyasaland).* Memoranda of the International African Institute, No. 16. London, 1938.

Rey, Pierre Philippe. "Articulation des modes de dépendance et des modes de production dans deux sociétés lignagères (Punuet Kunyi du Congo-Brazzaville). *Cahiers d'Etudes Africaines* 9 (1969): 415–40.

———. *Colonialisme, neo-colonialisme et transition au capitalisme.* Paris: Maspero, 1971.

———. *Les Alliances des classes.* Paris: Maspero, 1973.

———. "The lineage mode of production." *Critique of Anthropology* 3 (1975): 27–79.

Richards, A. I. *Land Labour and Diet in Northern Rhodesia.* London: Oxford University Press, 1939.

———. *Bemba Marriage and Present Economic Conditions.* Rhodes-Livingston Papers, No. 4 (1940).

———. *Economic Development and Tribal Change.* Cambridge: Heffer, 1955.

———. *East African Chiefs.* New York: Praeger: London: Faber, 1959.

———. "African Systems of Thought: An Anglo-French Dialogue." *Man,* n.s. 2, no. 2 (1967): 286–98.

Rigby, Peter. *Cattle and Kinship among the Gogo.* Ithaca: Cornell University Press, 1969.

———. "Pastors and Pastoralists: The Differential Penetration of Christianity among East African Cattle Herders." *Comparative Studies in Society and History* 23 (1981): 96–129.

Riley, Bernard W., and Brokensha, David. *The Mbeere of Kenya.* Lanham, London: University Press of America for the Institute for Development Anthropology, 1988.

Robertson, A. F. *The Dynamics of Productive Relationships: African Share Contracts in Comparative Perspective.* Cambridge: Cambridge University Press, 1987.

Ruel, M. *Leopards and Leaders.* London: Tavistock, 1969.

Sargent, Carolyn Fishel. *Maternity, Medicine and Power.* Berkeley and Los Angeles: University of California Press, 1989.

Schapera, Isaac. "Economic Changes in South African Native Life." *Africa* 1 (1928): 170–88.

———. *A Handbook of Tswana Law and Custom.* London: Oxford University Press, 1938.

———. *Married Life in an African Tribe*. London: Faber and Faber, 1940.

———. *Migrant Labor and Tribal Life*. London: Oxford University Press, 1947.

———. *Government and Politics in Tribal Societies*. London: Watts, 1956.

Seligman, C. G. and B. Z. *A Survey of the Pagan Tribes of the Nilotic Sudan*. London: Routledge, 1932.

———. *Races of Africa*. 3d ed. London: Oxford University Press, 1957.

Shipton, Parker. "The Kenyan Land Tenure Reform." In *Land and Society in Contemporary Africa*, edited by R. E. Downs and S. P. Reyna. Hanover and London: University Press of New England, 1988.

———. *Bitter Money: Cultural Economy and Some African Meanings of Forbidden Commodities*. American Ethnological Society Monograph Series 1. Washington D.C.: American Anthropological Association, 1989.

———. "African Famines and Food Security: Anthropological Perspectives." *Annual Review of Anthropology* 19. Palo Alto, Calif.: Annual Reviews, 1990.

Smith, E. W., and Dale, A. *The Ila-speaking Peoples of Northern Rhodesia*. London: Macmillan, 1920.

Smith, M. G. *The Economy of the Hausa Communities of Zaria*. London: HMSO, 1955.

———. "On Segmentary Lineage Systems." *Journal of the Royal Anthropological Institute* 86 (1956): 39–80.

———. *Government in Zazzau*. London: Oxford University Press, 1960.

Snyder, Francis. *Capitalism and Legal Change*. New York: Academic Press, 1981.

Southall, Aidan. *Alur Society*. Cambridge: Cambridge University Press, 1954.

———. *Social Change in Modern Africa*. London: Oxford University Press, 1961.

———. "The Illusion of Tribe." *Journal of African and Asian Studies* 5 (1970): 28–50.

———. *Urban Anthropology*. New York: Oxford University Press, 1973.

———. "The Contribution of Anthropology to African Studies." *African Studies Review* 26, Sept./Dec. (1983): 63–76.

———. "The Segmentary State in Africa and Asia." *Comparative Studies in Society and History*. Vol. 30, no. 1, pp. 52–88. Cambridge: Cambridge University Press, 1988.

Southall, Aidan, and Gutkind, Peter C. W. *Townsmen in the Making*. Kampala, Uganda: East African Institute of Social Research, 1957.

Southwold, Martin. *Bureaucracy and Chiefship in Buganda*, East African Studies, No. 14. London: Kegan Paul for the East African Institute of Social Research, 1960.

Spencer, P. *The Samburu*. London: Routledge and Kegan Paul, 1965.

———. *Nomads in Alliance*. London: Oxford University Press for the School of Oriental and African Studies, 1973.

Sperber, D. *Rethinking Symbolism*. Cambridge: Cambridge University Press, 1974.

Stewart, Frank. *Fundamentals of Age-Group Systems*. London: Academic Press, 1977.

Stocking, George W. *Victorian Anthropology*. New York and London: Free Press, Macmillan, 1987.

Swantz, Marja-Liisa. *Women in Development, a Creative Role Denied: The Case of Tanzania*. London: C. Hurst; New York: St. Martin's Press, 1985.

Talbot, Percy A. *Woman's Mysteries of a Primitive People (Ibibio)*. London, 1915.

———. *Life in Southern Nigeria*. London: Macmillan, 1923.

———. *Peoples of Southern Nigeria*. 4 vols. London: H. Milford, 1926.

Tambiah, Stanley J. *Magic, Science, Religion and the Scope of Rationality*. Cambridge: Cambridge University Press, 1990.

Terray, Emmanuel. *L'Organisation sociale des Dida de Cote d'Ivoire*. Annals de l'Universite d'Abidjan, Serie F, Tome 1, fasc. 2 (1969*a*).

———. *Le Marsixme devant les societes primitives*. Paris: Maspero, 1969*b*.

———. *Marxism and Primitive Societies*. New York: Monthly Review Press, 1972.

———. "Long-Distance Exchange and the Formation of the State: The Case of the Abron Kingdom of Gyaman." *Economy and Society* 3, no. 3 (1974): 315–45.

Thomas, C. Northcote. *Report on the Ibo-speaking Peoples of Nigeria*. London: Harrison and Sons, 1912.

———. *Law and Custom of the Timne and Other Tribes*. London: Harrison, 1916.

Thornton, Robert. *Space, Time and Culture among the Iraqw of Tanzania*. New York: Academic Press, 1980.

Tonkin, Elizabeth. "West African Ethnographic Traditions." In *Localizing Strategies: Regional Traditions of Ethnographic Writing*, edited by Richard Fardon, pp. 137–51. Edinburgh: Scottish Academic Press; Washington: Smithsonian Institution Press, 1990.

Turner, Victor. *Schism and Continuity in an African Society: A Study of Ndembu Village Life*. New York: Humanities Press; Manchester: Manchester University Press, 1957.

Van Binsbergen, W. M., and Geschière, P., eds. *Old Modes of Production and Capitalist Encroachment: Anthropological Explorations in Africa*. London and New York: Kegan Paul International, 1985.

Vaughan, Megan. *Curing Their Ills: Colonial Power and African Illness*. Stanford, Calif.: Stanford University Press, 1991.

Vincent, Joan. *Teso in Transition: The Political Economy of Peasant and*

Class in East Africa. Berkeley and Los Angeles: University of California Press, 1982.

———. *Political Anthropology*. Tucson: University of Arizona Press, 1990.

Watson, William. *Tribal Cohesion in a Money Economy*. Manchester: Manchester University Press, 1958.

Werbner, Richard, ed. *Regional Cults*. ASA Monograph 16. London: Academic Press, 1977.

———. "The Manchester School in South-Central Africa." *Annual Review of Anthropology* 13, pp. 157–85. Palo Alto, Calif.: Annual Reviews, 1984.

Willis, Roy. *Man and Beast*. New York: Basic Books, 1974.

Wilson, Godfrey. "The Economics of Detribalization in Northern Rhodesia" (1942). Reprint. Rhodes Livingston Papers, Nos. 5 and 6, 1968.

Wilson, Godfrey, and Wilson, Monica. *The Analysis of Social Change*. Cambridge: Cambridge University Press, 1945.

Wilson, Monica. *Good Company: A Study of Nyakyusa Age Villages*. London: Oxford University Press, 1952.

———. *Rituals of Kinship among the Nyakyusa*. London: Oxford University Press, 1957.

———. *Communal Rituals of the Nyakyusa*. London: Oxford University Press, 1959.

———. *For Men and Elders: Change in the Relation of Generations and of Men and Women among the Nyakyusa-Ngon People, 1875–1971*. New York: Africana, 1982.

Wissler, Clark. *The American Indian: An Introduction to the Anthropology of the New World*. New York: D. C. McMurtrie, 1917.

2

Africa and the Study of Economics

PAUL COLLIER

> "Few things should be more interesting to a civilised economic theorist than the opportunity to observe the interplay between social institutions and economic behaviour over time and place."
> Robert Solow (1986)

1. Introduction

As SOLOW IMPLIES, observation of the world is the stimulus to creative economic theory. Africa is a gold mine to economists because its economic history has been so extreme: booms, busts, famines, migrations. Because there are so many African countries, often following radically different economic policies, Africa offers a diversity ideally suited to the comparative approach which is the economist's best substitute for the controlled experiment. Until recently this potential has not been realized. Limitations of data have tended to confine analysis to the explanation of broad stylized facts. However, the situation is rapidly changing. This paper will describe recent advances that place African research at the forefront of several major developments in the discipline.

During the 1960s a flood of subsequently eminent economists worked in and on Africa. Particularly notable was the concentration of scholars at the Institute of Development Studies, Nairobi, which included James Tobin, Joseph E. Stiglitz, Peter Diamond, Gary Fields, John Harris and Michael P. Todaro. However, as of the 1960s, the economies of Africa could only be perceived murkily because of the lack of data. At the macroeconomic level, national accounts were rudimentary and available only for a few years. At the microeconomic level, there were few large-scale sample surveys other than for expenditure patterns of urban households. As a result, the major contributions of visiting scholars tended to be analytic explanations of a few features taken to be 'stylized facts' of African economies, notably unemployment and migration. This research was not, on the whole, sustained during the 1970s, and the study of Africa gained the reputation of being both difficult, because of data shortages, and of low quality. The latter damaged the reputation of the subject, and for a while it appeared that Gresham's Law might hold: bad currency driving out good. However, during the 1980s there has been a dramatic improvement in the quantity and quality of African data, especially at the micro level. National statistical bureaus and international agencies, often in collaboration with local and foreign academics, have built up the survey infrastructure essential for quantitative analysis. A few top scholars have really used this opportunity. For example, Professor A. Deaton (Princeton) based the prestigious Oxford Clarendon Lectures (1991) on two data sets which best tested his propositions on the central topic of consumption behavior; one was from the United States, the other from the Côte d'Ivoire. This is indeed part of a wider phenomenon, the upgrading of the economics of development. Scholars of the caliber of Robert Lucas, Willem H. Buiter, and Stanley Fischer are now working in what has previously been regarded as a backwater. However, at present, while containing analytically fascinating and socially important problems, researchable with current data sets, Africa is little studied. This temporary wrinkle in the market—abnormally high returns to research—will presumably make the reputations of some of those scholars who enter the field during the next decade. This essay reviews the past and current contribution of the study of Africa to economics, taking in turn the three major areas of the discipline: macroeconomics, microeconomics, and political economy. In concluding, it will also discuss the potential research agenda.

2. Macroeconomics

After a few remarks on the data, I will focus primarily on the analytic insights provided by work done on the macroeconomics of Africa.

National accounting techniques for Africa were pioneered in the early 1950s: in Southern Africa by Phyllis Deane (1953), in West Africa by A. R. Prest and I. G. Stewart (1954), and in East Africa by A. T. Peacock and D. Dosser (1958). However, consistent series of annual observations are generally only available from the early 1960s onwards. Since the error-correction mechanisms incorporated into much modern time series econometrics typically require around thirty observations, these powerful techniques will become deployable on African economies for the first time during the early 1990s. For some countries, the collection of macroeconomic data improved sufficiently so that from the early 1970s many quarterly series are also available. For example, for Kenya, which has the best macroeconomic data of the African countries, it is now possible to use error correction techniques on around sixty observations of quarterly data. Hence, Africa offers the imminent prospect to applied macroeconomics of perhaps thirty national time series data sets currently virtually unexplored by best-practice techniques.

I now turn to the analytic contribution. At the macroeconomic level the nations of Africa are all *small open economies:* price takers which experience large exogenous external shocks. Among the developed economies there is a profound distinction between those which, like the United States, Japan, and the major European economies, are so substantial in their export markets that they influence the price, and those which are small and therefore price takers. The latter group includes Scandinavia, Australia, the Netherlands, Ireland, and similar countries. Since an analytic macroeconomic model is a radical simplification of reality, a good model must discard huge amounts of detail and capture essentials. For these two types of economy, the "essential" is quite different, and so different macroeconomic models tend to apply. It is notable that the core macroeconomic models which were developed in pre-1939 Britain and in the United States until around 1970 were generally of closed economies: international trade was too small to be worth including. The small open economies model, which makes trade integral, was largely pioneered by economists living in small open economies. Harry Johnson was Canadian, W. Max Corden is Australian, J. P. Neary is Irish, Gus Edgren is Swedish, and Sweder Van Wijnbergen and Jan Willem Gunning are Dutch. The initiating article which formulated the "Salter model" was published in an Australian journal. Of course, the small open economies model has now provided fundamental insights. It is no longer merely used for peripheral economies; rather, it is one of the core macroeconomic models.[1] What has happened is that the particular and distinct economic conditions prevailing outside America and Britain where well over 90% of published economics is written have provoked insights which have been absorbed into the mainstream. The reason for elaborating upon the origins of the small open economies model is that African macroeconomic circumstances are similarly stimulating. The case for this does not rest on an argument by mere analogy but because African conditions highlight precise deficiencies in the small open economies model. When these are rectified we have a richer, more insightful model. Here I will focus on two aspects of African economies which invite extensions of the basic small open economies model.

First, African economies are heavily regulated. International trade is severely restricted by taxes and quantitative restrictions; financial markets are subject to very low interest rate ceilings and sometimes very high minimum liquidity ratios; and labour markets are subject to minimum wages. All of these features can be found to a lesser extent in all economies, including the United States. However, in most economies they can be ignored as a first approximation. In the macroeconomic analysis of Africa it is not possible to ignore the control regime. The key controls must be incorporated into the macroeconomic model. For example, if trade restrictions are actively used, tradable goods cannot be treated as a single aggregate as in the small open economies model since they are no longer a "composite commodity." Importables and exportables must be distinguished separately. There has already been considerable headway in augmenting the small open economies model to incorporate these characteristics and then using it to analyze particular episodes. David Greenaway and Chris Milner (1988) apply the model to the Côte d'Ivoire. D. L. Bevan et al. (1990) apply it to Tanzania and Kenya; T. A. Oyejide Ademola (1986) applies it to Nigeria; and Shantay Devarajan and Jaime de Melo (1987) apply it to the Cameroons. To contrast the augmented small open economies model with the original, consider the impact of a favorable external shock. There are two logical possibilities: trade policy is either exogenous or endogenous. In the former case it might seem that we are back with the original small open economies model. However, this depends upon how trade policy is specified. In most African economies the primary source of trade restrictions is import quotas rather than tariffs. If the import quotas are held constant in the face of the external shock, then the 'implicit tariff' (that tariff rate which would have an equivalent effect on imports to the quota) will change. One bizarre result of the augmented small open economies model is that in this case a favorable external shock will necessarily reduce the volume of exports, whereas in the original model export volumes are likely to increase. However, in many African countries trade policy has been endogenous to the macroeconomic environment: it has been used instead of the exchange rate to maintain a sustainable current account. In this case a favorable external shock induces a trade liberalization, so that the export and nontradable sectors are doubly favored. Recall that in the standard small open economies model, the export sector benefits directly from the terms of trade improvement, and the nontradables sector, from the increase in incomes and hence demand. In the augmented model there is an additional effect as liberalization shifts resources out of the import-substitute sector.

An analogous liberalization can occur in financial markets. Ever since R. McKinnon (1973) and E. Shaw (1973), the concept of financial repression has been a central building block of our understanding of the effect of government regulation of interest rates and cash ratios in financial markets. However, it is in the context of Africa's shock-prone economies that this has been extended to endogenous financial liberalization (Collier and Mayer 1989). A favorable shock increases the savings rate; when combined with inconvertibility this increases the supply of base money. Domestic banks become extremely able to expand their lending, and this drives down the market-clearing interest rate. Bevan et al. (1990) show that in Kenya during the coffee boom the financial system thereby floated off repression as market-clearing rates sank well below official ceilings and bank liquidity rose way above official floors.

So far I have discussed how the standard small open economies model has been augmented to incorporate various aspects of the control regimes common to Africa. As with the original small open economies model, the applicability of the innovations is not confined to the region which inspired them. While a model without an account of the control regime makes no sense in African conditions, whereas in developed countries it offers a passable account of reality, trade and financial controls are clearly endemic to all economies to some degree. I now turn to a second direction in which the small open economies model has been augmented: namely, by taking into account the evident temporariness of many of the shocks which have been a predominant feature of Africa's economies. The small open economies model came into its own for the analysis of a particular shock: the 1973 oil price rise. However, at the time this was perceived as permanent (or very long lasting). By contrast, the shocks which hit Africa in the late 1970s were largely perceived as temporary. New work by A. Deaton and G. Laroque (1990) establishes that the world prices of primary commodities experience occasional price spikes. More than any other region, Africa's economies are highly dependent upon a narrow range of these primary commodity exports and so experience temporary booms. A complete list of the temporary commodity booms experienced by post-Independence Africa would be very long, but some of the salient ones include: phosphates (Morocco), coffee (Kenya, Côte d'Ivoire, Tanzania, Uganda), cocoa (Ghana), tea (Malawi, Kenya), copper (Zambia), groundnuts (Senegal), uranium (Niger), and gold (South Africa). Temporary favorable trade shocks give rise to construction booms as the demand for nontraded capital goods rises. The analytic work on this has been contributed in part by economists working on small open economies other than Africa (for example, Bruno and Sachs 1982); but African experience has also been a major stimulus (Hill 1991, Bevan et al. 1990, Oyejide 1991, Aron 1991, Wetzel 1991, Devarajan 1991, Harrigan 1991, Hill and Knight 1991, Azam 1991, Azam and Chambas 1991).

Finally, when the endogeny of the control regime is combined with the perceived temporariness of external shocks, the outcome is anticipated policy change. For example, consider a temporary boom in an economy in which the government is known to be operating an endogenous trade policy rule. Private agents will therefore be able to anticipate that the resulting trade liberalization is temporary. Recent innovations in the economic theory of temporary liberalizations inspired by Latin American experience (Calvo 1987, 1988), which predict speculative hoarding of inventories as a consequence, can then be incorporated. We arrive at a theory which predicts speculative inventory accumulation in economies subject to volatile export prices, should a particular (and common) policy rule be adopted. This theory is testable, and once established, is clearly pertinent to policy makers. It is currently at the cutting edge of research in the international economics of development (see Collier and Gunning 1992 for a recent survey). Recall the antecedents of this cutting edge. An econometric and theoretical analysis of commodity prices (Deaton and Laroque) was combined with an Africa-inspired theory of endogenous trade policy (Bevan et al.) and a Latin America-inspired theory of anticipated trade liberalization (Calvo). This interaction of data, technique, and observation of an area is surely the core process of analytic innovation.

The small open economies model is not the only area of macroeconomics to have been augmented by African experience. The important advances in fix-price macroeconomic theory presented in Edmond Malinvaud (1977), J. Muellbauer and R. Portes (1978) and J. P. Neary and J. E. Stiglitz (1983) were originally designed to analyze unemployment: hence the title of Malinvaud's book *The Theory of Unemployment Reconsidered*. However, as a by-product, the analysis provided a more general classification of disequilibria, including excess demand: "repressed inflation." African countries, with their widespread price controls, provided a good example of economies with excess demand in the goods market, somewhat akin to Eastern Europe but more readily researchable. A substantial literature has built up, partly analytic (Besley 1988, van der Willigen 1986, Bevan et al. 1987, 1990) and partly empirical (Azam and Faucher 1988, Morrisson and Berthelemy 1987, Bevan et al. 1987a, 1989, Maton et al. 1989). The analytic literature generated some powerful testable corollaries of the theory of repressed inflation. One is that during periods of shortage, supply response will be determined by expectations of the availability of consumer goods. A second is that shortages change the demand for money, as households choose to build up precautionary balances to take advantage of unpredictable opportunities to make purchases during stochastic rationing. A third is that the resulting changes in the demand for money feed back upon supply response: households sell crops in order to achieve these desired money balances. A fourth is that supply response to price can be perverse. These corollaries have all been sustained on Tanzanian data, encompassing conventional supply response equations (see, for example, Bevan et al. 1992). A final and most spectacular corollary is that the repressed inflation phase is unstable, giving rise to an implosion in marketed output. This provides a fresh insight into the rapid decline of the Tanzanian economy in the early 1980s. It also offers insight into the economies of Eastern Europe, both their collapse and the prospective transitions. Professor Max Corden, in his review of *Controlled Open Economies* (Bevan et al. 1990) noted:

> This book is a valuable contribution to development economics and also, even though the authors did not intend it, to the economic theory of socialist decline and transition from socialism. . . . This study was researched and written well before 1989, but reads incredibly like a model designed for the Soviet experience, and should be noted as an early and very useful contribution to the "socialist decline and transition" literature. [W. Max Corden, in *Journal of Development Economics,* 1991]

The extraordinary reductions in the volume of imports which occurred in Africa during the early 1980s and the subsequent large contractions in public expenditure raised the issues of whether production in the private sector was dependent upon them. Did import compression assist manufacturing by reducing competition or damage it through lack of inputs? Did a reduction in public investment increase private investment through "crowding out" effects or reduce it due to complementarities: that is, could public investment "crowd in" private investment? The research on this was pioneered by Professor Benno Ndulu (Dar es Salaam) and subsequently taken up by Professor Lance Taylor (MIT). (See also Besley and Collier 1991.)

3. Microeconomics

During the 1950s there was a debate as to whether the fundamental maximizing assumptions of microeconomics were applicable to Africa. The "substantivist" view that production and consumption behavior were so dominated by reciprocity as to invalidate microeconomics was gradually demolished, a milestone being W. O. Jones' article "Economic Man in Africa" (1960). The application of microeconomic theory to African experience could begin. The discussion of microeconomics is organized into factor markets, product markets, and household economics.

Factor Markets

Africa's labor, credit, and land markets have provided a rich source for economic analysis. They are highly diverse, and so offer great potential for comparison between countries. They are highly dynamic because of population growth (the highest in the world), the very rapid expansion of education, and the monetization of the rural economy with a consequent emergence of credit markets. They offer remarkable contrasts between highly interventionist regulation of some transactions and the complete absence of regulation of others, often in the same market. Hence, they are an excellent test-bed for the theory of regulatory policy. I consider the labor, credit, and land markets in turn.

During the 1950s the study of the African labor market was pioneered by W. Elkan (1956, 1957, 1960). His work constituted the stimulus for an explosion of interest during the next decade. Minimum wage laws, unemployment, and migration inspired major theoretical innovations such as the Harris-Todaro (1977), labor turnover (Stiglitz 1974), and bumping (Fields 1975) models, together with an applied literature which tested the propositions of these models (Barnum and Sabot 1977, and Collier and Lal 1986). The basic puzzle confronting Harris and Todaro, both of whom were in Kenya in the mid-1960s, was the juxtaposition of high urban employment rates with continuing rural-to-urban migration. Their famous solution started from the postulate that urban wages were above the supply price of labor due to minimum wage laws. Whether wages were high for institutional or profit-maximizing reasons, the second postulate of the Harris-Todaro model was that migration and unemployment were motivated by expected earnings. Firms recruited randomly from among the unemployed. The rate of unemployment was therefore the endogenous, equilibrating variable. Although this was a great advance, it was challenged on the grounds that it did not really fit the Kenyan facts too well. Stiglitz, who was in Kenya in the late 1960s, challenged the first postulate. In Kenya, as in several other parts of Africa, urban minimum wages had been increased very substantially during the 1950s and early 1960s due largely to the political circumstances of the run-up to, and realization of, independence. Hence, this seemed a reasonable stylized fact. Stiglitz, however, argued that firms chose to set wage rates high in order to reduce labor turnover. This proved a very influential contribution both for the specific emphasis upon labor turnover and skill formation and, more generally, for its intent to move away from explanations of labor market behavior which invoked institutions as an exogenous "black box" to explanations rooted in optimizing behavior. Evidence that most workers in the Kenyan formal sector earned well in excess of the minimum wage seemed to bear Stiglitz out. The second postulate received some support in econometric tests of migration in Tanzania. Again the authors, N. H. Barnum and R. H. Sabot, were basing their results upon their own time spent in Africa. However, independently, both Sabot, working in Tanzania, and Fields, working in

Kenya, came to the conclusion that firms were not hiring randomly but were using education as a screening device. This was a very early application of fundamental theory developed by A. M. Spence. Implications were soon drawn that the private demand for education would be socially excessive, and this accorded well with the explosive growth in Kenyan private education. In an alternative analysis of the Kenyan labor market, P. Collier and Deepak Lal (1986) argued that real wages were far more flexible than had been credited by the earlier analyses. Whereas real wages had indeed risen massively during the 1950s, Stiglitz and Harris and Todaro et al. were observing not a structural feature of the market but a temporary feature associated with independence. They showed that after the mid-1960s, real wages had continuously fallen to a substantial extent up to the end of their data (1980). This view of flexibility was subsequently confirmed when during the negative external shocks of the 1980s, real wages in Africa fell at quite amazing rates. A new comparative study of the world's labor markets (Horton et al. 1992) finds real wages to be more flexible in Africa than any other major region. This suggests not only that economies change but that "stylized facts" based on casual observation may not bear close scrutiny. Collier and Lal accepted that, in the late 1960s, there was temporarily an excess supply of educated labor, with resulting unemployment, but argued that this reflected not the niceties of probabilistic job search but rather a temporary informational disequilibrium. Using labor force survey data, and an analysis of job advertisements, they showed that employers responded to the sudden increase in the supply of educated labor by paying attention to examination performance. They found that over a period of six years the unemployment rate of those who failed the leaving examination fell from being far higher than those with any sort of pass, to being lower even than those with top passes. The information that employers had raised and the intensified selection criteria had evidently quite rapidly filtered down to school leavers, radically reducing the size of the group for whom employment prospects were probabilistic. Just as the bumping model had been a revision of the Harris-Todaro model in the light of the educational data observed by Fields, so this thesis served as a revision of the bumping model.

At precisely the time when the Kenyan secondary schooling system was expanding explosively, that in neighboring Tanzania was being drastically restricted. If the screening model of the labor market postulated by Spence and Fields was an accurate characterization, this restriction was soundly based. Kenya was squandering very scarce resources while households pursued a beggar-my-neighbor strategy of giving their children an advantage which depended, by hypothesis, upon one child getting more education than another. One child's gain in acquiring a characteristic (namely, education) which improved the chances of employment, was another child's loss. The rival to the screening theory was the human capital account of the labor market. In this theory, education was useful because it conferred skills rather than preferential treatment. On the human capital account of the labor market, Kenya was wisely investing in its skill base and the Tanzanian policy was grossly misguided. This remarkable difference between Kenyan and Tanzanian educational policies has constituted a perfect 'natural experiment' in economic policy. John B. Knight (Oxford) and R. H. Sabot (Williams) recognized that this provided the ideal context for the testing of the screening versus the human capital model. In pioneering work, Knight and Sabot (1987a, 1987b, 1990), and Boissiere, Knight, and Sabot (1985) conducted matched surveys in Nairobi and Dar es Salaam. Their data set included cognitive testing and so was able to distinguish between inherited and educationally acquired characteristics. This and other features led a reviewer to describe their work as being the best of its kind in the entire human capital literature. Refuting the drift of the earlier work, their research strongly vindicated the human capital model, in the process suggesting that it was the Tanzanian rather than the Kenyan policy which had been misguided.

The "natural experiment" exploited so successfully by Knight and Sabot is illustrative of a general feature of Africa: policy diversity in otherwise similar economies. There are numerous cases of pairs of countries with radically different responses to common events, some of which have been analyzed and some neglected. To give some examples, the Ghana–Côte d'Ivoire comparison is a rich one for beverage booms and slumps under different macroeconomic policies. The Kenya-Tanzania pairing has been used not just by Knight and Sabot but by Bevan et al. (1989, 1990) due to radically different taxation of exports. Malawi and Madagascar have been paired by F. Pryor (Swarthmore) because of radically different approaches to poverty alleviation and growth in economies dominated by peasant agriculture. Only from a great distance do African economies appear uniform. Africa's policy diversity can be as valuable to the economist as its ecological diversity is to the botanist.

Whereas there has been a long tradition of research on labor markets, that on African financial markets is more rudimentary. This is surprising because Africa offers one of the great "natural experiments" in financial policy, analogous to the Kenya-Tanzania natural experiment in educational policy. The financial experiment is the contrast of the fixed and fully convertible hard currency of the Franc zone with the inconvertible and periodically devalued currencies of Anglophone Africa. The Franc zone, being a grouping of thirteen countries, additionally provides a rare example of currency union. The recent attempts at currency union in Europe have attracted huge research attention; the union which has existed in Africa for over forty years has been little studied. Reviewing African economic studies in 1965, W. T. Newlyn lamented: "African economic studies within each language area have proceeded almost completely independently" (p. 37). With a few exceptions the same could be said today, the major exceptions being work at Harvard by Professor Devarajan (1987, 1991) and by the group at CERDI, University of Clermont-Ferrand, under Professors Guillaumont (1988, 1989). The essence of the Franc zone is that adherence to a rule specifying fiscal discipline has as its quid pro quo an undertaking from the French Treasury to finance balance of payments deficits should they arise. Countries forego national central banks and so are unable to resort to money printing. This clear and permanent rule-based conditionality can be contrasted with the ad hoc, discretionary conditionality of donor lending to developing countries. During the 1980s the Franc zone has encountered severe problems. Real money demand fell because of the negative external shocks, and some member governments managed to evade budgetary controls by subverting the banking system, both generating large payments deficits. However, donor conditionality cannot be regarded as a success either, and arguably, the Franc zone in some modified form offers a more secure basis for the maintenance of sound macroeconomic policies. The evaluation of these essentially alternative systems of policy restraint will be one of the central research tasks of the 1990s.

African financial markets also offer intriguing puzzles at the microlevel. The absence of informal deposit-taking institutions was one the phenomena explained by Hans Binswanger and colleagues in influential theoretical work (Binswanger and MacIntyre 1987) which sought to incorporate the specific conditions facing households in semiarid agriculture. His hypothesis, that the high covariance of withdrawals would require such deposit-takers to retain a very high cash-to-deposits ratio and so be uneconomic, is plausible but remains to be tested empirically. The structure of West African rotating savings and credit associations (Roscas) has similarly attracted the attention of Professor T. J. Besley at Princeton University. The theoretical work (1993) has been directly inspired by field trips to West Africa. Extensive fieldwork in Northern Nigeria has enabled Professor C. Udry of Northwestern University (1990) to challenge the conventional view of rural credit markets as using collateral and interlocking of contracts to overcome informational asymmetries between borrowers and lenders. As a result of an attachment to the Department of Agricultural Economics at Ahmadu Bello University, he was able to conduct fieldwork refuting the importance of informational asymmetries in his study area. The extended kinship group served as an effective information channel and obviated the need for either interlinked contracts or collateral.[2]

The economics of land markets and land reform has been a major area of research with Asia as its primary focus. Again, the study of African experience is valuable both because it is significantly different from Asia and because within Africa there is such rich diversity. As with several of the other studies discussed above, African diversity has been harnessed by means of a comparative approach, an excellent instance being the new study of rural factor markets and agricultural policy directed by Professor Uma Lele (1989). Whereas in Asia, sharecropping is common, in Eastern and Southern Africa it is virtually nonexistent, other forms of tenancy also being rare. The original explanation for this is land abundance. However, with rapidly rising population densities, parts of Africa are experiencing a dramatic switch into land scarcity. They provide a laboratory experiment in the economics of rapidly changing factor proportions and the emergence of marketable property rights. The reasons for failure in the land market and its costs in terms of allocative efficiency have received a little analysis (Collier 1983, 1989). A primarily theoretical analysis was both triggered and tested by East African data.

The weakness of East African land and credit markets have left some households badly placed to respond to the rapid changes brought about by population growth and new agricultural opportunities, such as tea and improved livestock. Recent analysis (Bevan et al. 1989) suggests that there is a ladder of activities offering radically different economic returns. Poverty is associated with being confined to low-yielding activities such as grain production. Households appear to be constrained to these low-return activities because of an inability to borrow or to rent land, and because of the limited mechanisms for the spread of information.

In addition to the stress on land allocation generated by rapid population growth, Africa has had some truly remarkable policy experiments towards land allocation. Perhaps the most notable single experiment was the Ujamaa villagization initiative in Tanzania during the 1970s. Around two-thirds of the rural population was resettled from scattered dwellings into villages. By the early 1980s the Tanzanian experiment was attracting very widespread media and academic interest and being held up as a model for other developing countries. The cooperative agriculture experiment was studied by Professor L. Putterman (1986) in work which elegantly combined a theoretical analysis of the principal-agent problem with empirical material. Further research by Professor S. Wangwe of the University of Dar es Salaam, Samir Radwan of the ILO, and myself, established an assessment of the ujamaa villages radically different from the popular image, in work which won the Edgar Graham prize for the best study of Asia or Africa (Collier, Radwan and Wangwe 1986). They found that the reform had reduced mean holding size. Since the population was no longer able to reside on the holding, villagization was creating localized land scarcities in the neighborhood of the village. They also found that despite the reform there was considerable intra-village inequality, attributable to differences in endowments of education, land, and access to wage employment.

Having reviewed the analyses of the labor, credit, and land markets, it is appropriate to discuss the major innovation in applied social cost benefit analysis which was primarily designed to take into account factor market distortions. During the 1960s, at precisely the time when there was a flood of interest in Africa and many top scholars were visiting (particularly Nairobi), a revolution in this branch of economic theory was taking place. I. Little and J. Mirrlees (1968) pioneered a new technique in social cost benefit analysis using the device of shadow pricing. The new technique would clearly stand or fall by whether it was applicable. Since the whole point of shadow pricing was to make allowances for distortions in markets, the technique could best be tested in economies where markets were believed to be distorted. Kenya was a natural choice for this work which attracted researchers of subsequent renown: N. Stern (1972), D. M. Newbery (1976), Maurice Scott (1976). Indeed, it is reasonable to say that the applied work carried out in Africa during the late 1960s and early 1970s laid the foundations for the social cost benefit analysis which has since been the standard technique for the public appraisal of projects.

Product Markets

Two features of African product markets have attracted research attention: the coexistence of official and parallel markets, and the large price fluctuations in the prices of agricultural commodities.

There has been a revival of interest in the economics of parallel markets. For example, a recent conference at Harvard has yielded a special issue of a journal (*World Development,* December 1989) and a book (Roemer and Jones 1991). Much of the material for this revival has been African. It could scarcely be more timely: the events in Eastern Europe have placed the issues discussed in that literature at the forefront of policy debate. As the economies of Eastern Europe liberalilze at different rates, cross-border smuggling is already becoming the massive phenomenon which it has long been in Africa. Economists attempting to research its Eastern European manifestation will get a head start by reading (among others) J. P. Azam's analysis (1992) of smuggling between Niger and Nigeria.

One of the important and long-running policy debates in economics has been on the stabilization of commodity prices. The national and international attempts by public agencies to stabilize prices have inspired major theoretical analyses of which Newbery and Stiglitz (1981) is perhaps the most celebrated. The underlying motivation for price stabilization was the notion, popular both in government and academic circles, that private agents would misread and/or misuse price shocks. As discussed above, recent work by Deaton and Laroque (1989) has established that most commodity price shocks tend to be short, sharp booms (reflecting stock-outs) rather than crashes. Hence, the empirical question implicitly answered by this notion was how private agents, most notably peasant farmers, would respond to temporary windfall price increases. The recent work on the Kenyan coffee boom (Bevan et al. 1989) established from survey data that Kenyan coffee farmers had saved around 70% of the income windfall. Not only was this a very high rate by any standards, it far exceeded that of the Kenyan government from that part of the windfall which it acquired. Hence, empirical work from Africa called into question a long held but essentially untested view which had been highly influential in the determination of policy.

In important recent work on the role on marketing boards, A. Powell (1990) and C. L. Gilbert (1991) advocate that the boards could avoid incentive compatibility problems and yet provide a useful function by offering preannounced floor prices financed by buying exchange put options. Powell's doctoral thesis followed the pattern of theoretical innovation stimulated by and informing an African experience so successfully adopted by C. Udry.

Household Economics

The economics of the rural household has become a particularly exciting area. Because it combines production, labor supply, consumption, and asset decisions, it offers rich extensions of the fundamental household model (of which Deaton and Muellbauer 1980 and Singh, Squire, and Strauss 1986 are perhaps the classic statements). Since large parts of Africa are semiarid, risk is likely to play a central role in behavior. In a highly influential study of famines in Africa and Asia, Amartya Kumar Sen (1981) demonstrated that the phenomenon of famine was best understood as the consequence of income collapse at the level of particular households rather than as a decline in food availability at the level of the society. However, agricultural conditions in Africa and Asia are substantially different. Hans Binswanger and J. McIntyre (1987) derive analytically a set of postulates about rural markets, starting from the special features of the land-abundant, semiarid agriculture which characterizes much of Africa but little of Asia. Neither Sen nor Binswanger and McIntyre were able to supplement their analysis with analysis of large-sample African household data sets. However, during the 1980s such micro data sets were gathered in Africa which are now providing the basis for testing and refining hypotheses. Professor Deaton has led much of this work on savings behavior, on labor markets, and on testing for boy-girl discrimination in expenditure in Africa. Recent extensions by L. Haddad and J. F. Hoddinott (1991) establish that the pattern of household expenditure is influenced by the gender composition of the household: the greater the proportion of household income generated by women the greater the proportion of consumption which is on food. The most likely interpretation of this result is that female contribution to household income increases female influence over expenditure and so increases the weight placed upon female preferences. This has important implications for two branches of economics: the household as a decision unit and the measurement of poverty. A lengthy debate in economics has focused upon whether the household should be seen as the irreducible quantum of decision unit or whether it should be analyzed as a bargaining process between its members: the Haddad and Hoddinott evidence points to the latter, although the former has been far more common practice. This analysis could be replicated in developed countries, for example, to see whether transfer payments should be targeted to women. Recent developments in the measurement of poverty have suggested, using Asian data, that food consumption is the best indicator of household permanent income. But the Haddad and Hoddinott evidence suggests that food consumption may reflect the gender structure of income rather than simply its level. As with Udry, the Haddad and Hoddinott study is an example of a theoretical construct, which had been developed in the context of Asian data, coming to grief (or needing substantial refinement) when tested upon African data.

More generally, Africa has been at the forefront of the new economics of viewing household decisions as a bargaining process because in much of Africa there is no correspondence between the household and the nuclear family: the household is manifestly multicentered. In developed countries the analogous split within the household is multigenerational; hence Becker's "rotten kid" theorem (for an African application see Hoddinott 1992). However, the division of the household into gender-based rather than generation-based decision units opens far wider scope for principal-agent problems: in effect the whole realm of production.

The importance of incorporating the gender distinction into analysis is illustrated by a recent study of the spread of agricultural innovation in Kenya (Appleton et al., forthcoming). Since the acquisition of information is costly, agents copy others. Copying can take two forms: people can observe the outcomes of the innovations adopted by pioneers and, if those outcomes appear favorable, themselves follow suit. In effect, the experiences of pioneers are cheap additions to the information sets of others. Additionally, agents can observe the decision of pioneers to innovate. If the innovators are thought by the agent to be sufficiently like him or herself, then the agent may choose to imitate the decision without incurring the costs of gathering information and calculating the returns: the agent free-rides on the decisions of pioneers. Appleton et al. were able to show that both these processes of imitation were significant in the adoption of tree crops in Kenya: people copied their neighbors. Because tree crops take several years to mature, it was possible to distinguish between imitation induced by mature trees (where the economic returns could be observed) and that induced by new plantings (where only the decision to plant could be observed). Further, in work which appears to be innovative, they were able to show that the imitation of neighbors was gender-specific: male-headed households only copied other male-headed households, female-headed households only copied other female-headed households. A likely interpretation of this result is that the informational value of observed behavior depends upon the extent to which the potential imitator regards the potential role model as being in similar circumstances, for only then is copying appropriate. This research is of both methodological and policy interest. It could be applied to characteristics of self-identification other than gender, such as income, race, or education. In the specific case of Kenyan tree crops, it suggests that the public process of information dissemination, namely, the extension service, needs to be targeted towards female-headed households (a sizeable group), leaving the private process of copying to complete the spread of innovation among male-headed households.

4. Political Economy

Political economy was for some years primarily the domain of Marxists. Within this tradition, Africa provided interesting scope for the extension of the Marxist framework. For example, a reviewer of Kitching's 1980 study on the making of an Africa petit bourgeoisie rated it as so innovative that Marx himself would have been interested! However, the study of political economy has more recently come back into the mainstream of economic analysis, notably through the rise of public choice theory. Those economists with experience of South Africa made early contributions to the modern approach to political economy through formal analyses of apartheid (for example, Knight and MacGrath 1977, 1987).

Many of the hypotheses of political economy cannot be tested statistically because of a shortage of observations. This is, of course, particularly acute in the analysis of a single episode in a single country. For this reason, much of the recent work in political economy has been comparative, based on samples of countries which if not large enough for statistical testing, have still proved illuminating. The scholars who have directed these research programs have looked, when commissioning country studies, for interesting variation. African experience has figured prominently because it offers wide variety of both government policies and economic structures, due to the very large number of states. A major new study of the political economy of poverty, equity, and growth by Professors D. Lal (UCLA) and Myint (LSE) has drawn heavily upon African experience (see Lal and Myint, forthcoming). Volumes were commissioned on Ghana (Rimmer 1991), Malawi and Madagascar (Pryor 1990), and Nigeria (Bevan et al. 1992). Lal's central thesis draws particularly heavily upon the Ghana study. He argues that the dirigiste state "withers away" not as a matter of choice but through overexploitation of its tax base. As this continues, a point is reached at which, in order to reassert control, the state must liberalize. Hence, deregulation is not the "rolling back" of the state but an essential step in its reemergence. The deregulation in Ghana appears to accord with this account: certainly, by the time of the policy change in 1983, the share of government revenue in GDP had eroded to a remarkable extent, despite very high tax rates. Since the reforms, this revenue base has to some extent been restored.

A second new study of political economy, focused on the problems of transition from dirigisme, directed by R. Bates and A. Krueger (Duke), also chose to commission two of its six case studies on African experience—Ghana and Zambia (see Bates and Krueger, eds. 1992). The Zambian reform attempts provided an ideal test-bed for theories of policy formation. A sweeping reform program had been adopted by the government in 1985 only to be abandoned eighteen months later and then readopted in 1989. During 1990 the state moved from a single party to a multiparty system. The interplay between the interests of donors, labor unions, the business community, the parastatal companies, the political party, and different regions which determined these outcomes provided fertile material for collaborative research between political science and economics.

Because the key agents of observation in political economy are usually governments (and the interests which operate upon them), Africa with its multiplicity of states is likely to figure prominently in the resurgence of this subject.

5. Conclusion

Writing in 1966, Douglas Rimmer reviewed the economic study of Africa. Although his review was confined to British work, his fundamental assessment was sadly accurate for the entire field:

> The study of African economies . . . lies in the hands of a small number of relatively isolated individuals. . . . Their work lies very much on the fringe of British economic studies. [Rimmer 1966, p. 88]

This assessment could equally have been made twenty years later. During the intervening years there were fine, sustained contributions by S. K. Helleiner, Carl Eicher and Carl Liedholm, Arthur Hazlewood, and Rimmer himself, but these did not amount to a critical mass. Today such an assessment would be quite untenable. Within Africa there is the large, well-organized, and vibrant African Economic Research Consortium. In universities around the world, Deaton and Besley at Princeton, Gersovitz at Michigan, Udry at Northwestern, Devarajan at Harvard, O'Connell at Swarthmore, Eicher and Liedholm at MSU, Lele at Florida, Sahn and Thorbecke at Cornell, Sabot at Williams, Behrman at Penn, Helleiner at Toronto, Gunning at Amsterdam, Azam and the Guillaumonts at Clermont-Ferrand, Bourguignon at Paris, Bigsten at Gothenburg, Sarris at Athens, Faini at Milan, Oyejide and Ajayi at Ibadan, Ndulu and Wangwe at Dar es Salaam, Kanbur and Elbadawi at the Research Department of the World Bank, and my own group at Oxford (plus the many names which are omitted) collectively constitute a substantial base from which the new wave of economic research on Africa is being launched. The skeptical reader will hesitate at the assertion of a "new wave," and so I turn to two current objective indicators. The lifeblood of economic research flows through journals: genuine new waves generate important specialist journals. In 1992 two new journals on African economies were launched, the *Journal of African Development and Finance* and the *Journal of African Economies,* published by Oxford University Press. The *JAE* is attracting support from the highest levels of the profession:

> Especially now, Africa's economic problems and progress need both more careful analysis and more discussion, in Africa and abroad. This new journal, with its high level international board of Editors, promises to be just what is needed: an outlet and a stimulant for a growing volume of applied research on Africa. [Professor Stanley Fischer (MIT)]

Interest in economic development issues has increasingly shifted to those that are dominant in Africa. The *Journal of African Economies* promises to perform an important function. It should not only publish some of the best economic research on Africa, but also provide important examples of high-quality research on applied African economic issues, and thus be a catalyst for improving the quality of future research on these issues. [Professor Jere Behrman (University of Pennsylvania)]

The lifeblood of economic research is financed through the research councils: genuine "new waves" win funding. In 1990 the British Economic and Social Research Council held a major contest, the first in a decade, to establish a new Designated Research Centre. All fields of social science were eligible and some 150 bids were entered. The Centre for the Study of African Economies, at Oxford University, was the winning submission. In the same year, the European Commission held a contest for the creation of collaborative European research networks in social science. A network of Africanist economists was among the winners. These are all objective indications of the expansion of high quality research which is now under way.

What is the agenda for this research? What will a paper such as this written a decade hence identify as the salient contributions? In macroeconomics I will suggest three areas. First, as in Eastern Europe, many African economies are facing the problems of transition from socialism. Many of the leading economics journals are currently including special issues or symposia on this transition, and it is to be expected that the subject will be a popular areas for research in the coming decade. As noted by Professor Corden above, the economics of Africa has already made a contribution to the study of this transition; however, African socialism was usually rather different from that in Eastern Europe. Markets were usually controlled, taxed, or subsidized rather than being suppressed. Property rights, though sometimes contestable, were seldom absent. African governments have generally been less credibly committed to policy change than in Eastern Europe because the impetus for reform is often external rather than grounded in domestic ideological revolution. The African transitions, more numerous, more nuanced, more complex, will prove to be the more rewarding laboratory in which "to observe the interplay between social institutions and economic behavior." A second area of macroeconomics which will, I suspect, be pioneered by Africanists will be the economics of the transition from war to peace. Of course, the notion of a "peace dividend" is happily widespread following the demise of most Communist regimes. However, the orders of magnitude of the peace dividend are often spectacularly higher in Africa. While NATO has been fighting a costly cold war, Africa has been fighting ruinous civil wars. In Uganda, Ethiopia, Angola, and Chad lengthy and destructive conflicts have recently ended. Conflicts continue, but with moves towards peace in Mozambique, Sudan, Liberia, and Somalia. The economics of rebuilding such economies, of reorienting budgets dominated by military expenditure, has not been explored since the 1940s. That is, it has not been analyzed subsequent to the technical revolution in the discipline. A third area of macroeconomics to which Africanists can be expected to make a key contribution is that of monetary union. The currently proposed European monetary union and the proliferation of new states in Eastern Europe and Central Asia place this topic high on the agenda on general interest. However, European experience with monetary union has been too limited for much systematic research. Africa offers several sustained examples of monetary union (the franc, rand, escudo, and sterling zones). Indeed, it offers many examples of most types of exchange-rate arrangement. Lacking the control experiment, economists will find this variety of researchable experience a highly valuable resource.

In microeconomics I will suggest two areas in which research on Africa will be pioneering. In agricultural economics, panel data sets will be constructed which will permit major advances in the analysis of the dynamics of the peasant household, in particular, behavior towards risk and behavior in the presence of credit market constraints. Because the peasant household is involved in both production and consumption decisions, such panel data sets are far richer bases for study than panel data sets on households or firms in developed economies. In industrial economics, Africa offers an excellent area for research on the growth and death of the micro-enterprise. Black Africa has a higher proportion of its laborforce as self-employed, small-scale entrepreneurs than any other region. New work by Carl Liedholm promises to tap the potential that the study of African enterprise has, to further our understanding of this fundamental aspect of the growth process.

In short, Africa is ceasing to be the great unexplored area of applied economics. African economic policy manifestly matters, and applied economics has an important role to play in its improvement. But over and above this, the combination of fruitful intellectual challenge and sheer fun will prove irresistible to the coming academic generation.

NOTES

1. For example, it is used extensively in the Dornbusch textbook *Open Economy Macroeconomics*.

2. It may be remarked that on leaving Yale, Urdy declined offers from MIT and Stanford, choosing Northwestern because of its investment in the study of

Africa. A similar career choice may be noted in respect of Professor Gersovitz, who on leaving Princeton chose Michigan because of its long-standing focus on the study of Africa.

REFERENCES

Appleton, S.; Berger, K.; Bevan, D.; Collier, P.; Gunning, J. W.; and Hoddinott, J. *Public Services and Household Allocation in Africa: Does Gender Matter?* Washington, D.C.: World Bank, forthcoming.

Aron, J. "Copper Price Shocks in Zambia: 1964–78." CSAE. Mimeographed. Oxford University, 1991.

Azam, J. P. "Niger and the Naira: Some Monetary Consequences of Cross-Border Trade with Nigeria." In *Economic Reform in Sub-Saharan Africa,* edited by A. Chhibber and S. Fischer. Washington, D.C.: World Bank, 1991.

———. "The Uranium Boom in Niger (1975–1982)." CERDI. Mimeographed. University of the Auvergne, 1991.

Azam, J. P., and Chambas, G. "The Groundnuts and Phosphates Boom in Senegal (1974–77)." CERDI. Mimeographed. University of the Auvergne, 1991.

Azam, J. P., and Faucher, J. J. "The Supply of Manufactured Goods and Agricultural Development: The Case of Mozambique." OCED. Development Centre, Paris, 1988.

Barnum, N. H., and Sabot, R. H. "Education, Employment Probabilities, and Rural-Urban Migration in Tanzania," *Oxford Bulletin of Economics and Statistics* 39 (1977).

Bates, R., and Krueger, A., eds. *Political and Economic Interactions in Economic Policy Reform,* Oxford: Basil Blackwell, 1993.

Besley, T. J. "Rationing Income Effects and Supply Responses: A Theoretical Note." *Oxford Economic Papers* 40, no. 2 (1988).

Besley, T., Coate, S., and Loury, G. "Rotating Savings and Credit Associations, Credit Markets and Economic Efficiency." *American Economic Review* 83 (1993).

Besley, T. J., and Collier, P. "Import Compression and Trade Policy." In *Trade Policy and African Development,* edited by R. Kanbur. CEPR. Manchester: Manchester University Press, 1991.

Bevan, D. L., Collier, P., and Gunning, J. W. *Peasants and Governments: An Economic Analysis.* Oxford: Clarendon Press, 1989.

———. *Controlled Open Economies: A Neoclassical Approach to Structuralism.* Oxford: Clarendon Press, 1990.

———. "Anatomy of an External Shock: The Kenyan Coffee Boom. *Journal of African Economies,* 1, no. 2 (1992).

———. *Agriculture and the Policy Environment: Kenya and Tanzania*. OCED. Paris, 1993.

Bevan, D. L., Bigsten, A., Collier, P., and Gunning, J. W. "Peasant Supply Response in Rationed Economies." *World Development* 15, no. 4 (1987).

———. *East African Lessons on Economic Liberalization*. London: Trade Policy Research Center, 1987*a*.

Binswanger, H. P., and McIntyre, J. "Behavioral and Material Determinants of Production Relations in Land-Abundant Tropical Agriculture." *Economic Development and Cultural Change* 36 (1987).

Boissiere, M., Knight, J. B., and Sabot, R. H. "Earnings, Schooling Ability, and Cognitive Skills." *American Economic Review* 75, no. 5 (1985).

Bruno, M., and Sachs, J. "Energy and Resource Allocation: A Dynamic Model of the 'Dutch Disease.'" *Review of Economic Studies* 49 (1982): 845–59.

Calvo, G. A. "On the Costs of Temporary Policy." *Journal of Development Economics* 27 (1987): 245–62.

———. "Costly Trade Liberalizations: Durable Goods and Capital Mobility." *IMF Staff Papers* 35, no. 3 (1988): 461–73.

Collier, P. "Malfunctioning of African Rural Factor Markets: Theory and a Kenyan Example." *Oxford Bulletin of Economics and Statistics* 45, no. 2 (1983).

———. "Oil Shocks and Food Security in Nigeria." *International Labour Review* 127, no. 6 (1988).

Collier, P., and Gunning, J. W. "Trade and Development: Protection, Shocks and Liberalisation." In *Surveys of International Trade Theory*, edited by D. Greenaway and A. Winters. London: Macmillan, 1992.

Collier, P., and Lal, D. *Labour and Poverty in Kenya 1900–1980*. Oxford: Clarendon Press, 1986.

Collier, P., and Mayer, C. "The Assessment: Financial Liberalization, Financial Systems, and Economic Growth." *Oxford Review of Economic Policy* 5, no. 4 (1989).

Collier, P., Radwan, S., and Wangwe, S. *Labour and Poverty in Rural Tanzania*. Oxford: Clarendon Press, 1986.

Deane, P. *Colonial Social Accounting*. Cambridge: Cambridge University Press, 1953.

Deaton, A., and Laroque, G. "On the Behavior of Commodity Prices." *Review of Economic Studies* 59, no. 4 (1989).

———. "Saving in Developing Countries: Theory and Review." In *Proceedings of the World Bank Annual Conference on Development Economics 1989*. Supplement to the *World Bank Economic Review* and the *World Bank Research Observer* (1990): 61–90.

———. "Saving and Income Smoothing in Côte d'Ivoire." *Journal of African Economies* 1, no. 1 (1992).

Deaton, Angus, and Muellbauer, John. *Economics and Consumer Behavior*. Cambridge: Cambridge University Press, 1980.

Devarajan, S., and de Melo, J. "Evaluating Participation in African Monetary Unions: A Statistical Analysis of the CFA Zone," *World Development* 15, no. 4 (1987).

———. "Membership in the CFA Zone: Odyssean Journey or Trojan Horse?" In *Economic Reform in Sub-Saharan Africa,* edited by A. Chhibber and S. Fischer. Washington, D.C.: World Bank, 1991.

Dornbusch, Rudiger. *Open Economy Macroeconomics.* New York: Basic Books, 1980.

Elkan, W. "An African Labour Force: Two Case Studies in East African Factory Employment." *East African Studies,* no. 7. EAISR. Kampala, 1956.

———, ed. *Economic Policy and Labour: A Study in Uganda's Economic History.* East African Studies, no. 10. EAISR. Kampala, 1957.

———. *Migrants and Proletarians: Urban Labour in the Economic Development of Uganda.* London: Oxford University Press, 1960.

Fields, G. "Rural-Urban Migration, Urban Unemployment and Under-Employment and Job-Search Activity in LDCs." *Journal of Development Economics* (June 1975).

Gilbert, C. L. "Domestic Price Stabilization Schemes for Developing Countries." Mimeographed. Queen Mary and Westfield College, University of London, 1991.

Greenaway, D., and Milner, C. "Intra Industry Trade and the Shifting of Protection Across Sectors." *European Economic Review* 32 (1988).

Guillaumont, P., and Guillaumont, S. "The Implications of European Monetary Union for African Countries." *Journal of Common Market Studies* 83, no. 2 (1989).

Guillaumont, P., Guillaumont, S., and Plane, P. "Participating in African Monetary Unions: an Alternative Evaluation." *World Development* 16, no. 5 (1988).

Haddad, L., and Hoddinott, J. F. "Gender Aspects of Household Expenditures and Resource Allocation in the Cote d'Ivoire." CSAE. Mimeographed. Oxford, 1991.

Harrigan, J. "From Boom to Bust: Malawi's Positive 1977–1979 Trade Shock." IDPM. Mimeographed. University of Manchester, 1991.

Harris, J., and Todaro, M. P. "Migration, Unemployment and Development: A Two-Sector Analysis." *American Economic Review* (1977).

Hill, C. B. "A Precautionary Demand for Savings and Tests of the Permanent Income Hypothesis in Botswana." Mimeographed. Williams College, 1991.

Hill, C. B., and Knight, J. B. "The Diamond Boom: Expectations and Economic Management in Botswana." Williams College and CSAE. Mimeographed. Oxford University, 1991.

Hoddinott, J. F. "Rotten Kids or Manipulative Parents: Are Children Old Age Security in Western Kenya?" *Economic Development and Cultural Change* 40, no. 3 (1992).

Horton, S., Kanbur, R., and Mazumdar, D., eds. *Labor Markets in Structural Adjustment*. EDI. Washington D.C.: World Bank, 1992.

Jones, W. O. "Economic Man in Africa." *Food Research Institute Studies* 1, no. 2 (May 1960): 107–34.

Kitching, G. *Class and Economic Change in Kenya: The Making of an African Petite-Bourgeoisie*. New Haven, Conn.: Yale University Press, 1980.

Knight, J. B., and McGrath, M. D. "An Analysis of Racial Wage Discrimination in South Africa." *Oxford Bulletin of Economics and Statistics* 39, no. 4 (1977).

———. "The Erosion of Apartheid in the South African Labour Market: Measures and Mechanisms." IES Discussion Paper 35 (1987).

Knight, J. B., and Sabot, R. H. "Educational Expansion, Government Policy and Wage Compression." *Journal of Development Economics* 26, no. 385 (1987a).

———. "Educational Policy and Labour Productivity: An Output Accounting Exercise." *Economic Journal* 97, no. 3 (1987b).

———. *Education, Productivity and Inequality*. Oxford: Oxford University Press, 1990.

Lal, D., and Myint, Hla. *Poverty, Equity and Growth in Developing Countries*. Forthcoming.

Lele, U. "Sources of Growth in East African Agriculture." *World Bank Economic Review* 3, no. 1 (1989).

Little, I., and Mirrlees, J. *A Manual of Project Appraisal in Developing Countries*. OECD. 1968.

McKinnon, R. *Money and Capital in Economic Development*. Washington D.C.: Brookings Institution, 1973.

Malinvaud, Edmond. *The Theory of Unemployment Reconsidered*. Oxford: Blackwell, 1977.

Maton, J. "The Case of Rwanda." *The Supply of Manufactured Goods and Agricultural Development*. Paris: OECD, 1989.

Morris, M. L., and Newman, M. D. "Official and Parallel Cereals Markets in Senegal: Empirical Evidence." *World Development* 17, no. 12 (1989).

Morrisson, C., and Berthelemy, J. C. "Manufactured Goods Supply and Cash Crops in Sub-Sarahan Africa." *World Development* 15, nos. 10/11 (1987): 1353–69.99.

Muellbauer, J., and Portes, R. "Macroeconomic Models with Quantity Rationing." *Economic Journal* 88 (1978).

Neary, J. P., and Stiglitz, J. E. "Towards a Reconstruction of Keynesian Economics: Expectations and Constrained Equilibria." *Quarterly Journal of Economics* 98 (1983).

Newbery, D. M., and Stiglitz, J. E. *The Theory of Commodity Price Stabilisation: A Study in the Economics of Risk*. Oxford: Clarendon Press, 1981.

Newlyn, W. T. "The Present State of African Economic Studies." *African Affairs*. Special issue. Spring (1965).

Oyejide, T. A. *The Effects of Trade and Exchange Rate Policies on Agriculture in Nigeria.* Research Report 55. IFPRI. Washington, D.C., 1986.

———. "Trade Shock, Oil Boom and the Nigerian Economy: 1973–83." Mimeographed. University of Ibadan, 1991.

Peacock, A. T., and Dosser, D. "The National Income of Tanganyika 1952–54." Colonial Research Studies, no. 26. HMSO. London, 1958.

Powell, A. "The Cost of Commodity Price Uncertainty." Mimeographed. Nuffield College, Oxford, 1990.

Prest, A. R., and Stewart, I. G. "The National Income of Nigeria 1950–51." Colonial Research Studies, no. 11. HMSO. London, 1954.

Pryor, F. *The Political Economy of Poverty, Equity and Growth in Malawi and Madagascar.* Oxford: Oxford University Press, 1990.

Putterman, L. *Peasants, Collectives and Choice: Economic Theory and Tanzania's Villages.* Greenwich, Conn.: GOOEY Press, 1986.

Rimmer, D. "The Present Position of African Economic Studies in Great Britain." In *Britische Afrikawisserchaft: Stand und Aufgaben,* edited by W. Manuhard. Bonn: Deutsche Afrika-Iesellshaaft, 1966.

———. *Poverty, Equity and Growth in Ghana.* Oxford:Pergamon Press, 1991.

Roemer, M., and Jones, C., *Markets in Developing Countries: Parallel, Fragmented and Black.* ICEG. San Francisco: ICS Press, 1991.

Scott, Maurice Fitzgerald, and Little, I. M. D. *Using Shadow Prices.* London: Heinemann, 1976.

Scott, Maurice Fitzgerald, MacArthur, J. D., and Newbery, D. M. G. *Project Appraisal in Practice: The Little-Mirrlees Method Applied in Kenya.* London: Heinemann, 1976.

Sen, Amartya Kumar. *Poverty and Famines.* Oxford: Oxford University Press, 1981.

Shaw, E. *Financial Deepening in Economic Development.* New York: Oxford University Press, 1973.

Singh, I., Squire, L., and Strauss, J., eds. *Agricultural Household Models: Extensions, Applications and Policy.* Johns Hopkins University Press, 1986.

Solow, R. "Economics: Is Something Missing?" In *Economic History and the Modern Economist,* edited by W. N. Parker. Oxford: Blackwell, 1986.

Stern, N. *An Appraisal of the Tea Production on Small Holdings in Kenya.* OECD. Paris, 1972.

Stiglitz, J. "Alternative Theories of Wage Determination: The Labour Turnover Model." *Quarterly Journal of Economics* (1974).

Udry, C. "Credit Markets in Northern Nigeria: Credit as Insurance in a Rural Economy." *World Bank Economic Review* 4, no. 3 (1990).

van der Willigen, T. A. "Cash Crop Production and the Balance of Trade in a Less Developed Economy: A Model of Temporary Equilibrium with Rationing." *Oxford Economic Papers* 38, no. 3 (1986).

Wetzel, D. "Temporary Trade Shocks in Developing Countries: A Case Study of the Ghanaian Cocoa Boom." Mimeographed. CSAE. Oxford, 1991.

3

The African Frontier for Political Science

RICHARD L. SKLAR

POLITICAL SCIENCE IS A FORMIDABLE PRESENCE in modern African studies. In 1990 there were more than 1,950 members of the African Studies Association (U.S.A.); political scientists accounted for more than 23 percent of them, the largest disciplinary grouping. Between 1974 and 1987, political science and economics each accounted for an identical 12.4 percent of all doctoral dissertations and master's theses on Africa completed in the United States and Canada; only one subject, education, accounted for more (National Council of Area Studies Associations 1991, pp. 2 and 8). Today, few leading departments of political science lack a specialist in African politics. However, few Africanists in the profession of political science are highly regarded for their ability to communicate to the heart of their discipline. By and large, Africanists in this discipline are esteemed mainly for their analyses of Africa's political experience. Their works are read by those who seek knowledge about Africa, itself, rather than knowledge of the discipline or its theory.

There have been exceptions: a few Africanists have illustrious disciplinary reputations. The theory of political modernization, having weathered recurrent storms of intellectual disapproval, would be far less durable than it has proven to be were it not for the subtle conceptualizations of David E. Apter (1965) and James Smoot Coleman (1968). In conjunction with other comparativists, Apter and Coleman taught a generation of scholars about the integral relationship between democracy, as an "evolutionary universal," and modernity.

Yet another important contribution to political science by an Africanist is Crawford Young's (1976) application of a pluralist theory of the state to non-Western societies. Similarly, political scientists in various fields have been sensitized to the universal implications of methodological individualism by the rationalist theories of Robert H. Bates

(1981, 1983). Notwithstanding these and other significant innovations by political scientists who are also Africanists, the vast majority of political scientists still classify research on African questions as a peripheral "area study" which is not essential to the discipline's scientific progress.

To be sure, cosmopolitan and "worldly" political scientists are conversant with Africanist contributions to their discipline. By itself, however, such awareness does not lead to a conviction that every political science department should include an Africanist scholar for disciplinary reasons. The theoretical contributions of Africanists, including their distinctive approaches to political modernization, comparative pluralism, and rational choice, are represented in political science departments by specialists on various subfields and regions of the world. In competitive appointment processes, Africanist scholarship does not enjoy a comparative advantage based on the disciplinary contributions of its practitioners. If the question is, "Why should we want an Africanist particularly?" no decisive reason, based on scientific or theoretical necessity, can be adduced. In fact, I cannot think of a widely recognized problem or theory, of concern to political scientists generally, that requires African area expertise to either explore scientifically or explain to students.

Proponents of cross-cultural education and research would respond that a "worldly" department of political science cannot afford to neglect the African political experience. But that is not an answer to the question posed for this exercise, which is concerned with disciplinary reasons to seek African area expertise regardless of competing claims to scarce resources. In the minds of those who normally make such decisions, scientific, as opposed to cultural, imperatives probably handicap Africanist contenders for appointment in departments of political science. Of course, that preconception would be challenged by cultural relativists and others who reject the proposition that it is often necessary to choose between professional disciplinary expertise and the study of politics in any part of the world. Why, they wonder, should a disciplinary focus prejudice the claim of any sector of humankind to scholarly attention? Specialists on specific regions, they contend, should be competitive with disciplinary generalists to the extent that they present empirical evidence for significant propositions about political behavior.

Nevertheless, it is a fact that regional area specialists make up a small minority of the leading conceptual or methodological innovators in political science. Few area specialists have been able to acquire and maintain recognized competence in cross-cultural scholarship in addition to mastery of, and leadership within, an increasingly scientific discipline. Moreover, the Africanist today is disadvantaged among regional specialists by the relative marginality of Africa itself to the mainstreams of economic, scientific, and technological intercourse among regions of the world. Africanists are also acutely aware of the logistical impediments to research in Africa, including comparatively greater uncertainties concerning personal health, security, travel, and expenses. For example, the immunization and other procedures for disease prevention required to travel to Africa are far more demanding than those for other major regions. To some extent, the adverse conditions that deter research in Africa can be expected to attract highly motivated scholars who would like their work to make a "difference" in the short run. On balance, however, Africa's own marginality to the mainstream of global exchanges is a professional liability. For Africanists to capitalize on that liability and convert it into a professional asset, they must adduce fresh empirical evidence for new propositions about political life. Under existing conditions, nothing else is likely to enhance their market value relative to other regional specialists.

Can we, as Africanists, identify significant issues or tendencies in political behavior that are more prominent and further developed in Africa than elsewhere in the modern world? Can we expunge the prejudicial premise of choice between disciplinary and cultural values by means of our discovery and exposition of particular aspects of African politics which will command broad attention for disciplinary reasons? Heretofore, the best-known and most carefully studied political problems in Africa have not been specifically or generically African problems. A representative list of such topics would include parasitic statism, militarism, dictatorship, public corruption, the insufficient accountability of public officials, ineffective political socialization, and differential incorporation of ethnic groups resulting in conflict, among many others. These and other topics of current research by Africanists are paralleled by the research interests of political scientists in other regions. The quest for new agenda-setting propositions may have to transcend research horizons that are familiar to political scientists in most, if not all, parts of the world.

A few Africanists, among whom Thomas M. Callaghy (1984) is foremost, have perceived historical parallels between Africa today and the age of absolutism in early modern Europe. Callaghy's thesis will be rebutted by some of those who are wary of deterministic presuppositions, like Karl Marx's famous unilinear aphorism, "The country that is more developed industrially only shows, to the less developed, the image of its own future," which conveys the same message. However, he does draw attention to historical antecedents as a fruitful source of inspiration (divination?) in the quest for knowledge. "Original" ideas often turn out to be old ideas rediscovered. While history does not really "repeat" itself (no specialist in African studies has ever even suggested any such thing), historical analyses often clarify present-day realities, as Callaghy contends. In accord with that spirit, I wish to propose an historical idea about government that could help to secure recognition for African political studies as a source of new and valuable political knowledge. The idea which may serve this purpose could be denominated mixed government.

In the history of political thought, the idea of mixed government has both an ancient and a modern provenance. However, I do not wish to use this idea as it is used by theorists in relation to either of those historical contexts. Rather, I shall allude to medieval political thought, where a similar idea was used for an epoch in transition between ancient and modern forms of mixed government. The ancient form, described by Plato, Aristotle, and Polybius, involved a mixture of political institutions created to protect the interests of the poor with mechanisms devised to safeguard the rich. Modern forms of mixed government, designed during the sixteenth and seventeenth centuries, provided for representation of the great "estates" of society. In France, the Estates-General assembled representatives of the clergy, nobles, and citizens of the towns; similarly in England, Lords Spiritual, Lords Temporal, and commoners were associated with the King through the institutions of "mixed monarchy."

In medieval Europe, political life was bifurcated in a manner that has something in common with the primary political cleavage of modern Africa. At that time, there was no such thing as a state in Europe. As the constitutional historian, Francis D. Wormuth (1949; following German scholarship) has observed, the leading political idea of medieval Europe was "double majesty." The most common arrangement was coexistence of two self-subsistent realms of government, at arm's length from one another, known to Latinists as *Princeps* and *Populus,* or the King, including his military organization, and the Kingdom, including judicial and municipal officials who were independent of the king. Sovereign, unified states did not emerge until the sixteenth century.

Heretofore, the term "mixed government" has not been used by scholars to identify dualistic forms of political authority. In the history of political thought, it has always referred to a unified, and sovereign, political system. For this very reason, I suggest that the concept of mixed government is appropriate for the present-day African condition of dualistic authority with a single, undisputed sovereign in each country. Political scientists have neglected to articulate the reality of this circumstance, although its manifestation in contemporary Africa is pervasive. As in previous (both ancient and modern) epochs of mixed government, African polities today are governed by unified sovereign authorities. However, there are also two separate dimensions of governmental authority, as there were in medieval Europe. These back-to-back domains of authority are readily identifiable as the realm of state sovereignty and the realm of traditional government; both systems effectively govern the same communities of citizen-subjects. Although dualistic systems of political authority can be found in other parts of the world, their establishment by combinations of custom and law in Africa is more comprehensive and systematic than elsewhere. Hence the utility of "mixed government" as a concept that draws attention to the comparative advantage of Africanist scholarship on a neglected subject that could be of general interest to political scientists.

Dual Authority

Broadly conceived, government signifies the regulation of social relations by means of authority. Authority, in turn, is a form of power that people accept as being right and proper, or legitimate. All government is founded on authority, or values held in common between those who make binding decisions and those who abide by them. Political scientists often distinguish between "private" and "public" governments; the latter include the governments of territorial states, their subdivisions, and international organizations created by territorial states. In our epoch, sovereignty is an attribute of territorial states; it cannot be acquired by other forms of public government.

In most parts of the world, the territorial state does not coexist with the institutions of a second state, or state-behind-the-state. In a sense, the modern state is normally one-dimensional. But African states were molded differently. In Africa, it is normal for auxiliary states to occupy a second dimension of political space behind the sovereign states. This condition is a consequence of Africa's colonial past and its cultural resilience.

The modern African states were constructed on precolonial foundations. (The term "precolonial" is meaningful in all African countries except Ethiopia and Liberia, where it would not be relevant.) Apart from Lesotho, Somalia, and Swaziland, all modern African states are "plural," or multinational and multilingual societies. Many of their citizens identify with traditional nations associated with ancestral cultures and languages. The political officials of the second states are known generally as traditional authorities. They can be identified as individuals who hold positions of public trust in accordance with customary, rather than statutory, rules. However, their appointments and functions are normally regulated by statutory law as well.

I shall examine the realm and role of traditional government in several African countries but mainly with reference to Nigeria, Africa's giant country of approximately 90 million people, which is about one-fifth of the total population of sub-Saharan Africa. The people of pre-colonial Nigeria were organized into numerous kingdoms, chiefdoms, and other, relatively decentralized, systems of government. In Northern Nigeria, Muslim people and their non-Muslim vassals were ruled by theocratic emirs who personified the fusion of political and religious authority. South of the emirate belt, kings personified the spiritual essences of their states; in their absence, government by the title-holders of local communities was prevalent. Everywhere in Nigeria, respect for traditional authority is a cultural norm even though its modern role is highly controversial and its impact on modern government varies greatly among peoples and sections of the country.

Consider this testament to the efficacy of traditional government from the pen of General (ret.) Olusegun Obasanjo, Nigeria's Head of State between 1976–79, subsequently active as a member of both Commonwealth and United Nations commissions. On October 1, 1979, he stepped down as Head of State, having presided over a complex transition from military to civilian/constitutional government. His memoir of the event, published in 1990, describes his reception by his traditional community at Abeokuta, the capital city of Egbaland, which is a traditional kingdom and section of the Yoruba-speaking people, who constitute over 20 percent of the national total. The Egba themselves number between three and four million. Here is an excerpt from his account of the reception and ceremony at Abeokuta.

> [W]e were stopped at Aro by the Egba Chiefs representing the Obas [kings], Chiefs and the people of Egbaland. . . . I was received with a short traditional rite and the convoy moved into the town. . . . At the cenotaph [ancestral shrine] I had to perform another traditional rite with an ancient Egba sword . . . paying homage to our ancestral Egba warriors. After that rite, a white charger was produced for me to mount from the cenotaph to Ake Palace [where] I dismounted to pay homage to the Alake [principal king of the Egbas], this time not as a Head of State but as an Egba chief and an Egba son. From there we moved together to St. Peter's Anglican Cathedral Church. . . . Bishop Adeniyi . . . delivered the sermon . . . thus:
>
>> Kabiyesi [Your Highness] Oba Oyebade Lipede, the Alake of Egbaland, Obas, Chiefs and my fellow countrymen. We are all gathered here to welcome back into this historic city our son General Olusegun Obasanjo. Our beloved Jagunmolu [his Egba title as the holder of a traditional office] we heartily welcome you back.

Later an address was read by the *Sereki* (a high official) of Egbaland in the name of the *Alake* himself. The address included this observation on the conferment of General Obasanjo's own title four years earlier: "in appreciation of your gallant efforts during the Nigerian Civil War [of 1967–70] and the credit which you brought to the Egbas through your performance, His Highness, the Alake of Egbaland, on behalf of the Egba people, conferred on you the title of Jagunmolu of Egbaland in the year 1975. That was a most fitting title" (Obasanjo 1990, pp. 207–12).

This brief excerpt from General Obasanjo's vivid memoir should allow the reader to glimpse the vitality and, more to the point, *gravitas* or deep significance of Egbaland's elaborate traditional government.

Literally hundreds of similar governments adorn Nigeria's political landscape. No one of them is more important in the national life of Nigeria than the Caliphate (domain of an orthodox Muslim ruler) of Sokoto. The Sultan of Sokoto is the religious leader of nearly forty million people who are also traditional subjects of more than thirty Muslim emirs in the northern states of Nigeria. He is also the traditional ruler of a domain inhabited by more than four million people in the State of Sokoto. Great as it is, the temporal authority of the Sultan in Sokoto is essentially extra-constitutional; his strictly constitutional role is to preside over a Traditional Council, which cannot exercise executive, legislative, or judicial power under the Constitution. The incumbent Sultan, Alhaji Ibrahim Dasuki, enthroned in 1989, is an impeccably modern traditionalist. His previous careers include diplomacy and banking; indeed, prior to his installation as Sultan, he was chairman of the Nigerian division of the notorious Bank of Commerce and Credit International. It would not occur to him to question the exclusive sovereignty of Nigeria's constitutional government. Yet he has been quoted by an American journalist thus: "Nigeria today is trying to blend military and civilian government. But the ordinary man still looks to the traditional institutions as his last resort" (Hiltzik 1991).

Consider another example of this deep layer of government in Nigeria. In April 1991, the governor of Benue State installed a new king of the four million Tiv people. His Royal Highness Alfred Akawe Torkula, Tor Tiv, is a linguist, trained in France. At the coronation ceremony, he "pledged," as reported authoritatively, "his support and that of his people to the service of Benue State and Nigeria within the framework of Tiv traditions and the Nigerian Constitution" (Audu 1991). He too personifies the African form of mixed government.

Yet another representative example of the modernity and vitality of tradition was reported by the American press in 1990. Dr. Joseph Edozien had retired from his position as dean of the Department of

Nutrition in the University of North Carolina, Chapel Hill, at the age of sixty-five, and had been selected by a traditional council as *Asagba* of Asaba, the traditional ruler of an Igbo-speaking people who number more than one million. His prospective contributions to the well-being of his own Asaba people during the years ahead may eventually rival his estimable contributions as a health scientist to human well-being.

In Nigeria, a role for traditional authority is sanctioned by the Constitution of 1989, which permits the thirty constituent states of the federation to establish Traditional Councils over which Traditional Rulers preside. Such councils are authorized to advise and assist Local Government Councils on various matters but without the right to exercise executive, legislative, or judicial powers (Federal Republic of Nigeria 1989). Critics of this arrangement deplore the illogical perpetuation of monarchical power within the body politic of a prospective Democratic Republic. Despite the acrimony of this debate, a common ground seems to have emerged: abolitionists concede that Traditional Councils and state-level Councils of Chiefs could function usefully as advisory bodies for the promotion of arts, culture, and community development, provided that appointment to such honorific office is made on the basis of exemplary service to society rather than dynastic, lineage, or other hereditary entitlement (Takaya 1990). On the other side, relatively few defenders of Traditional Authority seriously contemplate the restoration of monarchical power in an executive, legislative, or judicial form at any level of government. Traditional rulership under the auspices of a democratic republic may be illogical; yet, as Winston Churchill observed during a wartime debate on reconstruction of the House of Commons, which had been destroyed, "Logic is a poor guide compared with custom." Experience indicates that traditional institutions are more durable and resilient than newly constructed forms of government. Although its influence is pervasive, I would not describe traditional authority as a power behind the throne. There are several such powers in modern Nigerian politics; for example, the military, the civil service, big business, and banking. Rather, I would suggest that many thrones lend their support to the power of the modern state, which they also help to legitimate.

In 1950, the population of Nigeria was less than 40 million; by 2025, it is expected to exceed 200 million. This means that in the space of a single lifetime, Nigeria will experience a fivefold increase in the number of people to feed, clothe, educate, and socialize into a rapidly changing culture. Traditional governments, such as those of Asaba, Egbaland, Sokoto, Tivland, and hundreds of others in Nigeria will bear an immense burden of social responsibility during the difficult transitions that lie ahead. They are needed to help maintain civic morale and a necessary degree of social order.

Let us turn to the Republic of Botswana for a less elaborate but equally vivid example of the reality of mixed government in modern Africa. The Tswana people constitute 90 percent of the national population of 1.2 million. From time immemorial, Tswana chiefs have conducted public meetings, attended by adult males, for discussions of public affairs; known as *kgotla,* this institution has been liberalized during the postcolonial era; women and non-Tswana minority groups now participate as equals in principle, if not yet in practice. Michael Crowder (1988), a historian, identified the *kgotla* tradition as a fundamental reason for the survival of constitutionalism in Botswana. In a recent study, Patrick Molutsi and John Holm (1990, p. 334) reported that the government of Botswana "must run a gauntlet of *kgotlas* throughout the country on all issues which have grass roots impact." Evasion, they find, "would seriously compromise a programme's legitimacy." Furthermore, "some policies have gone through numerous reformulations because they could not pass muster in *kgotla* when it came to implementation." In this manner, many communities will have "bought into" legislative proposals before they become laws.

Although the government of Botswana has been controlled by one and the same political party since independence in 1966, competitive elections, based on freedom of association and expression, have been held regularly. In a thoughtful exposition of the role of chiefs in democratic Botswana, Chief Linchwe II has described the modernization of *kgotla* in his own district. In his opinion, it is his duty as chief to encourage women to attend and to assure their participation as equals. In his *kgotla* now, minutes are taken and decisions recorded. The chief, he says, has no more important role than to protect fundamental human rights. "Botswana," he contends, "needs to build a political structure in which the Westminster type of government and our traditional government coexist for preservation and development of our unique form of democracy" (Linchwe II 1989, p. 102).

Kgotlas are convened by traditional rulers in rural areas; they rarely meet in urban settings, where political meetings, known as "freedom squares," are common occurrences. Both forms of community-based political participation are crucial to the practice of democracy in Botswana; no one mistakes the one for the other. Freedom squares manifest the activities of political parties. In *kgotlas,* however, traditional authorities complement the system of republican office-holders without usurping their functions or infringing on their legal jurisdictions. *Kgotla* signifies the distinctively African synthesis of double majesty with mixed government. The key to comprehension of this combination is the word, used by Chief Linchwe, "coexist."

The architects of government in Africa are building new structures on traditional as well as modern foundations. Often, they appear to be constructing a new type of mixed government, one that conserves traditional authority as a resource which may serve to enhance the authority of the modern state. More often than not, mixed governments will be dual, rather than consolidated, systems of authority; for the most part, traditional rulers and title-holders have advisory, ceremonial, and extra-constitutional functions, rather than enumerated constitutional powers. In some countries, however, constitutions and fundamental laws have been devised to incorporate traditional authorities, either directly or indirectly, into the basic processes of modern government. In such cases, the state is "mixed" in two different ways: first, traditional office holders are entitled to participate in the exercise of sovereign authority on a privileged basis; second, the states-behind-the-state continue to function within their own domains in accordance with customary law and practice. The examples of Ghana and Lesotho, each embarked on a process of democratization, illustrate this major variation.

In 1987, the military government of Ghana decided to create 110 district assemblies, based on a combination of competitive election for two-thirds of the membership of each assembly and appointment of the remaining one-third. The law provides that appointed members will be chosen by the government "in consultation with the traditional authorities and organized productive economic groupings in the District"—in other words, on a corporatist basis (Republic of Ghana 1988). In Lesotho, the draft constitution of 1991 provides for a Senate, empowered to delay the enactment of legislation passed by the National Assembly; two-thirds of the Senate's membership shall consist of the Paramount Chiefs of the "sovereign democratic kingdom," or their designated representatives (Kingdom of Lesotho 1991). The circumscribed, yet significant, constitutional roles provided for traditional rulers in Ghana and Lesotho contrast with the virtual exclusion of traditional rulers from the machinery of constitutional government in both Botswana and Nigeria. An additional case of exclusion that warrants special mention is that of Senegal, where the dominant Socialist Party relies upon the political support of theocratic sufi marabouts, Muslim authorities who command the allegiance of the bulk of the peasantry. Donal B. Cruise O'Brien has described the *zawiya,* or sufi lodge, as a parallel government:

> The lodge is sited at the tomb of a revered saint, and apart from pious pilgrimage, it exists for the task of sacred instruction. But

the social purposes of the *zawiya* are wonderfully varied, a true functionalist utopia; an inn to accommodate the pious traveller, a school to instruct the faithful, a court to arbitrate differences sacred or profane, a market place and farm to provide for the material sustenance of the believers, a miniature welfare state for the distribution of alms, as well as a church and a final resting place for the bones of the devout. The conventional label of lodge seems inadequate to cover such a social range which, if anything, brings to mind the glories of the medieval Christian monastery. In political terms the *zawiya* can accommodate to hard times, to a surrounding anarchy or civil war, by a self-encapsulating autarchy: all the tasks of government are after all already included within its purposes. Under a secure state authority the *zawiya* can develop an intermediary political role and convert the faithful into a negotiable clientele. The sacredly sanctioned hierarchy of the sufi *zawiya* then becomes a parallel hierarchy of government, valuable to state authority as resting on a true popular devotion. In multi-party situations one can even see the *zawiya* converted to the political purposes of a party cell. [O'Brien 1986, pp. 74–75]

Since each of the three large sufi brotherhoods (*tariqa* in Arabic) in Senegal consists of many lodges, the mixed state there is asymmetrical and does not result in a clash of rival claimants to sovereignty.

The distinction between extraconstitutional traditional governments, as in Botswana, Nigeria, and Senegal, and those which have been incorporated partially into the constitutional system, as in Ghana and Lesotho, is not as clear-cut in practice as it is in theory. It will surely become even more nebulous with the adoption of innovative reforms designed to harness the energies of traditional rulers for democratic purposes. Thus Victor Ayeni's vision of "traditional rulers as ombudsmen" would be difficult for a constitutional democrat to fault (1985, pp. 305–19). However, one would be gravely mistaken to minimize the intensity of debates by African intellectuals about the abolition or preservation of traditional rulership. Abolitionists harp on the abuses of authority perpetrated by chiefs, many of whom are the heirs of rulers who were co-opted or installed and nurtured by foreign overlords during the colonial era. They allege that so-called traditional authority is really a form of social parasitism that corrupts the political process. For example, in Nigeria today, manipulative lords of the second state confer titles galore on prominent politicians. There and elsewhere, state officials pursue traditional titles for ulterior political reasons.

In several African states, abolitionists have won decisive victories; for example, chieftaincy in Tanzania was abolished in 1963, two years after independence. Yet David Brokensha, a former district officer, was impressed by the evidence of continuity as well as change when he returned for a visit to the rural Tanzanian district in which he had served, fourteen years after his departure and seven years after independence. His friend, a former chief, "was still the leader of his area, though now in a different role," that of divisional executive officer, to be addressed respectfully as *Bwana* (Mr.) rather than *zumbe* (chief). Brokensha found that his friend "did much the same work as he had as a chief, except for court cases; he discussed all disputes and, if he could not informally reconcile them, sent the disputing parties to the district magistrate." Writing as the professional anthropologist he had by then become, Brokensha concluded: "The dramatic changes at the centre will doubtless eventually be reflected in changes in Handeni, and in all the other remote rural districts; but in the meantime the imperatives of ecology and of society are still very strong" (Brokensha 1970, pp. 167–68). Today, two dozen years after Brokensha's return visit to rural Tanzania, an even more dramatic reversal of the revolutionary policies which had involved the abolition of chieftaincy is underway.

These observations introduce an idea about the form of government in Africa that addresses the importance of Africanist research for the discipline of political science. Systematic research comparing the roles of traditional political institutions in many African countries would be required to confirm the hypothesis of mixed government. Meanwhile, the auxiliary, or second, state in Africa, by whatever name it may be identified, is increasingly reckoned by Africans to be a political resource of inestimable value. Furthermore, the practical importance of traditional authority, its real significance, does not depend on the manner of its interpretation by social scientists. The *kgotla,* the *Alake* of Egbaland, and the marabouts of Senegal exert power in their societies regardless of one or another academic interpretation of their roles. Hence the concept of mixed government differs from concepts, such as statism, that refer to abstract objects of thought rather than concrete realities. The significance of the second state can be explained, but its real impact on society cannot be explained away.

The facts of dual authority in independent Africa have been kept in circulation by an undercurrent of political research for many years. In an early, yet prescient, assessment of the role of chieftaincy in postcolonial Africa, Leslie Rubin offered this observation:

> [T]he new African states cannot avoid confrontation with the demands of traditional concepts and institutions. The available evidence indicates . . . that the theoretical rejection of chieftaincy as a feudal institution incompatible with the needs of a modern state has not wiped out the influence of the chief. For the present at least, social stability would seem to demand the recognition of a

continuing role for the chief in societies otherwise determined to keep up with the pace of the nuclear age. The nature of that role would seem to be determined by the balance of modern and traditional political forces in the individual countries, resulting from their national histories and the influence of their leaders. [Rubin 1967, p. 128]

The classic study of political dualism in Africa is C. S. Whitaker's masterwork, *The Politics of Tradition: Continuity and Change in Northern Nigeria, 1946–1966* (1970). With incontrovertible evidence, Whitaker confirmed the social identity of modern and traditional elites. In their pursuit of office, he revealed, political actors shuttle back and forth between the parliamentary and the traditional systems of government. His paradoxical demonstration of institutional change with social continuity implies dual authority. In this paper, the African dualistic polity is rendered typologically as mixed government.

Whitaker's subtle analysis has been widely endorsed by African scholars themselves. For example, it was adopted by Yakubu Saaka in his study of "local government and political change" in Gonja, a rural district in Northern Ghana:

Professor Whitaker's characterization of the transitional system as "Confrontation Society" is one that seems to be very appropriate for the Gonja situation today. He used the conceptualization to describe situations in which aspects of political structures of different historical origins actually co-exist and interact. The relationship between the institution of chiefship and local government in Gonja typifies this situation.

In many ways Gonja is essentially a dual political system. There is, first, the secular system represented most vividly by the structures of modern local government. Along side it is the traditional system represented by chiefship. Undoubtedly the former is the superior of the two in terms of the authoritative control of political resources. Even though the latter is dependent on the former for its financial allocations (and thus, to that extent is inferior), technically there is supposed to be mutual accommodation of the other in the functions cut out for each. In fact, a large part of the story of local government in Ghana as a whole is the problem of how much actual authority chiefs should have in each revised system (that is, how accommodative the two parts can be in the confrontation society). [Saaka 1978, p. 101]

The condition of problematic accommodation, described by Saaka, persists in Ghana as a result of the decision to incorporate traditional authorities in the recently reorganized system of local government.

Peter P. Ekeh's influential thesis on "the existence of two publics" in Africa, "instead of one public, as in the West," complements Whitaker's conception of a durable symbiotic relationship between parallel political institutions with origins on either side of the historic imperial divide (Ekeh 1975). His further identification of the "primordial public" as "moral" while the "civic public" is "amoral" partially anticipated Richard A. Joseph's (1987) conception of "prebendal politics," a Weberian idea about the pursuit and conduct of public office mainly for the sake of private gain. In a lecture delivered on the occasion of his book's publication in Nigeria, Joseph endorsed a suggestion to the effect that Nigeria is a dualistic federation in transition:

> [T]here is the issue of . . . cultural federalism. This is a term suggested to me by Mallam Turi Muhammadu. . . . More fundamental than the boundaries of Nigeria's constitutional federalism, Turi Muhammadu claimed, was an informal federalism of cultural groups. Nigeria's constitutional federalism cannot forever chase after its protean cultural federalism. At a certain point, a national framework has to be accepted, and cultural changes and manifestations forced to find outlet in, through and around that constitutional mesh. When will an acceptable point of equilibrium between these two federalisms, one fairly permanent, and the other ever-changing, be reached? What factors will contribute to the reaching of a national consensus on the structural composition of the federation? These are questions to which answers must still be sought. [Joseph 1991]

Nigeria is one of the world's leading laboratories for the development of federal government. Joseph's image of a dualistic federation reflects the two-dimensional complexity of Nigeria's multinational state.

Metaphorically speaking, an undercurrent of political thought has begun to return from the deep as a new wave. Taken at the crest, it could stimulate ideas for coping with the flood of problems—demographic, ecological, nutritional, medical, educational, and social—that tend to produce recurrent episodes of social disorganization, including serious breakdowns of law and order. The African national governments are fragile, and there is great need for authority based on consent of the governed. In this circumstance, a separate source of authority, embedded in tradition, could powerfully reinforce social discipline without abandonment of democratic forms of government. The rejuvenation of traditional authority would not, then, imply a resurgence of either "feudalism" or political oligarchy.

The auxiliary or second state, behind-the-state, in Africa should not be misunderstood as an informal or quasi-private sphere of government which exerts control beyond "the reach of the state," whether it be with its tacit approval or illegally. So-called informal systems of authority, which supplement the activities of official governments, or compensate for their deficiencies, or compete with them, are commonplace the world over. In Africa, however, traditional authorities are unmistakably formal and part of the public domain. Furthermore, their existence is often recognized by national constitutions, and they are frequently incorporated into a constitutional order for the performance of specific functions. In every such case, the reality of a second state is suggested by shading, that is, an area of government which is not, strictly speaking, either mixed or unmixed. Shading is positive evidence for the existence of a second dimension of government, one that is so important in Africa, and so visible, that it ought to be studied systematically by political scientists. Anthropological research is invaluable; the relevant anthropological works should be mastered by political scientists, but they do not compensate for the absence of political studies which integrate the two dimensions.

It may be suggested that contrary to the logic of a dualistic conception of government, traditional authority will fade as the urban population overtakes that of rural Africa during the first quarter of the twenty-first century. Yet, many modern African cities have been built on bedrocks of older polities, originally formed by combinations of kinship groups and governed by traditional rulers. The contours of these communities are shaped to a great extent by their origins; traditional authority persists vibrantly within them, in modern forms.

In Africa, the notion of a rural-urban dichotomy is often misleading, particularly in relation to urban settlements that absorb many migrant workers and other recent arrivals from rural areas. For example, in South Africa's Transvaal Province, political conflict between partisans of the African National Congress (ANC) and the Zulu-based Inkatha Freedom Party is, in part, a product of antagonism between the residents of established township communities, on the one hand, and newcomers as well as those, mainly miners, who live in dormitories for employees, on the other hand. In an effort to end the violent clashes of 1990, both the traditional king of the Zulu and a traditional ruler of Xhosa-speaking people toured the embattled townships where they made joint appeals for peace. Calls to conscience from the traditional thrones of "second" states could become more, rather than less, imperative in South Africa as the pace of political change accelerates. Indeed constitutional guidelines formulated by the ANC in 1988 provide for the adaptation, rather than abolition, of traditional rulers in a democratic South Africa:

> The institution of hereditary rulers and chiefs shall be transformed
> to serve the interests of the people as a whole in conformity
> with the democratic principles embodied in the Constitution.
> [Rugege 1990, p. 166]

The question of traditional authority came to the fore suddenly, in December 1991, at the historic first meeting of the Convention for a Democratic South Africa (CODESA). A request for recognition as a participant in the Convention was submitted by a delegation led by the Zulu king; subsequently, a broadly based Congress of Traditional Leaders, allied to the ANC, also asked for recognition as a participating organization. Neither the ANC nor its principal adversary and partner in these negotiations, the National Party, support the claims of "internal nations" for representation, as such, in the CODESA process. Both requests were referred to the CODESA management committee and placed on the agenda of crucial questions for the architects of democracy in South Africa.

Afrocentricity

The concept of dual authority did not occur to me as a result of my own thinking in the course of research. It was precipitated in my thought by a brief yet intense exchange of views among a group of Nigerian scholars and diplomats at a conference that I attended at the Hoover Institution, Stanford University, in 1990. Before then, I had been aware of the public debate in Nigeria on the question of participation by traditional rulers in the prospective Third Republic, due to be inaugurated in 1993 (Federal Republic of Nigeria 1987, pp. 142–47). However, I had not paid much attention to that issue and did not attach much importance to it. During a recess, I was asked by a Nigerian colleague of many years' standing where I stood on this question. I replied that I did not have a position because I always tried to be impartial on questions involving cultural practices and religion. My friend was obviously disappointed by my response. "You should have a position on this question," he said. Only then did I begin to think seriously about the ramifications of traditional authority in African politics. I doubt that my friend would either agree with my current views or countenance my notion of mixed government. But he had admonished me, in effect, to act in accordance with a precept to which I, myself, subscribed in principle but had neglected to respect in practice: that the student of African politics should not simply disregard political issues that Africans themselves describe and identify as being fundamental.

My friend's justifiable rebuke of my withdrawal from engagement in the debate about traditional rulers was an expression of Afrocentricity. I do not mean to suggest that he necessarily believed that I could contribute usefully to that discourse; he may or may not have thought so. In any case, the role of people like me (I am a Jewish-American) in African studies is, itself, an issue in the debate about Afrocentric scholarship. Whatever position one may adopt on the latter issue, my statement of withdrawal from the arena of responsible deliberation about the political role of traditional rulers on the ground that the subject was somehow too "cultural" for me to "butt in" undermines whatever claim I may have to study African politics objectively. I now recognize that the question of traditional authority in African politics demonstrates the salience of Afrocentricity as a methodological principle for political scientists in this field. More generally, it involves the Africanist scholar in an especially topical version of the debate about "an enduring issue, namely, the antinomy of universalism vs. relativism." James S. Coleman and C. R. D. Halisi (1983, p. 25), whose words are quoted here, adopted this perspective to examine the encounter between Africa and American political science. Others have since identified Afrocentricity as the specific form of methodological relativism in African (including African diaspora) studies.

The idea of Afrocentricity and its methodological corollaries have been misunderstood and trivialized by polemicists, who have either endorsed or disparaged highly debatable arguments for the presumptive African origins of various other civilizations. Occasionally, polemicists have alleged that African people have been harmed by the effects of biased research conducted by non-Africans. These and similar manifestations of polemical Afrocentricity have obscured a crucial methodological imperative of Afrocentric scholarship, one which is entirely compatible with standard practice in the social sciences. Essentially, methodological Afrocentricity ordains that those who interpret Africa should acquire a sympathetic understanding of African thought and values. As C. S. Whitaker, an African-American political scientist and proponent of Afrocentricity, has written:

> Properly invoked, Afrocentricity is an analytical imperative, not a sentimental gesture. Its importance derives from fundamental issues of comprehension in the wake of powerful intellectual legacies that tend to discount the capacity of African cultures and societies to act rationally and constructively in the face of historic realities. It suggests, importantly, that these realities, not Africans, are the source of problematic conditions.

And,

> Like all precepts, Afrocentricity is also liable to promote distortion and misuse if it is uncritically invoked. In the course of

trying to render sensitively and accurately the data of African politics, obscurantism and exoticism are no less dangers than in other
scholarly arenas. A sound corollary of authenticity is that novelty
of treatment is not an end in itself. [1991, pp. 359 and 361]

Not a few proponents of Afrocentricity do contend that cultural
and racial qualifications are sometimes required for Afrocentric research on certain topics. Convictions of that kind, espoused by serious
intellectuals, will challenge and test the ability of scholars to reconcile
their universalist methodologies with Afrocentric values. A credible effort is represented by David D. Laitin's study of politics and religion in
the Yoruba city of Ile-Ife, Nigeria (1986). Over a period of fifteen
months, Laitin, a Jewish-American, regularly attended religious services
at both an Anglican church and the city's central mosque. He compiled
histories of both congregations and formally interviewed thirty-five
members of each. A specialist on the relationship between language and
politics in Africa, Laitin has studied both the Yoruba language and, in
connection with his previous research, the Somali language. Among the
works of political scientists who use comparative methods of research
in African studies, it would be difficult to identify a body of work by a
single author that is more Afrocentric in its content than that produced
by Laitin.

If Afrocentricity is a desirable trait in Africanist scholarship, is linguistic expertise a necessary condition of genuine Afrocentric achievement? I think not; very few political scientists in African studies, apart
from those who speak an African language as their mother tongue, have
linguistic skills that would be adequate for the purpose of unassisted
research in an African language. In this regard, the field of African
studies is unlike either Asian or Middle Eastern studies. In African
studies, it is normal for researchers, other than native speakers, to rely
on the assistance of interpreters, even as they increase their comprehension of one or more African languages. In African political studies,
research-grade proficiency in an African language is rarely anticipated
or attained by individuals who are not native speakers of the language
concerned.

Why should this be so? The explanation lies in the extraordinarily
large number of African languages which are spoken as first languages
in everyday life. Approximately 800 languages are spoken in Africa,
excluding the Mediterranean region, where Arabic and Berber pre-
dominate. This conservative estimate, by the noted linguist, Pierre Alexandre (1972, p. 2), is much lower than the figure of 1,200 obtained
by aggregating the total number of entries in standard, complementary
classifications of African languages. In a large majority of the forty-

seven African countries, excluding the Mediterranean tier, no one language is spoken as a first language, or mother-tongue, by a majority of the people. The exceptions include several countries noted for their virtual linguistic homogeneity (Botswana, Burundi, Lesotho, Rwanda, Somalia, Swaziland) and other countries where linguistic divisions correspond to basic political cleavages, despite the fact that most citizens do share a common language. In Kenya and Tanzania, Swahili is both the national language and the second language-of-choice for most people, although English is indispensable for commerce and education. In Sudan, the northernmost states of Nigeria, and some of the Sahelian countries, Arabic is often the second language-of-choice. Everywhere else, the second language-of-choice is likely to be a European language, either English, French, Portuguese, or Spanish.

Undoubtedly, the multiplicity of languages in Africa does create a predisposition for those political scientists (and sociologists) who are not native speakers to favor universalist methodologies and theories, rather than relativistic approaches that require deep immersion in a culture and its linguistic expression. Yet relativism, based on the values of cultural particularity, is no less relevant to the political analysis of a multilingual society than it is to the ethnographic analysis of any one traditional community or people by itself. Afrocentricity is the name for relativism, either as epistemology or methodology, when its referent is the general field of African studies. The idea of dual authority, based on the coexistence of legally sovereign and traditional governments, is an Afrocentric hypothesis; to the extent that it corresponds to the African reality, it could help to explain the resiliency of constitutional forms of democracy in Africa. Other such hypotheses are implicit in various doctrines and practices which have been analyzed deeply by political scientists. I will comment briefly on a few examples merely to indicate potential horizons for research in African studies that might attract far wider attention.

Perhaps the best known example of Afrocentricity in social thought is the francophone philosophy of *négritude*, formulated, during the 1930s, by intellectuals of African descent, to affirm the distinctive and self-subsistent attributes of African culture. One of the principal expositors of *négritude*, Leopold Sedar Senghor, eventually became president of Senegal. His beliefs were highly controversial among African intellectuals because they appeared to deemphasize the significance of economic and political imperialism by comparison with cultural imperialism. In other words, he argued that it was far more important for Africa to affirm its cultural independence than to either separate itself from world capitalism or oppose, rather than cooperate with, the former colonial powers. Senghor's immense personal influence, and that of the *négritude* doctrine, in Senegal could help to explain the relative weakness of Marxism-Leninism there, compared with several other states in francophone Africa that, like Senegal, have also been inclined toward socialism. This hypothesis also draws attention to the agency of thought itself as a causal factor in social action.

Yet another manifestation of Afrocentricity in postcolonial Africa is a tendency in thought and practice known as African Socialism. Motivated by the ideas of Julius K. Nyerere, Tanzania has represented the leading example of mildly doctrinaire "African," as opposed to Marxist-Leninist, socialism in practice. Despite a dismal economic record, attributable in large part to ill-conceived policies adopted in the name of socialism, Tanzanians still evince a more durable commitment to socialist values than shown by the citizens of countries where avowedly socialist regimes were directly discredited by the debacle of European Leninism. Tanzania's self-motivated and self-directed socialist experiment could be significant for the discovery of practical mixtures of capitalism and socialism, unrelated to dogmas, such as revolutionary class struggle, which have negative economic and social effects.

Finally, in South Africa, a cultural and political movement, known as Black Consciousness, was created by intellectuals in the latter 1960s. A successor to the older, uniracial "Africanist" movement, Black Consciousness proclaimed the solidarity of all oppressed races in South Africa, including both Indians and people of mixed racial descent as well as the indigenous African majority. Strictly speaking, Black Consciousness is not exclusively Afrocentric. Furthermore, the research of C. R. D. Halisi (1991) demonstrates its affinity with New Left thinking in Europe and the United States.

> Consistent with New-Left thought, the Black Consciousness Movement offered a critique of capitalism that was both radical, without being explicitly Marxist, and democratic without yielding to the Eurocentric pressures of South African liberalism.

Halisi's interpretation of Black Consciousness suggests that Afrocentricity should be viewed as a stage in the evolution of thought toward truly universal theories of society, unencumbered by ethnocentrism. Few political studies offer a more dramatic view of the enduring dialogue between universalist and relativist thought.

Mixed Methodologies

Each of the Afrocentric hypotheses to which reference has been made in this discussion—traditional government as a research horizon; *négritude,* African socialism, and Black Consciousness as themes in African social thought—refers to an aspect of intellectual, political, or social life in Africa. It is important to distinguish between such hypotheses, which can be tested in the crucible of research, and Afrocentric methodologies, which rely on African perspectives to formulate questions for research.

Critics of so-called Western scholarship on Africa often allege that prejudice, detrimental to Africa, pervades the agenda of intercontinental research. Regardless of the merit of that accusation, it would be a mistake to conclude that scholarship based on African values is at all disadvantaged in the marketplace of ideas. The formulation of questions for research is a subjective exercise. Those who dislike the existing choice of questions are at liberty to formulate and display their own. Experience shows that Afrocentric questions hold their own in competition with Eurocentric and other subjective varieties.

Yet there is another, real threat to Afrocentric, or relativist, scholarship. It arises when subjective methodologies are confronted by methodologies based on the canons of formal logic and mathematical proof. A growing number of political scientists subscribe to such methodologies. In their eyes, Afrocentric and all other subjective methodologies are problematic and presumptively unsuitable for scientific purposes. This issue is not more salient in African political studies than in other subject areas, regional or topical, of political science. Yet African area specialists may actually enjoy a comparative advantage in the quest for a resolution of this methodological issue.

Consider an example from the recent work of Robert H. Bates (1990), who is prominently identified with the scientific persuasion of methodological individualism and rational choice. In an effort to explain the basis of ideological conflict in Africa, he describes a contrast between two different patterns of capital formation—one individualist, the other collectivist—at the household level. At bottom, he suggests, the divergence observed is attributable to differing environments of risk. Broadly, forest dwellers tend to favor private property while the inhabitants of harsh, savannah-type climes are more inclined to believe in shared property and "communal entitlements to assets." Bates identifies this culturalist explanation of economic behavior as the source of a lasting ideological divide in Africa. Regardless of the pros and cons that may be adduced when this hypothesis is debated, it is significant methodologically because it combines the universalist presuppositions of both rational choice and classical Marxism with Afrocentric, culturalist qualifiers. The Marxist teaching of a causal relationship between modes of production and ideology is modified by the addition of cultural and environmental factors as independent variables. Briefly stated, distinctively African conditions have prompted Bates to formulate a mixed methodology which may, with further development, have the potential to transcend Coleman and Halisi's "antinomy of universalism vs. relativism."

Yet another example is provided by David D. Laitin's study of politics and religion in Ile-Ife, noted previously for its Afrocentric merit. Laitin proposes a mixed methodology to assess the relative political importance of alternative cultural values. With insight derived from Antonio Gramsci's theory of ideology, Laitin adopts an historical approach that not only reveals the cultural basis of political choice but also clarifies the range of choice available to political actors. His method combines relativist and universalist methodologies in order to probe the nature and political effects of religious differentiation in a Yoruba community.

To the extent that African polities are really sustained by dual systems of authority, as suggested in this paper, cultural relativism may be expected to flourish as the sturdy companion of rationalist political economy. Bates and Laitin have reached this conclusion independently. The methodological tendency of their thought implies the use of subjective methods, including intuition, in connection with the analysis of culture. For example, in mixed (legally sovereign and traditional) governments, the "calculus of consent" is exceedingly complex. Scholars would be ill-advised to underestimate the intangible bonds of authority that regulate the second, or traditional, domain of political life. The force of traditional authority is far more difficult to render mathematically than that of modern governments which produce statistics. Most interactions between the two dimensions of government cannot be fathomed without the use of subjective methodologies.

In African planning for economic, political, and social development, constitutional reform is at, or near, the head of the agenda in many countries. Constitutions are bodies of rules that govern the operations of governments themselves. When a government, or system of authority is "mixed" in the sense of combining both legal and traditional authorities, it operates on the basis of multiple constitutions or bodies of rules. I wish to stress the word "multiple" because there are several, or many, distinct traditional polities "behind" the sovereign state in nearly ever case. (Lesotho and Swaziland, each with one traditional polity that is incorporated into the constitutional system, are notable exceptions.) In all cases, members of the judicial establishment of a sovereign state resolve disputes involving traditional law, including rules of succession to a throne. Indeed judiciaries link the two dimensions of government and regulate their relations. Judicial independence, a basic principle of constitutional government, is crucial to the vitality of mixed governments.

In addition to the potentially divisive effects produced by numerous traditional constitutions, African governments are endangered by the circumstance of their construction on shaky colonial foundations. The only exceptions to that generalization are Ethiopia, which has been independent since the first millennium B.C.E., and Liberia, which was, however, established by African-American settlers sponsored by the antebellum American Colonization Society. Hence the mixed constitutions of all African governments embody elements of law from two or more different cultures. In nearly all cases (prerevolutionary Ethiopia would be an exception) the sovereign government has been founded, mainly but not exclusively, on exogenous legal precepts, while coexisting traditional governments have been regulated, mainly but also not exclusively, by indigenous legal precepts. Furthermore, this mixture was produced by European conquest and with little regard for the constitutional principles of precolonial African governments.

Cobie K. Harris (1991) attributes the deterioration of governmental performance in postcolonial Africa mainly to the previous imposition of autocratic and paternalistic forms of colonial government. Inexorably, foreign authorities repressed and marginalized "all indigenous constitutional traditions and conventions." Africa's political revival, he contends, would be accelerated by the recovery of African constitutional traditions and their recombination with European and other exogenous constitutional precepts, insofar as they may be appropriate.

> [T]he urgent task for political leadership in the new African republics is to seize the idea of constitutionalism by limiting the power of the rulers, reconstituting the polity and engendering new forms of political solidarity that incorporate fragments of the African political tradition into a new constitutional framework.

Harris uses the metaphor "genetic code" to characterize "the relationship between cultures and constitutional practice." The translation of that relationship into legal norms, he believes, would enhance the legitimacy of national governments that are not deeply respected by their citizens at the present time. This is a problem that requires Afrocentric thought and analysis.

Mixed governments, as they have been described in this paper, are subject to serious conflicts between the principles of statutory and traditional laws. This too poses an Afrocentric challenge to legal theory. Conflicts between the expanding domain of human rights and the jurisdiction of restrictive customary laws are commonplace, particularly in cases involving family law and the rights of women. In a searching analysis of human rights in Commonwealth Africa, Rhoda Howard (1986; concurring with Jack Donnelly) differentiates between "extreme" and "weak" versions of cultural relativity. Although her own methodology (and moral philosophy) is firmly universalist, she would nonetheless countenance reasonable deviations from universal norms in the protection of human rights.

> [W]hile the principle of cultural relativity should not be raised to an absolute standard to excuse any and all deviations from international human rights standards, it may be used as a check on radical universalism in very carefully defined circumstances. [P. 17]

And, with particular reference to the personal rights of women, she observes:

> The customs of child betrothal, arranged marriage, bridewealth, and widow inheritance, all of which contravene United Nations provisions for human rights, are central to the organization of society. Marriages based on these principles are generally contracted in good faith, and the people who arrange the marriage are attempting to obtain a satisfactory outcome both for the individuals concerned and for the lineages that are allied by the particular marriage.
>
> The best position to take regarding this dilemma is one of "weak" cultural relativity. That is to say, a sensitive understanding of the meaning and value of custom should temper any imposition of universal norms of human rights that, although philosophically valid, are not yet fully accepted by ordinary people (as opposed to the ruling class) in a society. Weak cultural relativism cannot be used to deny the existence of any right in principle. It can, however, be used to modify the implementation of a right so as not to offend the basic integrative norms of a society, as long as it is understood that those norms may well change, thus requiring the full implementation of a right under dispute at a later date. Advocacy of immediate implementation in Commonwealth Africa of laws that conform to U.N. provisions for women's rights in the sphere of marriage and the family could be interpreted as an imposition of a secularized, individualistic view of human relations upon Africa. On the other hand, there is almost universal evidence that marriage customs are hinged on the subordination of women as a group to men as a group. Customs are neither immutable in time nor neutral in their impact. [Pp. 195–96]

As a jurisprudential principle, "weak relativity" strongly affects the everyday lives of citizens. For example, in 1987, the nature of the state in Kenya was reflected through the illuminating prism of a celebrated legal battle over the burial of a body. Briefly, a widow's attempt to bury her deceased husband as she wished, and in accordance with his own probable wish, was denied by jurists in deference to the burial custom of his clan, although the deceased man had been estranged from his clan community for many years. The traditionalist views of many Kenyans are summarized in Blaine Harden's report of what he was told by a Kenyan university professor. "Bringing the body home" to the land of his own tribal group, the professor argued, "would validate the African system of tribal obligation, a system he said held Kenya together."

> Tribal tradition, he said, anchored a continent dizzy with change. It redistributed wealth and lessened the destructive power of corrupt national leaders. It gave Africans a sense of continuity with their parents, their grandparents, and their largely unwritten precolonial history. [Harden 1990, p. 120]

In Kenya, as elsewhere in Africa, legal duality signifies political duality despite the reputed insignificance of traditional political authority in that country compared with many others on the continent.

As a methodological principle, relativism requires the social scientist to represent the attitudes and values of human subjects faithfully, regardless of their deviation from presumed universal norms. Subjective methods of cultural and behavioral analysis are indispensable for this purpose. They include both intuition and the exercise of judgment based on either participant observation or any other reliable source of personal knowledge. Increasingly, mixed methodologies, such as those suggested by Bates for political economy, Laitin for political culture, and Howard for the study of human rights, will be firmly supported on the ground of scientific necessity. Thus, in the subfield of African international relations, the utility of multiple, transborder, ethnic linkages for regional peace-keeping and security warrants attention. Such linkages could prove to have methodological as well as practical significance, given the transborder ramifications of mixed government.

In African political studies, the dialogue between proponents of universal and relativist methodologies is normally conciliatory and accommodating rather than antagonistic. There are few extremists and many seekers in quest of synthetic methodologies. Some of them may yet transcend the durable antinomies of scientific thought.

NOTE

I wish to thank Naomi Chazan, David Uru Iyam, Elwin V. Svenson, and Aliyu Modibbo Umar for sharing their thoughts about aspects of this essay.

REFERENCES

Alexandre, Pierre. *Languages and Language in Black Africa*. Evanston, Ill.: Northwestern University Press, 1972.

Apter, David E. *The Politics of Modernization*. Chicago and London: University of Chicago Press, 1965.

Audu, Felix D. V. "A Greater Tomorrow: Installation of Alfred Akame Torkula, Tor Tiv IV." *West Africa,* no. 3843 (1991): 648.

Ayeni, Victor. "Traditional Rulers as Ombudsmen: In Search of a Role for Natural Rulers in Contemporary Nigeria." In *Local Government and the Traditional Rulers in Nigeria,* edited by Oladimeji Aborisade. Ile-Ife: University of Ife Press, 1985.

Bates, Robert H. *Markets and States in Tropical Africa*. Berkeley, Los Angeles, and London: University of California Press, 1981.

—————. *Essays on the Political Economy of Rural Africa*. Berkeley, Los Angeles, and London: University of California Press, 1983.

—————. "Capital, Kinship, and Conflict: The Structuring Influence of Capital in Kinship Societies." *Canadian Journal of African Studies* 24 (1990): 151–64.

Brokensha, David. "Handeni Revisited." *African Affairs* 70 (1970): 159–68.

Callaghy, Thomas. *The State-Society Struggle: Zaire in Comparative Perspective*. New York: Columbia University Press, 1984.

Coleman, James S. "Modernization: Political Aspects." In *International Encyclopedia of the Social Sciences,* edited by David Sills. Vol. 10. New York: Crown Collier & Macmillan, 1968.

Coleman, James S., and Halisi, C. R. D. "American Political Science and Tropical Africa: Universalism vs. Relativism." *African Studies Review* 26, nos. 3/4 (1983): 25–62.

Crowder, Michael. "Botswana and the Survival of Liberal Democracy in Africa." In *Decolonization and African Independence: The Transfers of Power, 1960–1980,* edited by Prosser Gifford and Wm. Roger Louis. New Haven and London, Conn.: Yale University Press, 1988.

Ekeh, Peter P. "Colonialism and the Two Publics in Africa: A Theoretical Statement." *Comparative Studies in Society and History* 17 (1975): 91–112.

Federal Republic of Nigeria. *Report of the Political Bureau*. Lagos: Government Printer, 1987.

—————. *The Constitution of the Federal Republic of Nigeria (Promulgation) Decree 1989*. Sections 8 and 329; and Fourth Schedule, part 2, 1989.

Halisi, C. R. D. "Steve Biko and Black Consciousness Philosophy: An Interpretation." Manuscript. 1991.

Harden, Blaine. *Africa: Dispatches from a Fragile Continent*. New York: Norton, 1990.

Harris, Cobie K. "Constitutionalism: Genetic Code for Restoring the African

Polity." Paper presented at the Annual Meeting of the American Political Science Association, Washington, D.C. 1991.

Hiltzik, Michael A. "The Sultan of Sokoto Bridges Two Worlds in Nigeria." *Los Angeles Times*, 14 May 1991, sec. H.

Howard, Rhoda E. *Human Rights in Commonwealth Africa*. Totowa, N.J.: Rowland & Littlefield, 1986.

Joseph, Richard A. *Democracy and Prebendel Politics in Nigeria*. Cambridge: Cambridge University Press, 1987.

———. "Challenges of the Nigerian Third Republic." *Daily Times* (Lagos), 8 June 1991.

Kingdom of Lesotho, Ministry of Law, Constitutional and Parliamentary Affairs. *Preliminary Draft Constitution of Lesotho, 1991*, Sections 1 and 55, and Schedule 2. Maseru: Government Printer, 1991.

Laitin, David D. *Hegemony and Culture: Politics and Religious Change among the Yoruba*. Chicago: University of Chicago Press, 1986.

Linchwe II, Chief. "The Role a Chief Can Play in Botswana's Democracy." In *Democracy in Botswana*, edited by John Holm and Patrick Molutsi. Gaborone: Macmillan, 1989.

Molutsi, Patrick P., and Holm, John D. "Developing Democracy When Civil Society is Weak: The Case of Botswana." *African Affairs* 89 (1990): 323–40.

National Council of Area Studies Associations. *Prospects for Faculty in Area Studies*. Stanford, Calif., 1991.

Obasanjo, Olusegun. *Not My Will*. Ibadan: University Press, 1990.

O'Brien, Donal B. Cruise. "Wails and Whispers: The People's Voice in West African Muslim Politics." In *Political Domination in Africa*, edited by Patrick Chabal. Cambridge: Cambridge University Press, 1986.

Republic of Ghana. *Local Government Law*, Section 3, P.N.D.C. 207. 1988.

Rubin, Leslie. "Chieftaincy and the Adaptation of Customary Law in Ghana." In *Boston Papers on Africa: Transition in African Politics*, edited by Jeffrey Butler and A. Castagno. New York: Praeger, 1967.

Rugege, Sam. "The Future of 'Traditional' Hereditary Chieftaincy in a Democratic Southern Africa: The Case of Lesotho." In *Southern Africa after Apartheid*, edited by Sehoai Santho and Mafa Sejanamane. Harare: Southern Africa Political Economy Series Trust, 1990.

Saaka, Yakubu. *Local Government and Political Change in Northern Ghana*. Washington, D.C.: University Press of America, 1978.

Takaya, B. J. "Republican Monarchies'? An Assessment of the Relevance and Roles of Traditional Rulers in Nigeria's Third Republic." Presented at a Conference on Democratic Transition and Structural Adjustment in Nigeria, Hoover Institution, Stanford University, August 27–29, 1990.

Whitaker, C. S. "A Coda on Afrocentricity." In *African Politics and Problems in Development*, edited by Richard L. Sklar and C. S. Whitaker. Boulder, Colo.: Lynne Rienner, 1991.

Whitaker, C. S., Jr. *The Politics of Tradition: Continuity and Change in Northern Nigeria, 1946–1966*. Princeton, N.J.: Princeton University Press, 1970.

Wormuth, Francis D. *The Origins of Modern Constitutionalism*. New York: Harper and Brothers, 1949.

Young, Crawford. *The Politics of Cultural Pluralism*. Madison: University of Wisconsin Press, 1976.

PART TWO: THE HUMANITIES

4

The Impact of African Studies
on Philosophy

V. Y. MUDIMBE AND
KWAME ANTHONY APPIAH

THOSE OF US WHO ARE INTERESTED in the impact of African Studies on disciplines in the American academy do well to locate ourselves as much in the current history of those disciplines as in the current state of African Studies. And this seems to us especially true in the case of the discipline of philosophy, whose recent history in the United States, indeed in the English-speaking world, has been dominated by a certain important internal division.

We refer, of course, to the notorious "analytical-Continental" divide; and the importance of that divide for disciplinary interactions with African Studies resides in its almost exact correspondence to a division within African intellectual life, namely, that between Anglophone and Francophone states. For the division between analytical philosophy and Continental philosophy is in large measure a cleavage between those who trace their tradition to the British philosophers of Oxford and Cambridge in the mid-century, on the one hand, and those who trace a tradition back through certain French philosophers (most recently, for example, Jacques Derrida), on the other hand. Both of these histories end up in nineteenth-century German philosophy, and there is much overlapping of personnel on the way; but the stories that disciplines tell themselves of their ancestry, the family trees they construct, are an important part of their rhetoric and their method. Issues can be of contemporary importance in a tradition because they once mattered to people who still matter to that tradition. That Nietzsche worried about the possibility of eternal recurrence makes that problem a philosophical problem for a tradition that looks back to Nietzsche;

that Russell puzzled over definite descriptions makes them a problem in a tradition that looks back to him.

We begin, therefore, with a brief (and necessarily highly schematic) sketch of that history.

Part I: Recent American Philosophy

When, in the early part of this century, Frege replaced Hegel as the tutelary spirit of English philosophy, the ethos of Continental historicist modes of thought was largely extirpated from the philosophy faculties of English (though, curiously, not from Scottish) universities. In England, the most influential body of philosophical practice through the mid-century derived from the transfer, through such figures as Ludwig Wittgenstein and Alfred Ayer, of the logical positivism of the Vienna Circle to Oxford and Cambridge into the context provided by the critique of idealism which had been begun by Bertrand Russell. The tradition that resulted came to be known as "analytical philosophy."

This wind from Austria blew less vigorously in the United States, where pragmatism provided an indigenous alternative to the influences of the Vienna Circle. But W. V. O. Quine, one of the most potent figures in the formation of the modern idiom of American philosophy, had been influenced, like Ayer, by his contacts with the Viennese school, even if, as he acknowledged, pragmatism was another of his major influences. While Wittgenstein brought the gospel to Cambridge, the lectures of Moritz Schlick, a central figure in the organization of the Circle, and, above all, the work of Rudolf Carnap—from one perspective, the greatest systematic philosopher of the century—also left their impress on American academic philosophy.

For the many who resisted these strains of thought in the United States, the founding figure of their tradition remained not Frege but Hegel, and the most influential of the moderns were not Wittgenstein and Carnap but Husserl and Heidegger. Those in this tradition felt at ease with Sartre, who had introduced into French philosophy the influence of the German phenomenologists and turned it, as he claimed, to good existentialist use. They continued to read Schopenhauer. They rediscovered Nietzsche—decontaminated of his Nazi associations—after the Second World War. The analytical philosophers, meanwhile, were reading Russell and Moore and the early Wittgenstein—and later on Carnap and the later Wittgenstein and Quine—and spending more and more of their time on something called the "philosophy of language."

Far more striking to the casual observer than the differences in the groups' doctrines—for neither "Continental" nor "analytical" philosophy is easily characterized by a creed—are their differences in method and idiom. They share, of course, a vocabulary of key words which belong to the language of the Western philosophical tradition—"truth" and "meaning," for example, being familiar words for each—but they often put these shared words to radically different uses. Words like "being" (for the analyticals) and "reference" (for the Continentals), which were important for the other tradition, became for a period virtually taboo.

WE CAN CHARACTERIZE THE DIVIDED HOUSE of American academic philosophy not only by its double genealogy and its double idiom but also by a double self-image. Analytical philosophers think of themselves as on the side of logic, science, and method against superstition and on the side of a modest and careful search for truth against bombast. For them philosophy is often a technical subject, and a grasp of these technicalities is a condition of professional competence. Continentals believe that the issues they deal with are difficult and important and that their tradition is continuous with the best and deepest of the Western tradition of humanistic scholarship. They are likely to see philosophy as continuous not with the sciences but with literature and the arts. If they complain about the analyticals, they complain that their work is shallow, cold, dry, inconsequential; that they evade the difficulty of the central philosophical questions by reducing them to trivial, often semantic, debates; that they lack a sense of the historical development of the life of reason. And, in return, the analyticals are likely to object that Continentals mistake obscurantism for profundity.

These self- (and other-) images are, of course, stereotypes. Few, on either "side," express themselves as clearly and strongly as this; most analytical philosophers will agree that there is some interest in, say, Sartre's moral psychology, and most Continentals will agree that analytical philosophy of logic and language, while not nearly as important as it is supposed to be, is often the work of subtle and gifted minds. But though these images are stereotypes, they are not, in our view, caricatures.

In the United States this discourse of mutual incomprehension and distaste has become more complicated in the recent years. For many younger philosophers see little point in the labels. There is a tendency more and more to speak—as Williams does here—of differences of idiom and to hope for some sort of common ground. But in the academy, as in politics, true detente requires more than the regular expression of a desire for rapprochement.

Not only have the recent rapprochements made the work of European philosophers increasingly familiar to Anglo-American philosophers, but there is also in Europe a growing interest in the work of the British, North American, and Australian philosophers who constitute the canon of analytical philosophy. Nevertheless, for the first twenty-five years of the postwar era we must recognize two powerful and powerfully distinct philosophical traditions in the West. And it was in those decades that the philosophy departments of Anglophone and Francophone Africa were established.

INTO THIS HISTORY IN RECENT YEARS have come at least three further specific factors that are relevant for our own project. First, the account of analytical philosophy as the analysis of concepts fell victim to Quine's devastating attacks on the idea of conceptual truth (see, for example, Quine and Ullian 1970).[1] Lacking the old clear answer to the questions "What is a philosophical question?" and "What is a proper philosophical method"[2] analytical philosophers began to broaden their conceptions of the subject. Second, influenced by a receptiveness to Foucauldian genealogies of forms of knowledge, many "Continental" philosophers have become sensitive to the ways in which philosophy, far from being a "pure" uncorrupted realm that proceeds without the influence of social—and, more particularly, national—histories, is itself embedded in the social and political life around it.[3] Third (and most recently) a number of American philosophers—notably Richard Rorty, Stanley Cavell, Cornel West—have become preoccupied with questions about what is distinctively *American* about American philosophy—or distinctively European about the philosophical culture of Europe (see, for example, Cavell 1981, 1989, 1990; Rorty 1989; West 1989). In these circumstances the philosophical climate is ripe for lessons from African work: both because, in exploring the differences between philosophical practices in different places, one is able to approach the question that interests Cavell, Rorty, and West, and because there is a certain openness to new possibilities at the present moment as the result (in part) of the first two developments.[4]

Part II: The Context of Recent African Philosophy

The prospect of an African philosophy surely holds a great deal of promise. But the practice has so far not lived up to its potential. Furthermore, because it is a relatively recent idea, there is also a good deal of uncertainty about how to define its projects.

Still, the problem of African philosophy has a history, a context. It arises directly from a way of thinking about the nature of philosophy: an understanding of philosophy that defines it as, in principle, always explicit and systematic, always critical and self-critical, as bearing on particular human languages and experiences but never identifying with them. This ideal perspective is bound to exclude, as a matter of intellectual principle, such expressions as "Corsican philosophy," "American philosophy," or, for that matter, "Italian singers' philosophy." And what this understanding of philosophy presupposes is a sharp distinction between *Weltanschaungen* and the practice of philosophy as an intellectual discipline, between folk-philosophy and philosophy as a formal academic practice.

This distinction has not always been clearly understood. We should begin by recalling that the concept of African philosophy was generally used, during the nineteenth century and at the beginning of the twentieth—at least in the idiom of European anthropologists, missionaries, and travelers—to mean something like African *Weltanschaungen*. What they describe are cultural curiosities perceived and analyzed not as rational systems in their own right but rather as exotic and primitive exempla. Representative claims of this sort are to be found, for instance, in R. Baron's research on philosophical categories in Wolof, C. Delhaisse's description of Warega religious and philosophical categories, or B. Tanghe's article on Congolese philosophy (Baron 1829; Delhaisse 1909; Tanghe 1925). In the 1920s an ethnographer, specializing on the Kongo, the Belgian Van der Kercken, used the term "philosophical individualities," in the sense expounded later by P. Radin's "Primitive Man as Philosopher," to refer to individuals whose thinking has an impact on a particular *Weltanschauung* (see Radin 1927). This understanding led L. de Laggere in 1940 to discuss one Rwandan thinker—M. K. Sefu—as a philosopher (see Kinyongo 1989, p. 134).

On the whole, however, even when African local *Weltanschauungen* have been explored with sympathy, they have rarely been able to demonstrate their own rational coherence, since they have had to prove themselves against two theoretical assumptions: first, that African thought was backward, primitive; and second (correlatively) that Africans needed to be converted to a more civilized, more systematic order. Lévy-Bruhl's articulation of the difference between prelogical and logical mentalities, between primitive and civilized cultures, is witness to an intellectual configuration, which in his extreme version, identified philosophy and civilization with the reign of reason, and absence of philosophy and the fact of primitivism with mythical thinking.

Yet between the Lévy-Bruhl of *Les fonctions mentales dans les sociétés inférieures* (originally published in 1910) and the Lévy-Bruhl of *Les carnets* in the late 1940s, there is a discontinuity. And this radical change shows that African realities are no longer observed, perceived, described, and known in the old way. What we have here is a rupture.

And that rupture explains not only Lévy-Bruhl's recantation of the doctrine of the prelogical mentality but also, more generally, the progressive disintegration of evolutionist and reductionist models which led to the reorganization of disciplines and methods (anthropology, history, philosophy, theology, and so forth) and brought about the emergence of new metaphors. For example, what were once seen as signs of primitivism transmute themselves into elements of African cultures; "pagan" ideas are reinterpreted in the form of what come to be called African religions; and a continent whose history had been supposed to begin with the arrival of Europeans can finally designate and rewrite the complexity of her own histories.

The field of African Studies—and particularly that of philosophy in both its prehistory and history—witnesses and exemplifies this major epistemological discontinuity that has completely reorganized the domain of human sciences. This reversal can be seen, from a comparison of contemporary everyday intellectual practices with those of the beginning of this century in three main domains: first, the historicization of every culture and all human experiences; second, the questioning of evolutionary paradigms; and finally, the critical interrogation of the gap between the difference of the Other and the order of the Same.

What organizes the nineteenth-century *episteme* in anthropology is fundamentally a Western paradigm of knowledge: Western experience actualizes history, reason, and civilization. The colonizing vocation of the West (which was effective since the beginning of the expansion of European geography at the end of the fifteenth century) and its corollary, Christian missionizing,[5] posit a basic and curiously ethical necessity: to bring into conformity the variety of existing cultures and mentalities in the world. Among many others, Hume, Kant, and Hegel, in remarkably contemptuous pages on non-Westerners, had tried to provide a philosophical foundation for this Western right to colonization and exploitation of Africa, America, and Asia. Thus Lévy-Bruhl, a philosopher turned interpreter of ethnographic and anthropological materials is not an aberration (see Lévy-Bruhl 1912). He magnificently exemplifies an *episteme;* and he is a crucial exemplar of a philosophical tradition whose clearest moment in the nineteenth century was illustrated by Auguste Comte's law of three stages.

Thus, we have two opposed cultural universes: on the one hand, a primitive, summed up in a prelogical mentality—which does not actualize the principles of identity, noncontradiction and *tertium non datur*—functioning on the basis of a mythical thinking which, favoring its own tradition and past, would be, essentially, neophobic; and, on the other hand, an advanced, civilized mentality, promoting reason, logical rules and, by nature, neophile, that is facing positively the new and the unknown in order to apprehend and integrate it in its order of knowledge.

Evans-Pritchard is wrong, we fear, when he notes that "for various reasons most writers about primitive peoples have tended to lay stress on similarities, or what they supposed to be similarities, between ourselves and them; and Lévy-Bruhl thought it might be as well, for a change, to draw attention to the differences" (see Evans-Pritchard 1980, p. 80). For where, in fact, do we find the scholars who were able to challenge an epistemological tradition whose solidity is mirrored in the writings of Hume, Voltaire, Hegel, and Comte—indeed, in the whole library that justified both the slave trade and, some centuries later, the colonization of Africa? In the evolutionist library, concerned with the hierarchy of beings, as well as in a colonial library that was mainly interested in the right to colonize, otherness is a disease, an abnormality, a deviation.

Malinowski's functionalism and Lévi-Strauss' structuralism—applied to Central African myths in the 1950s and 1960s by Luc de Heusch, a former disciple of Marcel Griaule—privilege and mark a new rigor (see de Heusch 1971, 1972, 1981a, 1981b). But we must insist on the continuous accommodation that still records differences in terms of an evolutionary development of societies and cultures; we must confirm that the anthropological vocation combines an urge for knowledge with a romantic curiosity. Anthropology, as Malinowski put it himself, was, for him, a romantic flight from a standardized culture. Lévi-Strauss' confession in *Tristes Tropiques* can be similarly interpreted; and de Heusch would surely subscribe to it also.

Nevertheless, these works do exemplify a rupture: Malinowski's functionalism detaches itself from evolutionism. Its methods claim to apprehend otherness and its roots in such a way that it could account for any system. Lévi-Strauss' project accentuates such a different will to knowledge.[6] The order and equilibrium of Otherness in its multiple variations and transformations becomes a grid for reinterpreting the law and the grid of the Same—in fact describing universals from the margins of the Same, from the margins, that is, of the traditionally integrating schema.

The reversal is complete, and it occurs between 1920 and 1950.

Let us thus draw out the consequences of Michel Foucault's thesis about three epistemological regions:

—A biological region, situating the human being characterized by specific *functions* and who lives and acts accordingly to clear *norms* that allow him or her to live in a community;

—A socio-economic region, in which the human being is a being of needs and desire, caught between socio-economic *conflicts* and socially promulgated *rules;* and

—A linguistic region, in which human behavior is regulated by a body of *significations* and, on the other hand, by a philological and linguistic system.

As Foucault put it:

It might be possible to retrace the entire history of the human sciences, from the nineteenth century onward, on the basis of these three models. They have, in fact, covered the whole of that history, since we can follow the dynasty of their privileges for more than a century: first, the reign of the biological model (man, his psyche, his group, his society, the language he speaks—all these exist in the Romantic period as living beings and in so far as they were, in fact, alive; their mode of being is organic and is analyzed in terms of function); then comes the reign of the economic model (man and his entire activity are the locus of conflicts of which they are both the more or less manifest expression and the more or less successful solution); lastly—just as Freud comes after Comte and Marx—there begins the reign of the philological (when it is a matter of interpretation and the discovery of hidden meanings) and linguistic model (when it is a matter of giving a structure to and clarifying the signifying system). Thus a vast shift led the human sciences from a form more dense in living models to another more saturated with models borrowed from language. But this shift was paralleled by another: that which caused the first term in each of the constituent pairs (function, conflict, signification) to recede, and the second term (norm, rule, system) to emerge with a correspondingly greater intensity and importance: Goldstein, Mauss, Dumézil may be taken to represent, as near as makes no difference, the moment at which the reversal took place within each of the models. Such a reversal has two series of noteworthy consequences: as long as the functional point of view continued to carry more weight than the normative point of view (as long as it was not on the basis of the norm and the interior of the activity determining that norm that the attempt was made to understand how a function was performed), it was of course necessary, de facto, to share the normal functions with the non-normal; thus a pathological psychology was accepted side by side with normal psychology, but forming as it were an inverted image of it (hence the importance of the Jacksonian notion of disintegration in Ribot or Janet); in the same way, a pathology of societies (Durkheim), of irrational and quasi-morbid forms of belief (Lévy-Bruhl, Blondel) was also accepted; similarly, as long as the point of view of conflict carried more weight than that of the rule, it was supposed that certain conflicts could both be overcome, that individuals and societies ran the risk of destroying themselves by them; finally, as long as the point of view of signification carried more weight than that of system, a division was made between significant and non-significant: it was accepted that there was meaning in certain domains of human behavior or certain regions of the social area, but not in others. So that the human sciences laid down an essential division within their own field: they always extended between a positive pole and negative pole; they always designated an alterity (based, furthermore, on the continuity they were analyzing). When, on the other hand, the analysis was conducted from the point of view of the norm, the rule, and the system, each area provided its own coherence and its own validity; it was no longer possible to speak of "morbid consciousness" (even referring to the sick), of "primitive mentalities" (even with reference to societies left behind by history), or of "insignificant discourse" (even when referring to absurd stories, or to apparently incoherent legends). Everything may be thought within the order of the system, the rule, and the norm. By pluralizing itself—since systems are isolated, since rules form closed wholes, since norms are posited in their autonomy—the field of human sciences found itself unified: suddenly, it was no longer fissured along its former dichotomy of values. [Foucault 1973, pp. 359–61]

The prehistory and the history of African philosophy concretely illustrate Foucault's historical claims, and they provide at least three examples that had an enormous impact on social and human sciences in general: (a) the methodological preconceptions of the functional point of view made possible the scientific invention of the non-normal and the pathological, socially or individually, with, for example, Durkheim and Lévy-Bruhl; (b) the intellectual naiveté which postulated an absolute lack of coherence about social conflict in societies which did not conform to the normative rules conceived in the West; (c) finally, in terms of meaning, the political tension between positive and negative rationalities which justifies the right to colonize and underwrites both a philosophy and a theology of colonization.

Let us use some markers: Frazer and Lévy-Bruhl; Malinowski, Evans-Pritchard,[7] and Tempels; and finally, Crahay and Hountondji.

In the first paradigm, that of Frazer and Lévy-Bruhl, to be an African is to be ahistorical. In the second, it is to belong to a radical difference witnessing to its own localized functional achievements. Finally, with Crahay and Hountondji, the complex networks of African difference and the reality of African narratives—myths, cosmologies, rituals, social institutions, languages—give rise to a question: Is there such a thing as a philosophy that is a radical passage from sages (non-literate wise men and women) to philosophers? From an original experience to an opening up to something else?

The prehistory and the history of African philosophy raise two further important issues. The first is about the organic transformations of the field of African Studies. The second, which follows from the first, concerns the paradoxes of historicity. So far as the first issue is concerned, we should begin by admitting that African Studies has changed its paradigms—from evolution to diffusionism and functionalism first, and then to structuralism and post-structuralism—reflecting the successive discontinuities that have marked the social and human sciences in general.

To illustrate this, let us focus on the two moments of rupture represented by Tempels and Crahay. The first, Tempels, an intellectual disciple of Lévy-Bruhl who in the early 1930s was still convinced of his mission as a civilizing agent, questions his own evolutionary assumptions in his 1945 *La Philosophie Bantoue*.[8] Indeed, he comments on these assumptions as a basis for future work, participation, communion with the world, and prelogical mentality are converted. They become, for Tempels, axes in which a functional and implicit philosophy roots itself and from which one should think the future of African societies. Crahay, on the other hand, by transcending the local contingencies and underscoring the demand for the practice of philosophy in Africa, in the mid 1960s, was also applying a philosophical lesson, but a different one, expressed in an Aristotelian maxim: *aptum natum praedicari de multis* to be predicable, to be applicable to singulars.

It is clear Tempels marginalized Bantu *Weltanschauungen* in the name of their otherness (paradoxically, in order to make them respectable and universal) and Crahay negated what Tempels had called "Bantu philosophy" in the name of a philosophical practice. The whole history of African studies is summed up in this tension which, to go back to Foucault's thesis, is witness to a drift in the epistemological arrangement for which Freud is a useful symbol: "between positive and negative (between the normal and the pathological, the comprehensible and the incommunicable, the significant and the non-significant), it is easy to see how (Freud) prefigures the transition from an analysis in terms of functions, conflicts, and signification to an analysis in terms of norms, rules and systems: thus all this knowledge within which Western culture had given itself in one century a certain image of man, pivots on the work of Freud, though without, for all that, leaving its fundamental arrangement" (see Foucault 1973, p. 361).

Part III: Bringing the Two Together

The practice of philosophy in Africa, so far as it has distinguished itself from Anglophone philosophy in England or the United States or Francophone in France, has begun implicitly by answering the questions: first, is anything distinctive we can bring to the Western tradition from our own history and culture, our languages and traditions; and, second, what, in Africa, is the teaching and writing of Western-style philosophy for?

There have been many answers to these questions, but we would like to focus here on a body of work in recent African philosophy—by which we mean philosophical work guided by problems and issues raised particularly in contemporary African circumstances—that has already had a significant impact in British and American philosophy, and that provides one model for how that influence and impact can continue.

The problem that we are concerned with here is the question of the rationality of traditional magico-religious beliefs of a sort that are familiar in the ethnographies of Africa, such as Evans-Pritchard's, to which we have already referred.

Faced with such phenomena as Evans-Pritchard's Zande poison-oracles—in which whether or not a chicken dies when the oracle poison, *benge,* is administered, is taken to answer questions about important matters—many ethnographers and philosophers, like Lévy-Bruhl, essentially concluded that they were presented with deep irrationality. This was especially so because it seemed obvious to many European observers that belief in the oracle must be regularly contradicted by "experience." Evans-Pritchard, after living in Zandeland for some time, gave a classic account of the methods by which Zande people could maintain their belief in oracles against this charge. Towards the end of *Witchcraft, Oracles and Magic among the Azande,* he wrote:

> It may be asked why Azande do not perceive the futility of their magic. It would be easy to write at great length in answer to this question, but I will content myself with suggesting as shortly as possible a number of reasons.[9]

He then lists twenty-two such reasons. He mentions, for example, that since "magic is very largely employed against mystical powers . . . its action transcends experience" and thus "cannot easily be contradicted by experience,"[10] reinforcing a point made a few pages earlier:

> We shall not understand Zande magic . . . unless we realize that its main purpose is to combat other mystical powers rather than to produce changes favourable to man in the objective world.[11]

He says that the practices of witchcraft, oracles, and magic presuppose a coherent system of mutually supporting beliefs. "Death is proof of witchcraft. It is avenged by magic. . . . The accuracy of the poison oracle is determined by the king's oracle, which is above suspicion. . . . The results which magic is supposed to produce actually happen after the rites are performed. . . . Magic is only made to produce events which are likely to happen in any case . . . [and] is seldom asked to produce a result by itself but is associated with empirical action that does in fact produce it—e.g. a prince gives food to attract followers and does not rely on magic alone."[12] And, though he acknowledges that Azande notice failures of their witchcraft, he shows too how they have many ways to explain this failure: there may have been an error in executing the spell; there may be an unknown and countervailing magic; and so on.

It is the fact that it is possible to make exactly these sorts of moves in defense of traditional religious beliefs, that has led some to draw the conclusion that traditional religious belief should be interpreted as having the same purposes as those of modern natural science, which are summarized in the slogan "explanation, prediction, and control." For when scientific procedures fail, scientists do not normally react by saying that we must begin physics all over again. Rather, they offer explanations as to how the failure could have occurred consistently with the theory. Biochemists regularly ignore negative results, assuming that test tubes are dirty, or that samples are contaminated, or that in preparing the sample they have failed to take some precaution that is necessary to prevent the action of those enzymes that are always released when a cell is damaged. A skeptical Zande could well make the same sorts of observation about these procedures as Evans-Pritchard makes about Azande magic: "the perception of error in one mystical notion in a particular situation merely proves the correctness of another and equally mystical notion."

Philosophers of science have names for this: they say that theory is "underdetermined" by observation and that observation is "theory-laden." And they mean by underdetermination what the French philosopher-physicist, Pierre Duhem, noticed in the early part of this century: that the application of theory to particular cases relies on a whole host of other beliefs, not all of which can be checked at once.

By the theory-ladenness of observation, relatedly, they mean that our theories both contribute to forming our experience and give meaning to the language we use for reporting it. Karl Popper's claim that science should proceed by attempts at falsification, as we all know after reading Thomas Kuhn, is incorrect.[13] If we gave up every time an experiment failed, scientific theory would get nowhere. The underdetermination of our theories by our experience means that we are left even by the most unsuccessful experiment with room for maneuver. The trick is not to give up too soon or go on too long.

We have suggested that one might assimilate the theories that underlie traditional religion and magic with those that are engendered in the natural sciences because, in effect, the religious theories share the purposes of modern natural science, which we may summarize in the slogan "explanation, prediction, and control." It is his systematic development of the analogy between natural science and traditional religion that has made the work of Robin Horton so important in the philosophy of African traditional religions; and it will be useful to begin with him.[14]

Horton's basic point is just the one we made earlier: the fundamental character of these religious systems is that the practices arise from the belief, literal and not symbolic, in the powers of invisible agents. Horton argues persuasively that spirits and such function in explanation, prediction, and control, much as do other theoretical entities: they differ from those of natural science in being persons and not material forces and powers, but the logic of their function in explanation and prediction is the same.

Horton's view, then, is that religious beliefs of traditional peoples constitute explanatory theories and that traditional religious actions are reasonable attempts to pursue goals in the light of these beliefs— attempts, in other words, at prediction and control of the world. In these respects, Horton argues, traditional religious belief and action are like theory in the natural sciences and the actions based on it. As Meinrad Hebga, in the Francophone African tradition, says:

> While neither failing to recognize their limits nor restraining the march towards progress, theoretical understanding [science], and liberation, we must admit that African explanations of the phenomena of magic and sorcery are rational. Our popular beliefs are certainly disconcerting, sometimes false; but would it not be a serious methodological error to postulate irrationality at the beginning of the study of a society?[15]

Horton's thesis is not that traditional religion is a kind of science but that theories in the two domains are similar in these crucial respects.

The major *difference* in the contents of the theories, he argues, is that traditional religious theory is couched in terms of personal forces while natural scientific theory is couched in terms of impersonal forces. The basic claim strikes us as immensely plausible.

Yet various African philosophers have pointed out that there is in the analogy between natural science and traditional religion much to mislead also.[16] Kwasi Wiredu, for example, has pointed out that it is, on the surface, very odd to equate traditional religious belief in West Africa with modern Western scientific theory, when the obvious analogue is traditional Western religious belief (see Wiredu 1980). It will be obvious from what we have already said that there need be no contest here: for the explanatory function of religious beliefs in traditional Europe seems to be identical in its logic with that of scientific theory also.

What *is* misleading is not the assimilation of the logics of explanation of theories from religion and science but the assimilation of traditional religion and natural science as institutions. This is, first of all, misleading because of the sorts of changes—most notably an increasing demythologization—that have occurred in the last few centuries of Western religious life. For the modern Westerner to call something "religious" is to connote a great deal that is lacking in traditional religion and not to connote much that is present. But there is a much more fundamental reason why the equation of religion and science is misleading. And it is to do with the totally different social organization of enquiry in traditional and modern cultures. We shall return to this issue later.

HORTON HIMSELF IS, of course, aware that traditional religious beliefs are certainly unlike those of natural science in at least two important respects. First of all, as we have already insisted, he points out that the theoretical entities invoked are agents and not material forces. And he offers us an account of why this might be. He suggests that this difference arises out of the fundamental nature of explanation as the reduction of the unfamiliar to the familiar. In traditional cultures, nature, the wild, is untamed, alien, and a source of puzzlement and fear. Social relations and persons are, on the contrary, familiar and well understood. Explaining the behavior of nature in terms of agency is thus reducing the unfamiliar forces of the wild to the familiar explanatory categories of personal relations.

In the industrial world, on the other hand, industrialization and urbanization have made social relations puzzling and problematic. We move between social environments—the rural and the urban, the workplace and the home—in which different conventions operate; and in the new, urban, factory, market environment we deal with people whom we know only through our common productive projects. As a result the social is relatively unfamiliar. However, our relations with objects in the city are relations which remain relatively stable across all these differing social relations. Indeed, if factory workers move between factories, the skills they take with them are precisely those which depend on a familiarity not with other people but with the workings of material things. It is no longer natural to try to understand nature through social relations; rather we understand it through machines, through matter whose workings we find comfortably familiar. It is well known that the understanding of gases in the nineteenth century was modeled on the behavior of miniature billiard balls: for nineteenth-century scientists in Europe knew the billiard table better than they knew, for example, their servants. Alienation is widely held to be the characteristic state of modern man: the point can be overstated, but it cannot be denied.

> In complex, rapidly changing industrial societies, the human scene is in flux. Order, regularity, predictability, simplicity, all these seem lamentably absent. It is in the world of inanimate things that such qualities are most readily seen. And this . . . I suggest, is why the mind in quest of explanatory analogies turns most readily to the inanimate. In the traditional societies of Africa we find the situation reversed. The human scene is the locus *par excellence* of order, predictability, regularity. In the world of the inanimate, these qualities are far less evident . . . here, the mind in quest of explanatory analogies turns naturally to people and their relations.[17]

Horton relies here on a picture of the function of scientific theory as essentially concerned to develop models of the unified, simple, ordered, regular underlying features of reality in order to account for the diversity, complexity, disorder, and apparent lawlessness of ordinary experience.[18] His story works so well that it is hard not to feel that there is something right about it; and it would indeed explain the preference for agency over matter, the first of the major differences Horton acknowledges between traditional religion and science.

Horton in his original work made, as we have said, a second important claim for difference: he summarized it by calling the cognitive world of traditional cultures "closed" and that of modern cultures "open." "What I take to be the key difference is a very simple one," he writes. "It is that in traditional cultures there is no developed awareness of alternatives to the established body of theoretical tenets; whereas in scientifically oriented cultures, such an awareness is highly developed."[19] And it is here, when we turn from questions about the content and logic of traditional and scientific explanation to the social contexts in which those theories are constructed and mobilized, that Horton's account begins to seem less adequate.

Now Horton's account of the sense in which the traditional world view is closed has—rightly—been challenged. The complexities of war and trade, dominance and clientage, migration and diplomacy, in much of precolonial Africa are simply not consistent with the image of peoples unaware that there is a world elsewhere. As Catherine Coquery-Vidrovitch, a leading French historian of Africa, has pointed out:

> In fact, these reputedly stable societies rarely enjoyed the lovely equilibrium presumed to have been disrupted by the impact of colonialism. West Africa, for example, had been seething with activity ever since the eighteenth century waves of Fulani conquest and well before the creation of units of resistance to European influence. . . . The Congolese basin was the site of still more profound upheavals linked to commercial penetration. In such cases the revolution in production rocked the very foundations of the political structure. As for South Africa, the rise of the Zulus and their expansion had repercussions up into central Africa. How far back do we have to go to find the stability alleged to be "characteristic" of the precolonial period: before the Portuguese conquest, before the Islamic invasion, before the Bantu expansion? Each of these great turning points marked the reversal of long-term trends, within which a whole series of shorter cycles might in turn be identified, as, for example, the succession of Sudanic empires, or even such shorter cycles as the periods of recession (1724–1740, 1767–1782, 1795–1811, and so on) and the upswing of the slave-trade economy of Dahomey. In short, the static concept of "traditional" society cannot withstand the historian's analysis.[20]

In particular, African historians can trace changes in religious and other beliefs in many places long before the advent of Christian missionaries and colonial educators.[21] The Yoruba were aware of Islam before they were aware of England, of Dahomey before they heard of Britain. But Yoruba religion has many of the features that Horton proposed to explain by reference to a lack of awareness of just such alternatives.

It is also possible to find first-rate speculative thinkers in traditional societies, whose individual openness is not to be denied. We think here of Ogotemmeli, whose cosmology Griaule has captured in *Dieu d'Eau* (1948); and Barry Hallen has provided evidence from Nigerian sources of the existence, within African traditional modes of thought, of styles of reasoning which are open neither to Wiredu's stern strictures nor to Horton's milder ones.[22] In Yoruba culture many traditional intellectuals meet standards for being critical and reflective, which Hallen takes from Popper 1962 (a gesture all the more significant given the Popperian provenance of Horton's own open-closed dichotomy).

Hallen is right, we believe, to challenge the structure of Horton's original dichotomy of the open and the closed. On the one hand, there is in post-Kuhnian history and sociology of science a good deal of evidence that these Popperian desiderata are hardly met in physics, the heartland of Western theory. On the other hand, Horton's original stress on the "closed" nature of traditional modes of thought does look less adequate in the face of Africa's complex history of cultural exchanges and of Hallen's diviners and healers or in the presence of the extraordinary metaphysical synthesis of the Dogon elder, Ogotemmeli.[23] In a recent book, written with the Nigerian philosopher J. O. Sodipo, Hallen insists that among Yoruba doctors there exist theories of witchcraft rather different from those of their fellow countrymen (see Hallen and Sodipo 1986). Here, then, among the doctors, speculation inconsistent with ordinary folk belief occurs; and there is no reason to doubt that this *aspect* of contemporary Yoruba culture is, in *this* respect, like many precolonial cultures.

Horton has recently come—partly in response to Hallen's critique— to speak not of the closedness of traditional belief systems but, borrowing a term from Wole Soyinka, of their being "accommodative." He discusses work by students of Evans-Pritchard's which not only addresses the kind of static body of belief that is captured in Evans-Pritchard's picture of the Azande thought world, but which stresses the dynamic and, as Horton admits, "open" way in which they "devise explanations for novel elements in . . . experience" and "their capacity to borrow, rework and integrate alien ideas in the course of elaborating such explanations."

> Indeed it is this "open-ness" that has given the traditional cosmologies such tremendous durability in the face of the immense changes that the 20th century has brought to the African scene.

Horton contrasts this accommodative style with the "adversary" style of scientific theory, which is characterized by the way in which the main stimulus to change of belief is not "novel experience but rival theory."[24] And it seems to us that this change from the Popperian terminology of "open" and "closed" allows Horton to capture something important about the difference between traditional religion and science—something to do not with individual cognitive strategies but with social ones. If we want to understand the significance of social organization in differentiating traditional religion and natural science, we can do no better than to begin with those of Evans-Pritchard's answers to the question of why the Azande do not see the falsity of their magic beliefs that mention social facts about the organization of their beliefs.

"SCEPTICISM," EVANS-PRITCHARD WROTE, "far from being smothered, is recognized, even inculcated." He continued,

> But it is only about certain medicines and certain magicians. By contrast it tends to support other medicines and other magicians.
> . . . Each man and each kinship group acts without cognizance of the actions of others. People do not pool their ritual experiences.
> . . . They are not experimentally inclined.[25] . . . Not being experimentally inclined, they do not test the efficacy of their medicines.

And, he added, "Zande beliefs are generally vaguely formulated. A belief, to be easily contradicted by experience . . . must be clearly shared and intellectually developed."[26]

Whatever the practices of imperfect scientists are actually like, none of these things is supposed to be true of natural science. In our official picture of the sciences, skepticism *is* encouraged even about foundational questions: indeed that is where the best students are supposed to be directed. Scientific researchers conceive of themselves as a community which cuts across political boundaries as divisive as the (late and unlamented) cold war Iron Curtain; and results, "experiences," *are* shared. The scientific community *is* experimentally inclined, and, of course, scientific theory *is* formulated as precisely as possible in order that those experiments can be carried out in a controlled fashion.

That, of course, is only the *official* view. Three decades of work in the history and sociology of science since Kuhn's iconoclastic *The Structure of Scientific Revolutions* have left us with a picture of science as much more messy and muddled—in short, as a more human business. Yet while this work has had the effect of revising (one is inclined to say "tarnishing") our image of the institutions of scientific research, it has not revised the fundamental recognition that the production of scientific knowledge is organized around competing theoretical positions, and that the demand for publication to establish the success of laboratories and individual scientists exposes each competing theory to review by ambitious counter-theorists from other laboratories, with other positions. What we have learned, however (though it should have been obvious all along), is that there are serious limits placed on the range of positions that will be entertained.[27] The development of science is not a free-for-all with all the participants cheering each other on with the cry: "And may the best theory win." But science *is,* crucially, adversarial: the norms of publication and reproducibility of results, even though only imperfectly adhered to, are explicitly intended to lay theories and experimental claims open to attack by one's peers, and thus make competition from the adventurous "young Turk" possible.

More important than the hugely oversimplified contrast between an experimental, skeptical science and an unexperimental, "dogmatic," traditional mode of thought is the difference in images of knowledge that are represented in the differences in the social organization of enquiry in modern as opposed to "traditional" societies. Scientists, like the rest of us, hold on to theories longer than they may be entitled to; suppress, unconsciously or half-consciously, evidence they do not know how to handle; lie a little. In precolonial societies there were, we can be sure, individual doubters, who kept their own counsel, resisters against the local dogma. But what is interesting about modern modes of theorizing is that they are organized around an image of constant change: we expect new theories; we reward and encourage the search for them; we believe that today's best theories will be revised beyond recognition if the enterprise of science survives. The Azande never organized a specialized activity that was based around this thought. They knew that some people know more than others, and that there are things to be found out. But they do not seem to have thought it necessary to invest social effort in working out new theories of how the world works, not for some practical end (this they did constantly) but, as we say, for its own sake.

The differences between traditional religious theory and the theories of the sciences reside in the social organization of enquiry, as a systematic business, and it is differences in social organization that account both for the difference we feel in the character of natural scientific and traditional religious theory—they are the products of different kinds of social process—and for the spectacular expansion of the domain of successful prediction and control, an expansion that characterizes natural science but is notably absent in traditional society. Experimentation, the publication and reproduction of results, the systematic development of alternative theories in precise terms—all these ideals, however imperfectly they are realized in scientific practice, are intelligible only in an organized social enterprise of knowledge.

But what can have prompted this radically different approach to knowledge? Why have the practitioners of traditional religion, even the priests, who are the professionals, never developed the organized "adversarial" methods of the sciences? There are, no doubt, many historical sources. A few, familiar suggestions strike one immediately.

Social mobility leads to political individualism, of a kind that is rare in the traditional polity; political individualism allows cognitive authority to shift, also, from priest and king to commoner; and social mobility is a feature of industrial societies.

Or: In traditional societies, accommodating conflicting theoretical views is part of the general process of accommodation necessary for those who are bound to each other as neighbors for life. And this accommodating approach to daily interactions is part of the same range of attitudes that leads to theoretical accommodations.

We could think of more differences in social, economic, and ecological background, which together may help to account for this difference in approach to theory. But there is one other fundamental difference between traditional African cultures and the cultures of the industrial world, and it plays a fundamental role in explaining why the adversarial style never established itself in Africa. And it is that these cultures were largely nonliterate.

Now literacy has, as Jack Goody has pointed out in his influential book *The Domestication of the Savage Mind,* important consequences; and among them is that it permits a kind of consistency that oral culture cannot and does not demand. Write down a sentence and it is there, in principle, for ever; and that means that if you write down another sentence inconsistent with it, you can be caught out. It is this fact that is at the root of the possibility of the adversarial style. In the absence of written records, it is not possible to compare the ancestors' theories in their actual words with ours; nor, given the limitations of quantity imposed by oral transmission, do we have a detailed knowledge of what those theories were. We know more about the thought of Isaac Newton on one or two subjects than we know about the entire population of his Asante contemporaries.

The accommodative style is possible because there is no need for, indeed no possibility of, recognizing discrepancies. And so it is possible to have an image of knowledge as unchanging lore, handed down from the ancestors. It is no wonder, with this image of knowledge, that there is no systematic research: nobody need ever notice that the way that traditional theory is used requires inconsistent interpretations. It is literacy that makes possible the precise formulation of questions that we have just noticed as one of the characteristics of scientific theory, and it is precise formulation that points up inconsistency. This explanation, which we owe to Horton, is surely very plausible.

Given the orality of traditional culture, it is possible to see how the accommodative approach can be maintained. With widespread literacy, the image of knowledge as a body of truths always already given cannot survive. But the recognition of the failures of consistency of the traditional world view does not automatically lead to science; there are, as we have already observed, many other contributing factors. Without widespread literacy it is hard to see how science could have got started: it is not a sufficient condition for science, but it seems certainly necessary. What else, apart from a lot of luck, accounts for the beginnings of modern science? So many things: the Reformation, itself dependent not merely on literacy but also on printing and the wider dissemination of the Bible and other religious writings, with its transfer of cognitive authority from the Church to the individual; the experience with mechanism, with machinery, in agriculture and warfare; the development of universities. Our claim is not that literacy explains modern science (China is a standing refutation of that claim); it is that it was crucial to its possibility. And the very low level of its literacy shaped the intellectual possibilities of precolonial Africa.

Part IV: In Conclusion

We have pursued this African debate in some detail because it so well exemplifies the major point we want to make: (1) addressing questions that arise obviously for philosophy in Africa obliges you to address questions that are centrally philosophical in the American tradition. Not only does African philosophy thus inevitably connect with American (and European), it does so in ways that illuminate those "Western" discussions. This fact is demonstrated in the ways in which the Horton discussion that we have described has influenced the writings of philosophers of science and social science such as Bryan Wilson, Paul Feyerabend, and Peter Winch (see Feyerabend 1975; Hollis and Lukes 1982; Horton and Finnegan 1973; Wilson 1970; Winch 1972). Much reaction to Horton's work is summarized in Horton 1982.

In exercising its influence this work has also (2) shown the many intellectual benefits of the combination of historical, anthropological, and philosophical analysis that is characteristic of the humanities in African studies, generally, as well as of African philosophy more particularly; and thus (3) provides a model for interdisciplinary analysis in philosophical work. Furthermore, (4) in the interaction between Anglophone and Francophone philosophers around these questions, it has provided a model for dialogue among the divided analytical and Continental traditions. And, finally, in exemplifying the ways in which a philosophical culture both depends on and transcends its own context, (5) African philosophy can illuminate the currently important question—raised, as we said, in the works of Cavell, Rorty, and West—of the relations between philosophy and culture *elsewhere*.[28]

NOTES

1. Similar conclusions follow from Wittgenstein's notion of the inextricability of belief and meaning in his *Philosophical Investigations* (Wittgenstein 1968).

2. And, perhaps, bored by the limited interest of analysis of this sort.

3. See especially Foucault 1976. Kuhn's notion of a "paradigm," much taken up in the sociology and philosophy of science, has also played its role in causing analytical philosophers to reflect on the contingencies of method, subject-matter, and norm that define particular stages of philosophy. See Kuhn 1962.

4. We should not, however, ignore here the wider trend in the academy towards an interest in the issues that are broadly grouped under the label of "multiculturalism," which is also important in creating an openness to "other" cultures.

5. There is something paradoxical in the way Christian missionary activity presented itself before the eighteenth century as a divine duty, and thus elaborated a theology of colonization, which drew largely on a conception of natural law according to which the most advanced have the obligation to promote their inferior brethren; and, in the name of thus promoting them, allowed itself to dispossess non-Christian countries in order to exploit the wealth meant by God for the use of all humankind.

6. And, more particularly, its illustration in Luc de Heusch's works about Bantu mythology, and from a different and more empirical point of view, the work of Victor Turner.

7. Evans-Pritchard 1956.

8. Translated as *Bantu Philosophy* (Tempels 1959).

9. Evans-Pritchard 1976, p. 201.

10. Evans-Pritchard 1976.

11. Ibid., p. 199. By "mystical" notions Evans-Pritchard means, as he says, "patterns of thought that attribute to phenomena supra-sensible qualities which, or part of which, are not derived from observation or cannot logically be inferred from it, *and which they do not possess*" (ibid., p. 229; italics ours). It is the italicized phrase that does all the work here; the rest of this definition simply means that mystical predicates are theory-laden, which means, if recent philosophy of science is correct, that they are, in this respect, like every other empirical predicate (see Hanson 1958 and, for some reservations, Hacking 1983, pp. 171–76). (Hanson's term is "theory-loaded" but we—and others—use the expression "theory-laden.")

12. Evans-Pritchard 1976, pp. 201–3.

13. See Popper 1962, and Kuhn 1962.

14. Horton's most famous paper is his Horton 1967. See also Horton 1956, 1962, 1964, 1970, 1972, 1973*a*, 1973*b*, 1976, 1977, 1982. (We have

also relied on the three typescripts listed in the references.) See also Gjertsen 1980, Hallen 1977, Hallen and Sodipo 1986, and Pratt 1972. The philosophy journal *Second Order* is edited at Ife, Nigeria.

15. "Sans méconnaître ses limites ni freiner la marche vers le progrès, la science et la libération, il faut admettre que l'explication africaine des phéno-mènes de la magie et de la sorcellerie est rationelle. Nos croyances populaires sont déconcertantes certes, parfois fausses, mais ne serait-ce pas une faute méthodologique grave que de postuler l'irrationnel au point de départ de l'étude d'une société?" (Hebga 1979, p. 267).

16. See, e.g., Wiredu 1980; Gyekye 1987; Appiah 1992.

17. Horton 1967, p. 64.

18. Ibid., p. 51.

19. Wilson 1970, p. 53.

20. Coquery-Vidrovitch 1976, p. 91.

21. As Horton himself has insisted in Horton 1970.

22. See Hallen 1977. Wiredu, of course, does not deny the existence of skeptics in traditional cultures. See Wiredu 1980, pp. 20–21, 37, and 143.

23. Griaule 1948. And we might add, despite Horton's comments in the manuscript "African Thought-Patterns: The Case for a Comparative Ap-proach," that after Kuhn the "openness" of science is also in question; see Gjertsen 1980.

24. This work is in Horton typescript *c*.

25. This is not to say that they do not have the concepts necessary to un-derstand the idea of an experiment, merely to say that they are not interested in disinterested experimentation simply to find out how things work. For the Azande are very aware, for example, that an oracle needs to be run carefully if it is to be reliable. They therefore test its reliability on every occasion of its use. There are usually two tests: *bambata sima* and *gingo;* the first and second tests. Generally, in the first test, the question is asked so the death of a chicken means yes and in the second so that death means no; but it may be the other way round. Inconsistent results invalidate the procedure. The Azande also have a way of confirming that an oracle is not working; namely to ask it a question to which they already know the answer. Such failures can be explained by one of the many obstacles to an oracle's functioning properly: breach of taboo; witchcraft; the fact that the *benge* poison used in the oracle has been "spoiled" (as the Azande believe) because it has been near a menstruating woman.

26. Evans-Pritchard 1976, pp. 202–4.

27. In 1981, for example, when Rupert Sheldrake's *A New Science of Life* was published, a correspondent in *Nature* suggested it might usefully be burned. This was inconsistent with official ideology because Sheldrake, a for-mer research fellow of the Royal Society who had studied the philosophy of science, had constructed a proposal, which, though provocative, was deliber-ately couched in terms that made it subject to potential experimental test. Still, it outraged many biologists (and physicists) and if there had not been a chal-lenge from the *New Scientist* magazine to design experiments, his proposal, like most of those regarded as in one way or the other the work of a "crank," would probably simply have been ignored by his professional peers. (There is

some conclusion to be drawn from the fact that the copy of Sheldrake's book listed in the catalog at Duke University appears to be in the Divinity School library!)

28. We have not, by any means, discussed all the major movements in recent African philosophy, which are surveyed in Mudimbe 1988 and discussed in Appiah 1992, chap. 5. We would like to underline how much of the most interesting recent work in the field is by Africans or written by scholars working in Africa. For example, Appiah, Gyekye, Hebga, Houtondji, Kinyongo, Mudimbe, and Wiredu are Africans and have been members of African university faculties; Horton has worked in Nigeria since the 1950s; and Gjertsen was on the faculty of the University of Ghana at Legon. Equally important is the resonance between these issues in the work of Africanists and the work of those, like Cornel West, who are philosophically engaged with the African-American experience.

REFERENCE

Appiah, Kwame. *In My Father's House: Africa in the Philosophy of Culture.* New York: Oxford University Press, 1992.

Baron, R. *Recherches philosophiques sur la langue oulofe.* Paris, 1829.

Cavell, Stanley. *The Senses of Walden.* San Francisco: North Point Press, 1981.

———. *This New Yet Unapproachable America: Lectures after Emerson after Wittgenstein.* Albuquerque, N.M.: Living Batch Press, 1989.

———. *Conditions Handsome and Unhandsome: The Constitution of Emersonian Perfectionism.* Chicago: University of Chicago Press, 1990.

Coquery-Vidrovitch, Catherine. "The Political Economy of the African Peasantry and Modes of Production." In *The Political Economy of Contemporary Africa,* translated by Jeanne Mayo and edited by Peter C. W. Gutkind and Immanuel Wallerstein. Beverly Hills, Calif.: Sage Publications, 1976.

de Heusch, Luc. *Pourquoi l'épouser et autres essais.* Paris: Gallimard, 1971.

———. *Le roi ivre.* Paris: Gallimard, 1972.

———. *Why Marry Her?* translated by Janet Lloyd. Cambridge: Cambridge University Press, 1981a.

———. *The Drunken King,* translated and annotated by Roy Willis. Bloomington: Indiana University Press, 1981b.

Delhaisse, C. "Les Idées religieuse et philosophiques des Warega." *Mouvement Géographique* 29 (1909): 340–42.

Evans-Pritchard, Edward E. *Nuer Religion.* Oxford: Clarendon Press, 1956.

———. *Witchcraft, Oracles and Magic among the Azande,* edited and abridged by Eva Gillies. London: Oxford University Press, 1976.

———. *Theories of Primitive Religion.* Oxford: Oxford University Press, 1980.

Feyerabend, Paul K. *Against Method: Outline of an Anarchistic of Knowledge.* London: New Left Books, 1975.

Foucault, Michel. *The Order of Things.* New York: Pantheon, 1973.

————. *The Archaeology of Knowledge,* translated by A. M. Sheridan Smith. New York: Harper and Row, 1976.

Gjertsen, Derek. "Closed and Open Belief Systems." *Second Order* 7 (1980): 5–69.

Goody, Jack. *The Domestication of the Savage Mind.* Cambridge: Cambridge University Press, 1977.

Griaule, Marcel. *Dieu d'eau: Entretiens avec ogotemmeli.* Paris: Editions du Chêne, 1948.

Gyekye, Kwame. *African Philosophical Thought.* Cambridge: Cambridge University Press, 1987.

Hacking, Ian. *Representing and Intervening: Introductory Topics in the Philosophy of Science.* Cambridge: Cambridge University Press, 1983.

Hallen, Barry. "Robin Horton on Critical Philosophy and Traditional Thought." *Second Order* 6 (1977): 81–92.

Hallen, Barry, and Sodipo, J. O. *Knowledge, Belief and Witchcraft.* London: Ethnographica, 1986.

Hanson, Norwood Russel. *Patterns of Discovery: An Inquiry into the Conceptual Foundations of Science.* Cambridge: Cambridge University Press, 1958.

Hebga, Meinrad P. *Sorcellereie: Chimere dangereuse . . . ? Abidjan: INADES,* 1979.

Hollis, Martin, and Lukes, Steven. *Rationality and Relativism.* Oxford: Blackwell, 1982.

Horton, Robin. "God, Man and the Land in a Northern Ibo Village Group." *Africa* 26 (1956): 17–28.

————. "The Kalabari World View: An Outline and Interpretation." *Africa* 22 (1962): 197–220.

————. "Ritual Man in Africa." *Africa* 34 (1964): 85–104.

————. "African Traditional Religion and Western Science." *Africa* 37 (1967): 50–71 and 155–87. Reprinted, with changes, in Wilson 1970.

————. "A Hundred Years of Change in Kalabari Religion." In *Black Africa: Its Peoples and Their Cultures Today,* edited by John Middleton. London: Collier-Macmillan, 1970.

————. "Spiritual Beings and Elementary Particles: A Reply to Mr. Pratt." *Second Order* 1 (1972): 21–33.

————. "Paradox and Explanation: A Reply to Mr. Skorupski." *Philosophy of Social Sciences* 3 (1973*a*): 231–56.

————. Lévy-Bruhl, Durkheim and the Scientific Revolution." In *Modes of Thought,* edited by Robin Horton and Ruth Finnegan. London: Faber and Faber, 1973*b*.

————. "Understanding Traditional African Religion: A Reply to Professor Beattie." *Second Order* 3 (1976): 3–29.

————. "Traditional Thought and the Emerging African Philosophy Department: A Comment on the Current Debate." *Second Order* 6 (1977): 64–80.

————. "Tradition and Modernity Revisited." In *Rationality and Relativism,* edited by S. Lukes and M. Hollis. Oxford: Basil Blackwell, 1982.

————. "African Thought-Patterns: The Case for a Comparative Approach." Typescript *a*.

————. "Traditional Thought and the Emerging African Philosophy Department: A Reply to Dr. Hallen." Typescript *b*.

————. "African Thought Patterns: The Case for a Comparative Approach." Typescript *c*.

Horton, Robin, and Finnegan, Ruth. *Modes of Thought: Essays in Western and Non-Western Societies*. London: Faber and Faber, 1973.

Hountondji, Paulin. *African Philosophy: Myth and Reality,* translated by Henri Evans with Jonathan Rée. Introduction by Abiola Irele. Bloomington, Ind.: Indian University Press, 1983.

Kinyongo, J. *Epiphanies de la philosophie Africaine et Afro-Américane*. Munich-Kinshasa-Lumumbashi: Publications Universitaires Africaines, 1989.

Kuhn, Thomas S. *The Structure of Scientific Revolutions*. 2d ed. Chicago: University of Chicago Press, 1962.

Lévy-Bruhl, Lucien. *Les fonctions mentales dans les sociétés inférieures*. Paris: F. Alcan, 1912.

Mudimbe, V. Y. *The Invention of Africa*. Chicago: University of Chicago Press, 1988.

Popper, Karl. *Conjectures and Refutations: The Growth of Scientific Knowledge*. New York: Basic Books, 1962.

Pratt, Vernon. "Science and Traditional Religion. A Discussion of Some of Robin Horton's Views." *Second Order* 1 (1972): 7–20.

Quine, W. V. O., and Ullina, J. S. *The Web of Belief*. New York: Random House, 1970.

Radin, Paul. *Primitive Man as Philosopher*. New York: D. Appleton and Company, 1927.

Rorty, Richard. *Contingency, Irony and Solidarity*. New York: Cambridge University Press, 1989.

Sheldrake, Rupert. *A New Science of Life: The Hypothesis of Formative Causation*. London: Blond and Briggs, 1981.

Tanghe, B. "Une page de philosophie congolaise chez les Ngband.i." *Congo* 1, no. 6 (1925): 562–65.

Tempels, Placide. *Bantu Philosophy*. Paris: Présence Africaine, 1959.

West, Cornel. *The American Evasion of Philosophy: A Genealogy of Pragmatism*. Madison: University of Wisconsin Press, 1989.

Wilson, Bryan. *Rationality*. Oxford: Blackwell, 1970.

Winch, Peter. *Ethics and Action*. London: Routledge and Kegan Paul, 1972.

Wiredu, Kwasi. *Philosophy and an African Culture*. London: Cambridge University Press, 1980.

Wittgenstein, Ludwig. *Philosophical Investigations,* translated by G. E. M. Anscombe. Oxford: Basil Blackwell, 1968.

5

Truth and Seeing:
Magic, Custom, and Fetish
in Art History

SUZANNE PRESTON BLIER

> A remarkable feature of all artworks (or to be a bit more
> circumspect, *practically* all art works) is what I call, in a broad
> sense, their *fictive* character. This fictive character consists in a
> false seeming . . . in a purporting to be something it isn't, in
> putting on an act or show.
>
> Monroe Beardsley, *The Aesthetic Point of View*

"ANY TRAVELER'S TALE that claims to be a fruitful report," writes François Hartog with regard to the ancient Greeks in *The Mirror of Herodotus* (1988, pp. 230, 232), "must contain a category of *thoma*
(marvels, curiosities) . . . [objects or traditions which denote] the difference between what is here and what is there far away." The topics ex-
amined below are similarly concerned with marvels or *thoma* and the
framing of issues of cultural sameness and difference, here made somewhat more complex by the task at hand of addressing the question of
what African art historians can offer scholars dealing with other periods
and pieces. My aim is not to present an annotate compendium of recent
and interesting writing in the field of African art for the non-Africanist
to explore and mine for data or methodological insights. Related references may be found in four rather lengthy overview papers on African
art recently completed by Daniel Biebuyck (1983), Karen Barber
(1987), Monni Adams (1989), and Paula Ben-Amos (1989).

This essay instead is about the making and breaking of boundaries
and the construction of ideas of difference and sameness in the arts of
Europe and Africa. If the present analysis is more concerned with issues
and questions than with research as such, it is because, in my view, the
distinctions between African and European art scholarship lie as much

in the framing of associated discourse as in real or perceived questions of art or cultural distinctiveness in the two areas. In the pages below, I explore the language of these differences through an analysis of three key terms bearing on the construction of cultural otherness: "fetish," "magic," and "custom." By fetish, I refer to those ideas that one chooses to believe despite the irrationality (groundlessness, artificiality) of their foundation; by magic, I mean the common practice of privileging the strange as other and the other as strange; and by custom, I refer to the retention of ideas whether "invented" or "found" on which one hangs one's hat because they are said to have always been and to always be.

In the course of objectifying the field through a discussion of these terms, I hope to point out the tenuousness of some of our core assumptions of difference. At the same time I examine related concepts and rhetoric used by scholars historically to highlight the otherness of African art, I argue that comparable otherness concerns and issues are critical to the intellectual viability of the discipline at large. While this essay owes much to contemporary deconstructionist discourse with reference to the conceptualization of the Other—most importantly the work of Edward Said (1978), Hayden White (1978), Johannes Fabian (1983), Mikhail Bakhtin (1987), Roland Barthes (1974), Julia Kristeva (1986), Fredric Jameson (1988)—in the end I suggest that post-structuralist methodologies themselves may be inadequate for the examination of the unique issues raised by African art.

Beginning on a methodological note, I would argue that all art historians, present or past, positivist or nonpositivist, formalist or antiformalist, elitist or materialist, structuralist or deconstructionist, share an interest in questions of truth (truths, "truth," untruth, counter-truth, falsehood—however defined) and with those methodologies which in one way or another address related concerns. It is through this shared interest, I maintain, that scholars in African, European, and other world arts can fruitfully benefit from intellectual exchange. I would suggest in turn that the most important knowledge that we as teachers can convey to our students (and we as Africanists can impart to "others") is the primacy of the question—the delimiting and asking of what previously had remained unasked, the discerning of the unfamiliar in what has long been familiar, the learning how to productively address new theoretical models, but more importantly, the moving beyond, through, behind, and under both customary and new theoretical frames into unchartered seas. Because methodological issues enter into associated arguments in critical ways, before I turn to the specific questions raised by fetish, magic, and custom, in the next few pages I will take up related concerns in a well-known work of literary fiction, *Cat's Cradle* by Kurt Vonnegut.

On Ethnographic Truth, Fiction, and Otherness

"All the true things I am about to tell you are shameless lies," proclaims the Caribbean religious text, *The Books of Bokonon,* in Kurt Vonnegut's 1963 science fiction novel.[1] Picking up the central theme of this invented Bokonon text, Kurt Vonnegut asserts: "My Bokonist warning is this: Anyone unable to understand how a useful religion can be founded on lies will not understand this book either" (1963, p. 16). The subject of Kurt Vonnegut's fictional religion in *Cat's Cradle* has come to the fore recently as an intellectual frame for a chapter "On Ethnographic Truth" in the recent and highly regarded book, *Paths Toward a Clearing* by the anthropologist Michael Jackson (1989). As Jackson points out, what is of central importance in *Cat's Cradle* is the question Kurt Vonnegut poses regarding the viability of impartial observation, nonsubjectivity, and empiricism, as well as the concomitant issue of "whether . . . truths are invented or found, fictional or factual" (1989, p. 170). The present paper similarly is about questions of truth and untruth (nontruth). It is about how untruths are made useful, and how, through their very usefulness, they are made secure.

Michael Jackson's interest in the problem of truth in the Bokonon religion described in *Cat's Cradle* is conveyed in several distinct lines of inquiry; the first is textual—the question of whether Kurt Vonnegut's "Bokonon religion" itself is factual or fictional. What intrigued Michael Jackson in his search for *Cat's Cradle* sources was knowing that Kurt Vonnegut had pursued graduate studies in anthropology at the University of Chicago in the years following the Second World War. Michael Jackson writes:

> Sometime between [1963, the year *Cat's Cradle* was first published] . . . and now I am sure I read a Caribbean ethnography which gave details of a religious cult centered on a prophet called Bokonon. I have searched for that Caribbean ethnography in vain, cursed myself for not having made a note of the one detail which might now prove the critics wrong and Vonnegut slyly right, which would make *Cat's Cradle*—as the title itself suggests—a kind of ethnographic science fiction. [1989, p. 170]

What Michael Jackson wants to know, in other words, is whether *Cat's Cradle* is a work rooted in fact or fantasy, "truth" or "untruth."

With respect to the above, I will herein reaffirm Michael Jackson's hunch and recollection. Bokonon religion does exist. However, it is found not in the Caribbean[2] but in West Africa, among the Fon of the Danhomè kingdom (Dahomey—today the Republic of Benin), a people Kurt Vonnegut would certainly have known about in his graduate training since the most famous Africanist of the time not only had published extensively on Fon religion (and its Caribbean offshoots) but also was teaching anthropology up the road a bit at Northwestern University.[3] Moreover, Melville J. Herskovits was a strong proponent of cultural relativism, a theory which, as Michael Jackson points out, Kurt Vonnegut incorporates into his discussion of academic discourse in his later *Slaughterhouse 5* (1970). Cultural relativism with its positivist and non-value laden grounding is still for many the *sine qua non* of ethnographic "truth."

Interestingly, in light of the above, Melville and Frances Herskovits' 1958 publication *Dahomey Narrative* is filled with the sort of simple tales of vacillating between good and evil mostly deriving from Fa (Ifa) divination, a practice which would have intrigued the young Kurt Vonnegut, argues Michael Jackson (1989, p. 170), and even may have inspired his anthropology master's thesis on "Fluctuations between Good and Evil in Simple Tales." It was the rejection of this thesis, Michael Jackson suggests, that led to Vonnegut's departure from the University of Chicago and, I would add, perhaps his turning away from the pursuit of "truth" (the exclusive goal and model of academic anthropology at that time) towards a search for "untruth" ("fantasy," "fabrication," "falsehood"—the standard designation of literary fiction in that period).

Truth and falsehood also are critical issues with regard to the Danhomè belief system. The diviner or *bokonon* is not only the principal source of local tales of good and evil but also a key intermediary between gods and humans. This person, whose name means literally the one who is familiar (*non*) with knowledge (*ko*) of the mysterious powers (*bo*) at play in the world, is seen to be at once a revealer of truth and a source of potential "lies." The latter designation is based on the belief that no person, not even the *bokonon,* can ever know everything about the world, thus no one can ever really know "truth." Moreover, because the diviner serves as spokesman for a diversity of gods, many of whom, like humans, are wily and wicked, in divination as in life the revelation of falsehoods often naturally accompanies the disclosure of truth. Accordingly in ceremonies for deceased diviners one sings: "we are going to the reunion of the liars. If the *bokonon* does not know how to lie [*nuvu*—literally "unravel something"], he should stay at home."[4] In the Fa divination sign, Gbe Tu Mila, humans in turn are encouraged to lie in life as a means of escaping death.[5] Life, in other words, is predicated as much on "lies" as "truth."

It is not primarily the problem of "truth" and "untruth" in Danhomè philosophy, religion, and divination texts which is of concern to us here, however, but rather the questions raised by Kurt Vonnegut and the figure of the *bokonon* himself with regard to issues of veracity (truth, untruth, nontruth) generally and how they may relate to scholarly discourse. In our examination of Western terminologies used in the construction of otherness, critical questions of "truth" and "difference" in African and Western academic discussion are elucidated as well. The variant social and cultural values which scholars have accorded the fetish are particularly important in this regard.

Art Historical Fetish and Preoccupations with the Artificial

"Fetish" is a provocative term with a long and diffuse history in the West. While clearly distinct from the other terms discussed below of custom and magic, fetishes share essential qualities with the two. Like customs, fetishes are things that are valued (or just as frequently devalued) because of their identity with and/or disassociation from "one's own." Like magic, fetishes share important features of otherness as focuses of arcane or foreign belief. In the *Dictionary of Psychology* edited by Arthur S. Reber, it is suggested accordingly that, "Fetishes usually are articles used by *others* [emphasis mine], often but not always of the opposite sex (shoes, gloves, handkerchiefs), or parts of the body (hair, feet)" (1985, p. 273). Deviance also is important to fetish identity. Thus Sigmund Freud discusses the fetish *vis-à-vis* "sexual function" and the ". . . becoming dependent on special conditions of a perverse or fetishist nature" (1959, p. 14). Not surprisingly, the term fetish also has vital socio-political traces. Today it is linked not only to sexual aberrance but also to class difference. While historically linked to beliefs of the unschooled or ignorant masses, Karl Marx's famous dictum (1937) and the subsequent writings of Theodor W. Adorno (1961), Walter Benjamin (1973) and others, have identified fetishization with the upper classes, "fetish" connoting here the attachment with which the elite hold commodities.[6]

From the Latin *fasticious,* "artificial" or "manufactured," the term "fetish" in modern French, Portuguese, and English is identified with a range of other derogatory values. Webster's *New World Dictionary* (1966) accordingly defines "fetish" as "any object believed by Primitive people to have magic power; 2) hence anything held in unreasoning devotion: as she makes a fetish of dress." The *Oxford English Dictionary* definition (1971 edition) focuses more on Portuguese root associations of the word with "charms" or "sorcery," and identifies "fetish" (*feitiço*) as "originally any of the objects used by the negroes of the Guinea coast and the neighboring regions as amulets or means of enchantment or regarded by them with superstitious dread."[7]

In both its historic and current use, the term "fetish" conveys in this

way notions of superstition, unreality, falsehood, foreigners, and dero-
gation.[8] William Pietz notes in this light that as early as 1764, Kant

> . . . tried to formulate an aesthetic explanation for African fe-
> tish worship . . . [and] decided that such practices were founded
> on the principle of the 'trifling' (*läppisch*), the ultimate degen-
> eration of the beautiful because it lacked all sense of the sublime.
> [1985, p. 9]

This identity of the fetish with things lacking beauty and sublimity is of
considerable interest for the present discussion since, until recently, it
was especially the emotionally powerful or less-refined African works
such as Kongo *nkisi* figures, Danhomè *bocio* works, and Bamana *boili*
that were standardly identified as "fetishes." G. Hegel's view of fetishism is also interesting in its disparaging associations. He writes (1956,
p. 99) that Africans take up as Fetish

> the first thing that comes their way. . . . Such a Fetish has no
> independence as an object of religious worship; still less has it
> aesthetic independence as a work of art; it is merely a creation
> that expresses the arbitrary choice of its maker, and which always
> remains in his hands.[9]

In these statements by some of the most influential thinkers in the modern European period, we can see how both Africa and its objects of
worship are denegrated as at once "trifling," "arbitrary," and "irrational." Like the term "fetish" itself, however, such assertions are based
on presumptions which are pejorative and without grounding, hence
dependent on values which are at once "artificial" and "manufactured."

A masterful essay on the fetish by the historian Hayden White offers
further insight into the use of this word in the West. He defines fetishism as

> . . . at one and the same time, a kind of belief, a kind of devotion,
> and a kind of psychological set or posture. . . . From these three
> usages [of fetish] we derive the three senses of the term . . . : belief
> in magical fetishes, extravagant or irrational devotion, and patho-
> logical displacement of libidinal interest and satisfaction to a
> fetish. . . . fetishism here [is understood] as a fixation on the form
> of a thing as against its content or on the part of a thing as against
> the whole. [1978, p. 184, and p. 195 n. 2]

The "fetish," in other words, has a role not unlike that of synecdoche
or metonymy, with the part assuming essential values of the whole. In
this, the term's social and historical importance is widely felt. As Hayden White observes:

From the Renaissance to the end of the eighteenth century, Europeans tended to fetishize the native peoples with whom they came
into contact by viewing them simultaneously as monstrous forms
of humanity and as quintessential objects of desire. Whence the
alternative impulses to exterminate and to redeem the native
peoples. . . . When a given part of humanity compulsively defines
itself as the pure type of mankind in general and defines all other
parts of the human species as inferior, flawed, degenerate or
"savage" I call this an instance of fetishism. [1978, p. 194, and
p. 195 n. 2]

Fetishism, in other words, is contextualized wherever beliefs predicated
on untenable values or irrational tenets are firmly held. As noted above,
fetishes are as much a part of Western scholarly discourse as they are of
the "deviant" other.

Several "fetishes" to which art scholars historically have held seemingly "artificial" devotion in non-Africanist art history can be pointed
up as well. These include most importantly: (1) the primacy placed on
models of development, (2) the privileging of things past, and (3) the
identity of the artist as the principal source of artistic meaning. Although much of what scholars have come to call "new" art history has
been actively involved in the deconstruction of these "fetishistic" pearls,
African centrist art history offers both important additional insight into
the above as well as a range of alternative models.

One of the most widely held and powerful of the Western art historical "fetishes" is that of artistic progress or development, a model
long disavowed in our sister disciplines of history and literature. A
range of revisionist scholars, including, among others, Svetlana Alpers
(1979), have attacked the dominant metaphor of "progress" in European art traditions with its tracing of modern artistic foundations to
ancient Greece and Italy. This model sets forth Greek art to be an improvement over Egyptian, Italian Renaissance as a higher form of
Greek, Northern Renaissance as a stepchild of the Italian model, and
abstract art as an improvement over earlier naturalism. While such developmental models are renounced by most art scholars today, what this
developmental model still means in practical terms in most introductory
classes and texts is the joining or stringing of art forms and artists into
a single chain, leaving out (or awkwardly sandwiching in) those that do
not easily fit, and seeing those who do as in some way derivative or
departing from those which came immediately (or more distantly)
prior.[10] Here (as with myth) in the words of Susan Buck-Morss, "[T]he
passage of time takes the form of predetermination" (1989, p. 78).[11]

In the main, Africanists have had little possibility of formulating or
following comparable developmental models, not because (as some sug-

gest) Africa is without history, or is deficient in either an important sense of history or internal models of development, but rather because so little of its history is known. Lacking many conventional historical documents, other models and paradigms have had to be employed. Interestingly, while some African art scholars have turned to creating "histories of the present," many others have been more concerned with framing questions in new ways which lie outside the general rubrics of traditional historical discourse altogether. One wonders, accordingly, if by magic one could remove all the dates from European art, in what new ways would these works be approached? What insights would such a break bring about? Would Western art scholarship stop? I think not. Like African art scholars for whom specific dates are a rare luxury, other questions would be addressed, questions which no doubt would inform the art works and the discipline as a whole in new and important ways. To some degree, the recent interests of "new art historians" in issues of response, psychoanalysis, and museum presentation coincide with the above, for while grounded in time and place, the date of a particular work often is less central to the discourse than are other factors. Models similarly could enrich Western art discourse in critical ways.

Another result of the Western art historical, teleological "fetish" with prioritizing the past has been the widespread disinterest in the discipline with contemporary artistic production, whether for its own sake or for its potential insights into both future scholarship and research on earlier periods. Few scholars—including modernists—investigate contemporary art as a fertile field in which to test long standing theories about creativity, reception, perception, the production of meaning, patronage, and the like. There are several reasons for this. Dissertation advisers tend to push students to study things which they themselves know (generally past artists) and to utilize methodologies with which they are familiar (archival work usually or, increasingly, theoretical queries). Debates about "what is art" and "what is not art" also come into play. There are other factors as well, but the fetishization of the past is the preeminent one. It would seem thus, that a validation of the present could promote new avenues of innovative research and critical art historical insight potentially impinging not only on contemporary art but also on the scholarship of past, present, and future eras.[12] In this light, the sort of detailed, interview-rich, and data-filled studies that scholars do in Africa with regard to local art forms may provide important models for the study of contemporary art in the West.

Another dominant "fetish" in art historical scholarship has been the privileging of the voice of the artist above all others *vis-à-vis* the production of artistic meaning.[13] Although Roland Barthes' redolent proclamation (1989) that the author is dead rang through the university halls and offices of literary scholars over a decade ago, the ramifications of his statement are only now being addressed by art historians and principally in the form of studies centered on issues of viewership and reception (compare Andrée Hayun 1990, Jonathan Crary 1991, and David Freedberg 1991). African art scholarship again may offer insight as to alternatives to artist-centered meaning discourse. While the standard myth maintains that art in Africa is a collective, history-less, tradition-bound enterprise in which the artist—even if we knew his or her name—had (has) little real input into the work,[14] Africanists have been forced by their data to view meaning as far more complex than either artist- or reception-centered models often have acknowledged.

Field research has provided Africanists with opportunities to witness firsthand the complex interweave of individuals who both participate in the creative process as artists—diviners, ritual activators and the like—and bring signification to the work through their divergent roles as viewers, users, worshippers, and caretakers. I have argued (Blier 1988, 1987) that the artist and viewer (observer) represent only a small part of the larger meaning base. In this sense, there is much more than at first meets the eye in Roland Barthes' proclamation of the artist's demise. If by "magic" we could do away with all artists' names and identities in art history, innovative scholars would come up with new and vital questions to explore. For art history, thus, what this means is not loss but rather, in the end, scholarly gain and the realization that art works are richer than they first may appear.

The Necessity of Magic: Identifying the Familiar as Foreign

"Magic," like "fetish," is a term with rich semantic interest and vital connections to ideas of otherness. Used generally to designate a form of mysterious power or irrational belief, as with "fetish," the term "magic" is nuanced in important ways by socio-political concerns. Stated simply, magic also is the religion of the other. It is defined generally as a form of "irrational" belief held by those who remain at base "irrational." According to the *Oxford English Dictionary* (1971 edition) magic is: "The *pretended* art of influencing the course of events, and of producing marvelous physical phenomena, by processes *supposed to* owe their efficacy to their power of compelling the intervention of spiritual beings, or of bringing into operation some *occult* controlling principle of nature" (emphases mine).[15] Ironically, the term "magic" is used less in reference to African worship and religious practice as such, which is not all that different from ancient Greek or Roman traditions among others (compare Fustel de Coulanges 1956 with John Mbiti

1970). Instead, magic is used to signal those practices within the African religious realm which are perceived to be at variance with other religious forms. Moreover, in the above dictionary definition of "magic," if one removes the underlined pejoratives, the meaning of "magic" is strikingly similar to "orthodox" ritual and prayer in the West. In Catholicism, to give but one example, the mass, the Eucharist, and absolution are all understood by believers to be articles of faith and even mystery, but these individuals would never refer to them as religious "magic."[16] In Protestantism, similarly, baptism is accorded a value of individual empowerment and action equivalent in key respects to that associated with magic. Religious dogma among followers of other world religions—whether Judaism or Islam, Hindu or Buddhism—is similar. Yet in all these faiths, the term "magic" characteristically is used in reference only to the religious practices of others, to the beliefs and rituals of those individuals who are foreign, unschooled, and considered to be social outsiders.[17] The *Oxford English Dictionary* and other lexicons, accordingly, generally equate magic with "sorcery" and "witchcraft." R. Collingwood's discussion of "magic" is of special interest in this regard:

> The word "magic" as a rule carries no definite significance at all. It is used to denote certain practices current in "savage" societies and recognizable here and there in less "civilized" and less "educated" strata of our society, but it is used without any definite conception of what it connotes; and therefore, if someone asserts that, for example, the ceremonies of our own church are magical, neither he nor anyone else can say what the assertion means, except that it is evidently intended to be abusive; it cannot be described as true or false. [1977, p. 107][18]

Outside the West, the term "magic" has been applied to variant objects and acts, African and otherwise. The recent French exhibit *Magicians sur la terre* (Paris: Centre Georges Pompidou 1989), while seeking to elevate the status (élan and mystery) of third-world artists ironically labeled them as "producers of magic," thereby reinforcing their very otherness. Because of the term's decidedly derogatory associations, African art historians and curators over the years have been steadfastly removing it from texts and museum labels. Interestingly, however, while the word "magic" is eschewed by most Africanist scholars today because of its disparaging nature and "otherness" mystique, many still employ the term or its linguistic complements "charm" and "amulet" in reference to Islamic leather packets containing Koranic verse which are worn as dress elements in many parts of West Africa. This use, however, is an exception that proves the rule, for in African art discourse it is Islam that is the "othered" religion par excellence.

The concept of otherness in magic is reinforced in the long and interesting etymological history of the term in the West. The word derives from the Greek *magikos* (meaning "sorcery" or "wizardry") which in turn has its source in the old Persian *magush* or Iranian *magos*. This designated a member of a hereditary priestly class among the ancient Medes and Persians whose doctrines included belief in astrology. The above meaning has had continued relevance in Christianity, for, as is known to every young Christmas caroler, the *Magi* is a reference to the three (foreign) wise men from the East who were present at the birth of Jesus. To the ancient Greeks, similarly, the word *magikos* was employed to designate the religious practices of foreigners (called generally "barbarians"—Greek *barbaros*—"foreign," "strange," "ignorant"), whether they were country folk, folk from other countries, or city folk identified as others (generally, slaves).[19] Then, as in the present, just as everyone had an Other, everyone's Other was associated with belief in magic. As White has observed:

> In such a situation the tendency is to endow those parts of humanity which are, in effect, being denied any claim to the title of human with magical, even supernatural powers, as happened in the mythos of the Wild Man of the Middle Ages. If these magical or supernatural powers are fixed upon as desiderata for all men, including Europeans, then there will be a tendency to fetishize the imagined possessors of such powers, for example, the Noble Savage. [1978, p. 195 n. 2]

This framing of magic has been an important basis for the long-standing separation of Africa and its arts from Europe and the movement of Africa into taxonomic proximity with the Pacific Islands and Native America (compare Blier 1990*b*). In much of art historical writing, African art (along with Oceanic and Native American traditions) is likened to the Greek "barbarian" as something "foreign," "strange," and "ignorant" of the values accorded "high" art. Interestingly, African art also is widely seen to stand in relationship to Western art as woman to man in phallocentric psychoanalytic texts. Stated simply, African art is held to signify a lack, and accordingly is widely believed to lack: artists (at least those who are truly capable of making innovative changes and having intellectual insights); an interest in foreign cultures and universality; a concept of art apart from social setting; a perception of art outside of nature and the material world; and a valuation of history (and a "real" understanding of historical primacy).[20]

One could continue, but what is important to emphasize is that coupled with this sense of deprivation or lack is an assumption of surplus as Africa and African art are generally seen to display at the same time qualities of heightened sensitivity (emotional power) and danger.[21]

Here, too, psychoanalytic parallels with women are apt. As Kaja Silverman notes for the presentation of the woman in film: "As usual her body provides the means for representing this deprivation. She simultaneously attracts the gaze—appeals to the senses and represents castration" (1983, p. 223). In both gender discourse and views of Africa, a considerable amount of illogic (and indeed magic) goes to support these premises of simultaneous lack and longing, repulsion and attraction.

Moreover, in truth, it has been far easier politically and intellectually for art historians and others to follow the lead of both Africa-centrists and Europe-centrists in seeing Africa as Other. Technologically and economically, however, at the time of Africa's first encounter with Europe (during the late fifteenth to seventeenth centuries) sub-Saharan Africa was thought to be strikingly similar to its preindustrial neighbors north of the Mediterranean, a fact underscored by the degree of (favorable) surprise and lavish praise accorded sub-Saharan African cities and states by the early European visitors. The city of Benin, in one of the more frequently cited examples, was compared positively by the seventeenth-century Dutchman Olfert Dapper (1686) to the Dutch city of Harlem. In turn, with respect to art and cultural traditions generally, Africa shares far more in common with preindustrial Europe than it does (or ever did) with either Native America or Oceania (those areas with which African art is generally cojoined), a finding that should not surprise anyone with a cursory knowledge of world history and a map.

What has held these three areas together in art historical discourse is at once a form of retentive cultural Darwinism (promoted still today in H. W. Janson's widely used introductory survey, *History of Art* [1986]) and (paradoxically) a grossly simplistic sociological model of art history which sees these three areas as in some way sharing similar social, political, economic, technical, and even religious features in a strange (magical and fallacious), cross-cultural, trans-historical union of widely disparate political forms and geographic entities.[22] To be fair, Janson's ideas are grounded in late nineteenth-century theories of social and artistic evolutionary development which subsequent editors of the popular (and remunerative) text have never felt compelled to revise. In turn, most sociologically oriented art historians today would be quick to eschew such a mixed bag of art historical otherness with its veneer of materiality and pretexts of artistic and socio-technological similitude. The fact remains, however, that Africanists and Europeanists alike have found this fiction (untruth) useful and for this reason continue to promote it even while disavowing the more denegrating "primitive" nomenclature as they cojoin these disparate areas in introductory texts, surveys, and museum halls. By continuing to frame the Other as strange in this way, ideas of African differentness are continually reinforced.

Yet, were we able by magic to dislodge and disempower the longstand-
ing traditions of "us" and "them," scholars of European art might be
less hesitant to draw from African models in exploring in different ways
their own works.

After having pointed out the problematic basis of magic as an othered taxonomy, in the next few paragraphs I would like to shift focus
and suggest its potential importance for academic discussion generally.
The concept (if not language) of magic, I suggest, has critical methodological significance for art historians of various fields. In my view there
are two basic ways to go about doing art historical research. One involves the sort of careful, time-consuming, archival (and/or field) research many scholars in the discipline have done, wherein one hopes to
chance upon a meaty tidbit of new information which subsequently will
allow one to discuss the work in a different way, whether this involves
finding a previously unknown collection inventory, a letter from a pa-
tron, an overlooked religious text, an unexplored scientific treatise, or
whatever. The other method entails the same sort of meticulous, time-
consuming research, but in this case grounded in premises, questions,
or theories, which through the course of their exploration (and affir-
mation in associated data) place the object in a different light. Although
scholars on both sides are often critical of the other, each accusing the
opposition of framing research questions in such a way as to predeter-
mine potential answers, these two avenues of scholarly inquiry are never
mutually exclusive. Most of the best scholars do both, or at least are
aware of the extent to which the questions they ask and the theories
they employ may effect the answers they arrive at, to some degree quali-
fying those answers. If the second scholarly approach has gained ascen-
dency in "new art history," however, it is also much harder to "explain"
or even "teach," both because preestablished models are very hard to
break (and as Thomas Kuhn has pointed out [1970] there is a tendency
in every discipline to follow the accepted paradigm) and because once
one has approached something in a new (different) way, it is no longer
truly "new" or "different." African art research here too may offer important insight.

With this in mind, accordingly, I would like to reintroduce the importance of "magic" into the framing of academic discourse. One of the
most productive ways I have found to see in a long familiar work something that is new, is by identifying the familiar elements in it as if they
are in some way foreign. One needs to try to see in the most obvious
and accepted details, that which is strange, that which is different, striving to view them in some way as "other," as visual or linguistic equiv-
alents to "magic." In seeing the familiar as foreign, in this way, it is also
essential to explore the basis for their very otherness. Fieldwork gener-

ally presents Africanists with the same dilemma but in reverse. Coming as most of us do from non-African cultures, there is the probability (borne out over and over again by experience) that much of what we see will be foreign to us. To "succeed" in this research it is encumbent upon us to translate the very foreignness we see into something familiar (if only because we must write in our own language and describe or analyze what we see and hear in a form in some way comprehensible to both our own and the "other" culture). At the same time we must not lose the essence of what exactly is foreign about what we are witnessing. With this in mind, we continue to pose questions with which we hope to both illuminate differentness and explicate elements of sameness. Through these various ways, African art scholars often have had to develop a keen ability to "sense" the presence and the roots of otherness and familiarity.

What Africanists can offer other art historians in this way is a valuation of magic (and a concomitant privileging of strangeness) as well as an appreciation of the complex interpretative issues which magic raises. This is not to say that historians of Egyptian, Greek, Roman, Carolingian, Italian Renaissance, or other arts are not keenly aware that the (now dead) societies that they are studying also are very different from their own, but rather that the cultural and historical values of continuity and sameness in the West are far more pervasive and difficult to break. Field work in a living foreign culture often provides ready evidence of difference and distance. And, as many of us soon learn, the degree of discomfort (strangeness) which one may feel with a given tradition, belief, or argument often is to some degree correlatable with the potential insights (magic) provided by pursuing that inquiry.[23]

Custom: On the Invention of Tradition

"Custom" and "tradition" are words that one hears frequently in the context of African societies and art. African art texts and label captions proclaim proudly that this or that work is "traditional," conveying through this means a sense of formal and iconologic continuity with some remote and "idyllic" past. This point is reinforced by the fact that the term "tradition" is still used today to differentiate certain locally defined but clearly modern (that is, nineteenth-twentieth century) art works which show some form of European influence (the use of foreign-derived tools, glass beads, imported pigments, factory made cloth, or external metals) from others displaying a more prominent influence from the West (new genres, "tourist art," and so forth), the latter of which are generally labeled "contemporary." In Africa as in the West, "tradition" and "custom" are mottoes of choice, both for those seeking to rigidify mores or practices which are (and have always been) evolving (changing) and for those who wish to legitimate (and proscribe) newly established traditions (generally defined in this context as a return to some "real" or "imagined" past).

Deriving from the Latin *com*, "with," and *suescare* (from *suus*), "one's own," "custom" denotes in this way ideas of familiarity: it demarks a sense of valuation and validation based on accordance with one's own ways and ideas. "Custom" comprises accordingly those things or notions (invented or found) which one maintains (guards, esteems) because one has become accustomed to (used to, comfortable with) them. In art historical and other scholarship, both the following and the breaking of custom and traditions are to some degree suicidal.[24] Accordingly, to follow custom too closely is to wear blinders which prevent one from seeing new questions (and answers); to break from custom too far (too much) is often to incur the wrath of the larger discipline and/or to marginalize one's research because it cannot be fit into preexisting paradigms.

"Tradition," from the Latin *traditio*, "surrender" or "delivery," has different etymological roots. Originally tradition was associated with ideas of relinquishment and betrayal of valued ideas which were revealed to a third party. The association of tradition today with the handing down (usually orally) of practices or beliefs, however, retains little of its earlier pejorative identity. Nonetheless, both custom and tradition denote a valuation of the past as a source of beliefs and practices surrendered or delivered up from some bygone era.

Like fetish and magic, custom (and tradition) frequently denote a fictive frame, a means of legitimization for things defined as much or more by fancy (yearnings, recollection) as by fact. In Africa this is also the case. Accordingly, one of the answers that one frequently hears in the course of African interviews in response to a difficult question of why a given object takes a particular form, or why a specific practice is undertaken in a certain way is that *it is customary* (or *traditional*) that it is done this way because it has always been done in this fashion. That such a response often is provided in those cases in which the person interviewed feels at a loss for a better answer, serves to underscore the slippery scholarly terrain with which "custom" and "tradition" are identified. Both terms accordingly are words of enormous "thickness" (as Clifford Geertz might describe it [1973]); they are terms which bear considerable weight. When used by local personages in the context of interviews, they mean: Do not search further; Ask no more questions; It is the way it is because it is the way it has always been.

While important in the West, in Africa values of "custom" and "tradition" are deemed to be even more predominant.[25] Thus when Europeans visited the court of the Danhomè kings and witnessed the lavish yearly new years' ceremonies (called *huetanu*, "ceremony [thing] at the head of the year"), which many of them not only attended but also described in exhaustive detail, they referred to these as local "customs." This word (*coutumes* in French) today still is employed when discussing these rites with Western visitors. The fact that the *huetanu* ceremonies were a relatively new invention in Danhomé (dating to the reign of Agaja—1708–1740) made no difference to these foreign visitors. However new, these ceremonies were perceived to be "customary" and "traditional."

As can be seen in the above, the terms "custom" and "tradition," whether used in African or other contexts, connote more than they appear to at first glance. They constitute in key respects a form of Legal Fiction (to use Henry Maine's term [1963])—a fiction which is believed, a "lie" which has become to many "truth." That the words "custom" and "tradition" are brought up in field interviews only as a last resort when a more viable or better answer is not known, underscores this distinctive aspect of their character as lie-truth. Custom and tradition have similar associations in art historical scholarship in the West. A case in point is the desire expressed by some scholars today to return to the discipline's "customary" or "traditional" interests with artists, periods, regions, media, iconographic problems, and questions of art making, rather than issues of theory and methodology. Similar debates are found in many disciplines currently, where terms like "custom" and "tradition" also are employed to convey a sense of legitimacy based on a valued past. Here, too, such terms serve as Legal Fictions or lies-truths. As Susan Buck-Morss points out for myths, they ". . . give answers to why the world is as it is when an empirical cause and effect cannot be seen, or when it cannot be remembered" (1989, p. 78).

There are numerous examples of the problems generated by custom or tradition following in both African and other art scholarship, but because the African art field is younger and custom or tradition is less firmly entrenched, the breaking of custom here is somewhat easier. Moreover, since certain art historical customs by their nature are impossible to follow in African art scholarship (for example, the domination of written texts, the privileging of particular media and oeuvres, and the primacy of developmental models), alternatives frequently have arisen which have encouraged new ways of thinking about old issues and accustomed ideas.

Another reason why custom-breaking is relatively common in African art scholarship is that African art itself in many contexts is a living art, fully entrenched in the variant and varying societal roots which make and frame it. This has meant that scholars working in this field often have had to train themselves in a wide range of other disciplines in order to carry out effective research. The vast majority of one's time in turn generally is spent learning about society broadly rather than art more narrowly defined. Accordingly, the prototypical first comment by a returning African art Ph.D. student is: "I learned a lot about the culture, but about the art I 'got' almost nothing." For them and, to a somewhat lesser extent, their advisers, this presents a problem because ultimately the point is to complete a study of the art, however broadly socially framed. For the African art field this "problem" in the end often proves to be a distinct advantage, for what these students have witnessed (and in turn explore in various ways in their dissertations and later writings) is the integral grounding of art in life.[26]

African art scholars in turn often are both beleaguered and blessed by the fact that life and art within the cultures they are studying are not readily (or already) classified, categorized, and defined according to pre-existing (read "customary") style, genre, or other taxonomies. While early African art scholars sought to follow the Western taxonomic orientations of their European colleagues in defining key typologies, in the end the less than satisfying results of this enterprise lead many to move away from such concerns.[27] Along the way they threw out concepts such as "tribe" and "tribal style," not only because of the latter's derogatory associations (and lack of comparative use for comparable contexts in the West)[28] but also and equally importantly because in large areas of Africa such labels have little real historical, socio-cultural, or stylistic value (René Bravmann 1973; Sidney Kasfir 1984).[29]

While the concept of "tribe" has had no similar importance in Western art historical taxonomies, there do exist certain "customary" methods of categorization which may mitigate against creative thinking. Long held stylistic rubrics are one example. Following African research models, it might be fruitful to think about breaking from "custom" in reevaluating some of these classificatory frames. Giotto, for example, in my early art history classes generally was accorded the label of the "first" major artist to forge a path toward the Renaissance. What would happen if Giotto instead (or also) was discussed as a late and "deviant" artist of the Byzantine? By shifting identities in this way, might we not see both the Byzantine and Giotto in a new light? So too, although we have grown accustomed to viewing medieval art as an outgrowth, development, or somewhat delinquent stepchild of ancient Rome, its pointed arches and flying buttresses derivative of southern vaulting, might there not also be interesting insights (following Alois Riegl 1901) in wrenching the Gothic from its long-heralded Italian roots? Might it rather be explored as a vibrant early form of northern Renaissance, looking for its principal ideational and aesthetic foundations in the (albeit few) extant works of sculpture and architecture which survived the destruction of colonial Roman forces? As disquieting as these suggestions may be, what really lies behind my argument is a claim for the necessity of looking at the familiar in an unfamiliar way. Questions of custom-breaking also emerge with respect to traditions of object hierarchies. African scholars perforce often have been obliged to break "customary" (for the West—and then generally post-Romanticism) ways of framing and valuing materials and object types.[30] If we understand "custom" and "tradition" in the above to delimit ideas or lines of inquiry with which scholars have become comfortable (for better or worse), what African art scholars may offer our Western colleagues are not only models for custom-breaking but also, and equally important, ways of discerning and acknowledging custom for what it is (that is, practice) rather than for what it purports to be (truth).

In light of the above issues, can it be said that African art scholarship is beginning to have an effect within the discipline as a whole? I would like to say yes, but my answer has to be no. Unlike many other fields—anthropology, history, and political science, for example—the canon has remained so rigidly fixed that any larger discussion of the arts of different areas or interests has been virtually impossible. A few medievalists may be reading Victor Turner (particularly on pilgrimage) and others may look at African travelers' accounts to bolster theories of universal responses to art, but African art scholarship as such generally is avoided. That the standard introduction to art history, Janson's *History of Art*, discusses African artistic form in a chapter on Primitive (sic) art which is filled with derogatory statements and egregious factual errors, no doubt plays a role in encouraging both teachers and students to avoid the subject all together. And, because African art is so rarely taught in art history departments in this country and in Europe, most students and scholars are never given the chance to form an alternative opinion.

Envoie: Deconstructionism and Formalism in African Art

When it comes to framing questions, few experiences are as difficult and rewarding as ethnographic field work. Such research not only is physically and emotionally demanding, but more so it constitutes a scholarly and intellectual challenge of the highest order. In such work there is rarely any of the sublime, contemplative silence of the Western archive library or museum. Even the most shy and reticent researcher necessarily must become extraverted and intrusive. Research of this type continually necessitates decisions not only regarding paths to take at a particular crossing but also when to forge entirely new paths without ever really knowing where one would like one's final destination to be. Even on an "easy" day, field research is like trying to follow a maze in which the hedge borders are so wholly overgrown that boundary and path are indistinguishable. It is the kind of research in which, like this same maze, essential findings are often achieved through trial and error. It is an art one can only learn by doing. Each situation is unique. There is no model or customary way of proceeding. Interviewing, one of the most important field research techniques, in turn is a complex and often frustrating craft, particular when, as a foreigner, one frequently has no idea of what answer one is looking for and what line of questioning will achieve it. Despite the challenges and difficulties of the fieldwork enterprise, I know of no better way of both getting at the richness of art and culture and critically examining variant theoretical forms and methodologies.

Deconstructionism is a case in point. While academia as a whole and African art specifically has gained considerably through an examination of the larger issues raised by deconstructionism, by no means can its principal tenets be considered a panacea for African art or art history generally. Despite provocative examples of related scholarship—most importantly in Africa by scholars such as Ilona Szombati-Fabian and Johannes Fabian 1976; Johannes Fabian 1983; V. Y. Mudimbe 1986, 1988; Bogumil Jewsiewicki 1988; Michael Jackson 1989; and Anthony Appiah 1991—which have pressed scholars to recognize the complexity of "truth" and the political roots of what was hitherto thought to be "apolitical" positivist history, in some respects deconstructionism also has limitations when it comes to studying African art generally. What deconstructionism often has meant for Africa is the replacement of one form of "othered" identity with another. In the deconstructionist proclivity to privilege colonial history and Western perspective (bias) over all others, the distinctive pasts and identities of local cultures—both precolonial and modern—often have been trivialized or supplanted within the larger colonizer-colonialized dialectic.

Equally important, Africa and other "third world" cultures usually are mixed together in the same "global market" pot, the implications being not only that everyone is touched equally by global forces but also that their identities are so overpowered by these influences that little if any of their own distinctive cultural values remain. Africa (like Japan, India, and many other areas) indeed offers vital contemporary evidence to the contrary. At base, many such studies, however insightful and well intentioned, represent a new type of cultural hierarchy where self (the colonizer, the collector, the researcher, the writer) is again accorded the principal, privileged, and exclusive voice. Probably influenced in part by the recent best-selling books by Sally Price (1989) and

Marianna Torgovnick (1990), as well as the many insightful critiques by scholars such as George Marcus and Michael Fischer (1986), James Clifford and George Marcus (1986), George Stocking (1987), James Clifford (1988), Clifford Geertz (1988), and Adam Kuper (1988) to name but a few, armchair overviews of Othered art are becoming the genre of choice for some art scholars wishing to do creative scholarship without the expense or difficulty of additional in-depth fieldwork. While a welcome addition, in many respects, if such studies portend a general movement of African art research away from field research-based analyses, for the many reasons cited above, much may be lost in the process.

Peering around the corner, I see formalism, both resuscitated ("old") or reconstructed ("new") to be on the rise in art history and academics at large, each proposing to rectify (realign) some of deconstructionism's more radical tenets (nihilistic tendencies, some insist). Both forms of formalism offer many of the same intellectual and practical advantages (and difficulties) of deconstructionism. Each allows for a more distanced (nonfield based) approach to the "subject" arts and cultures. Advocates of a new formalism—Gilles Deleuze 1990 among others—however, in their search for unity and a sense of structure to replace the characteristic cacophony of postmodernist critique, have frequently substituted new myths or fictions for old ones still being aggressively fought for by Africanists of both positivist and deconstructionist stripes. The tendency of new formalists to press for hierarchical and developmentally based world system perspectives, in turn, while complementing deconstructionist global market orientations, undoubtedly will prove problematic for African art because, again, the African continent either will be relegated to the lower rung or elevated to a new mythic "noble savage" stature.

With "old" formalism, similar potentialities and problems come into play. While offering a (to some refreshing) return to the object, associated studies often have harbored assumptions that content can be discerned exclusively by visual appraisal and careful "looking." As Africanists who have done extensive field research know well, the very way one "sees" an object and comes to "understand" it usually is dependent on considerations outside the work itself, by factors of context, viewership, and society generally. To understand art, particularly that of a foreign culture (and one could argue in a way that all art is to some degree foreign), involves much more than formal looking, describing, and intuiting, however carefully and perceptively it is done. Again what African art can offer art historical discourse generally is not only a testing field for examining new and old approaches and theories, but also access to an extraordinarily rich and still understudied living and historic art. If, in turn, African art is seen to offer insightful and instructive *thoma* ("marvels," "curiosities") for Western art scholarship—to use François Hartog's term—it is the clarity with which, through this art, one is able to illuminate the relative truths and untruths (counter-truths, lies, artificialities) of Western conceptual traditions such as magic, custom, and fetish which in the end will be of greatest significance. To paraphrase the Bokonon text in Kurt Vonnegut's *Cat's Cradle:* Even useful theory may be founded on untruth.

NOTES

The research and writing of this paper was undertaken in the course of my recent residence at the Getty Center for the History of Art and the Humanities which I gratefully acknowledge. Among the scholars that year were several whose writings and conversation no doubt have had an impact on this essay, most especially Johannes Fabian, Thomas Y. Levin, and Hayden White. I also wish to thank Richard Brilliant, Johanna Drucker, and Eunei Lee for reading and commenting on earlier drafts.

1. In Haiti, however, the name *boko* or *bokon* is used to refer to someone skilled in the making of power objects, identified by many with "black magic." Many Haitian religious traditions derive from Danhomè (Alfred Métraux 1972, p. 267).

2. For a discussion of Melville and Frances Herskovits and the study of Dahomey art, see Suzanne Blier 1988, 1989.

3. For a discussion of the *bokonon* and Fa divination practice among the Fon, see Melville Herskovits 1967, Bernard Maupoil 1981, and Suzanne Blier 1990, 1991. Related traditions of Ifa divination are practiced among the Yoruba. See William Bascom 1969.

4. Interview with Ayido Gnanwisi of Sodohome (March 23, 1986).

5. Ibid. (April 25, 1986).

6. As Buck-Morss notes (1989, p. 24) following Walter Benjamin, "[T]he *fetish* is the keyword of the commodity as mythic phantasmagoria, the arrested form of history, it corresponds to the reified form of new nature, condemned to the modern Hell of the new as the always-the-same." Adorno explains in turn (1961, p. 42) that Karl Marx set out key differences between the static and the dynamic within his critique of fetishism, after situating the origin of fetishism in the realm of values we attach to commodities. Hayden White's perspectives on class and fetish also are of interest:

> But even more basic in the European consciousness of this time was the tendency to fetishize the European type of humanity as the sole possible form that humanity in general could take. This race fetishism was soon transformed, however, into another and more virulent form: the fetishism of class, which has provided the bases of most of the social conflicts of Europe since the French Revolution. [1978, pp. 194–95]

7. Paradoxically, fetishes of this type were particularly associated with early eighteenth century Ouidah (cf. William Bosman 1967), then the sea port of the Danhomè kingdom, the place in which "Bokonon religion" also is practiced.

8. Other individuals who have discussed ideas of fetish and fetishism include, among others, Gilles Deleuze 1972, Maurice Merleau-Ponty 1969, Susan Stewart 1984, pp. 163–64, William Pietz 1985, James Clifford 1988. In key respects fetishism also fits in closely with Edward Said's ideas of *monocentrism* (in Harari 1979, p. 188):

> Monocentrism is practiced when we mistake one idea as the only idea, instead of recognizing that an idea in history is always one among many. Monocentrism denies plurality, it totalizes structure . . . it decrees the centricity of Western culture instead of its eccentricity.

9. Freud's discussion of African "fetishes" which is similar in fundamental ways to that of both Immanuel Kant and G. Hegel is derisive as well. He writes (1961, p. 74) that, "It is remarkable how differently primitive man behaves. If he is met with a misfortune, he does not throw the blame on himself but on his fetish, which has obviously not done its duty, and he gives it a thrashing instead of punishing himself."

10. One scholar I know, seeking to move outside the fetishistic teleological canon, taught the introductory survey in reverse—much to the disgruntlement of both students and teaching assistants. The premise of this change, I would argue, also is problematic for reversal at base remains a form of reification and reaffirmation of the original model. What needs to be done instead is to step completely outside this model, a task made all the more difficult because as a discipline we are so accustomed to this particular way of perceiving and proceeding.

11. The fetishizing of the past is also evidenced in African art in the once ubiquitous catalog labels demarcating "ancestor figures" or the frequent peppering of the literature with the term "traditional," both descriptions, like "custom," having no real relevance except as labels for art works about which we have no known history. Both have served to convey an image of African art as in some way primeval.

12. The late African art scholar, Arnold Rubin, once taught a Los Angeles based fieldwork course for graduate students in art history. My own experience in teaching a graduate seminar at Columbia University called "New York Art Worlds: Studying Art Ethnographically" also has convinced me of the enormous potential for such a course in contemporary art studies generally.

13. See, however, Svetlana Alpers 1977.

14. In Africa this is compounded by the fact that then, as now, usually no one bothered to ask the artist's name.

15. In Webster's *New World Dictionary* (1966) magic is identified similarly as "the *pretended* art of producing effects or controlling events by charms, spells, and rituals supposed to govern certain natural or supernatural forces; sorcery; witchcraft" (emphasis mine). The circus magician similarly frames his performance with smoke, spells (hocus pocus), and a range of ritualistic props.

16. Interestingly, contemporary "witches" in the West and other religious outsiders wishing to emphasize their own positions as Others, often go out of their way to identify themselves with the use of magic.

17. In Judaism, magic also is identified with insiders who act dangerously. I thank Richard Brilliant for this insight.

18. R. Collingwood adds:

... positivistic philosophy which ignored man's emotional nature and reduced everything in human experience in terms of intellect ... further ignored every kind of intellectual activity except those which, according to the same philosophy, went to the making of natural science. This prejudice led them to compare the magical practices of the "savage" (civilized men, they ... assumed, had none, except for certain anomalous things which these anthropologists called survivals) with the practices of civilized man when he uses his scientific knowledge in order to control nature. [1977, p. 107]

19. The barbarian, in essence, thus was defined as anyone who was *not* Greek. Other in this sense must be seen to include not only those who are "not us" but also those who are "not like us." The following point by Lucy Mair is interesting in light of the above:

Apuleius, the author of *The Golden Ass,* when he was put on trial for practicing magic, remarked that the Magi were priests in their own country, and this brings home the point that an activity which in one context has all the sanction of authority may be treated as a crime if it is practiced without this authority. [1969, p. 25]

20. Hegel's negative presuppositions about Africa (1956, pp. 93 and 99) are still widely held today. As he has written in *The Philosophy of History:* "The peculiarity of the African character [is its lack of] ... the principle which naturally accompanies all *our* ideas—the category of Universality" (1956, p. 93). Hegel then goes on to discuss other assumed lacks. Africa, he writes,

is no historical part of the World, it has no movement or development to exhibit. ... What we properly understand by Africa, is the Unhistorical, Undeveloped Spirit, still involved in the conditions of mere nature, and which has to be presented here as the threshold of the World's History. [1956, p. 99]

21. The lack/desire of psychoanalytic discourse (especially Lacanian) is based on the notion of possibility that lack "produces" a sense of longing or desire, thus the simultaneous attraction/repulsion (see also Said 1979). And, it is Africa's perceived inferiority that can be seen to parallel this lack.

22. To suggest that Africa with its complex variety of kingdoms, states, cities, rural farming communities, and hunting cultures as a single economic, technical, political or religious identity which is comparable to those of the distant Pacific islands or native America is illogical as well.

23. By way of example, one can cite an issue of importance to both Africanists and Europeanists. It is already so deeply embroiled in a "hornet's nest" of feelings and scholarly discord, that rational academic interchange is virtually impossible. I am speaking, of course, of Martin Bernal's query into the

philosophical links between Egypt and Europe in his controversial book *Black Athena*. I will not enter into the thick of the fray by discussing the relative merits or demerits of the work, but suffice it to say that I have heard amply and angrily from both sides. And even if I did have the expertise in both Egyptian and Classics to be able to give an informed opinion, my observations would be far more important at this point in time for their assumed political worth than for their scholarly merit. My past field work experience with issues of art, belief, and societal change suggests that because of the vitriolic tenor of the associated debates, *Black Athena* clearly must deal with a subject of vital scholarly importance. This assumption is based not only on the heat and discomfort it has generated, but also and most importantly on the fact that the associated discourse is grounded in vital questions of taxonomic definition and positioning. Although not generally framed in this way, one of the essential undercurrents in the above dispute is that of relative Egyptian and Greek otherness and sameness and the degree to which "magic" (here "self" and "other" philosophical doctrine) is being identified with each.

24. This situation is made all the more paradoxical in light of the fact that both custom and suicide derive from the same Latin root—*suis*.

25. The erroneous assumption is that in Africa the weight of custom or tradition is so great that no internal change is possible.

26. For a discussion of the complex world in which art revolves, see Howard Becker 1987.

27. Early African art scholars followed nineteenth-century botanists' endeavors to label and classify unknown flora (Blier 1988–89).

28. In Great Britain, for example, one could classify in a similar way the Scots, Irish, English, and Welsh; in eastern Europe, Serbs, Croatians, and other groups could be included. In the Middle East comparisons are equally apt.

29. Among others, these include the "Poro" groups of Liberia and the Ivory Coast, the Cross River area of Nigeria, the grasslands region of Cameroons, and the Masai and neighboring cattle-herding cultures of Kenya.

30. See also Zerner 1982. Although recent Western art scholars have turned their attention to issues (and subjects) of "high" and "low" (the recent Museum of Modern Art exhibit exemplifying this trend), generally in this discourse one of the two is privileged as either source or receptacle of the other. Related discourse and criticism as Richard Brilliant has pointed out, however, goes back to the eighteenth and nineteenth centuries. Even when breaking with custom in the West, in other words, customary hierarchic and developmental values, perceptions and thinking are retained.

REFERENCES

Adams, Monni. "African Visual Arts from an Art Historical Perspective." *African Studies Review* 32, no. 2 (1989): 55–103.

Adorno, Theodor W. "'Static' and 'Dynamic' as Sociological Categories." *Diogenes* 33 (1961): 26–49.

Alpers, Svetlana. "Is Art History?" *Daedalus* 106 (1977): 1–13.

———. "Style Is What You Make of It: The Visual Arts Once Again." In *The Concept of Style,* edited by Berel Lang. Philadelphia: University of Pennsylvania Press, 1979.

Appiah, Kwame Anthony. "Is the Post- in Postmodernism the Post- in Postcolonial." *Critical Inquiry* 17 (1991): 336–57.

Asad, Talal, ed. *Anthropology and the Colonial Encounter.* London: Ithaca Press, 1973.

Bakhtin, M. M. *The Dialogic Imagination,* translated by Caryl Emerson and Michael Holquist. Austin: University of Texas Press, 1987.

Barber, Karen. "Popular Arts in Africa." *African Studies Review* 30 (1987): 1–78, 113–32.

Barthes, Roland. "The Death of the Author." In *The Rustle of Language,* translated by Richard Howard. Reprint. Berkeley: University of California Press, 1989.

Bascom, William. *Ifa Divination: Communication between Gods and Men in West Africa.* Bloomington: Indiana University Press, 1969.

Beardsley, Monroe C. *The Aesthetic Point of View: Selected Essays,* edited by Michael J. Wreen and Donald M. Callen. Ithaca: Cornell University Press, 1982.

Becker, Howard. *Art Worlds.* Berkeley: University of California Press, 1982.

Ben-Amos, Paula Girschick. 1989. "African Visual Arts from a Social Perspective." *African Studies Review* 32, no. 2 (1989): 1–54.

Benjamin, Walter. *Illuminations,* translated by Harry Zohn, ed. New York: Harcourt, Brace, and World, 1968.

Bernal, Martin. *Black Athena: The Afroasiatic Roots of Classical Civilization.* Vol. 1 of *The Fabrication of Ancient Greece 1785–1985.* New Brunswick, N.J.: Rutgers University Press, 1987.

Biebuyck, Daniel P. "African Art Studies since 1957: Achievements and Directions." *African Studies Review* 26, nos. 3–4 (1983): 99–118.

Blier, Suzanne Preston. *The Anatomy of Architecture: Ontology and Metaphor in Batammaliba Architectural Expression.* New York: Cambridge University Press, 1987.

———. "Melville J. Herskovits and the Arts of Ancient Dahomey." *Res: Anthropology and Art* 16 (1988): 124–42.

———. "Words about Words about Icons: Iconologology and the Study of African Art." *College Art Journal* 47 (1988): 75–87.

———. "Art Systems and Semiotics: The Question of Art, Craft and Colonial Taxonomies in Africa." *American Journal of Semiotics* 6, no. 1 (1988–89): 7–18.

———. "Field Days: Melville J. Herskovits in Dahomey." *History in Africa* 16 (1989): 1–22.

———. "African Art Studies at the Cross Roads: An American Perspective." In *African Art Studies: The State of the Discipline.* Smithsonian Institution. Washington, D.C., 1990.

————. "King Glele of Danhomè: Divination Portraits of a Lion King and Man of Iron (Part I)." *African Arts* 23, no. 4 (1990): 42–53, 93–94.

————. "King Glele of Danhomè: Dynasty and Destiny (Part II)." *African Arts* 24, no. 1 (1991): 44–55, 101–3.

Bosman, William. *A New and Accurate Description of the Coast of Guinea.* Reprint. London: Cass, 1967 [1704].

Bravmann, René A. *Open Frontiers: The Mobility of Art in Black Africa.* Seattle: University of Washington, 1973.

Buck-Morss, Susan. *The Dialectics of Seeing: Walter Benjamin and the Arcades Project.* Studies in Contemporary German Social Thought. Cambridge, Mass.: M.I.T. Press, 1989.

Clifford, James. *The Predicament of Culture: Twentieth-Century Ethnography, Literature, and Art.* Cambridge, Mass.: Harvard University Press, 1988.

Clifford, James, and Marcus, George, eds. *Writing Culture.* Berkeley: University of California Press, 1986.

Collingwood, R. G. *The Principles of Art.* In *Aesthetics: A Critical Anthology,* edited by Dickie et al. 2d ed. Reprint. New York: St. Martin's Press, 1977.

Crary, Jonathan. *Techniques of the Observer: On Vision and Modernity in the Nineteenth Century.* Cambridge, Mass.: M.I.T. Press, 1990.

Dapper, Olfert. *Naukeurige beschrijvinge der afrikaensche gewesten van Egypten, Barbaryen, Lybien, Biledulgerid, Negroslant, Guinea, Ethiopien, Abyssinie.* 2nd ed. Amsterdam: Jacob van Meurs, 1676.

Deleuze, Gilles. *Différence et répétition.* Paris: Presses Universitaire de France, 1972.

————. *The Logic of Sense.* Translated by Mark Lester; edited by Constantin V. Boundas, Reprint. New York: Columbia University Press, 1990 [1969].

Deleuze, Gilles, and Guattari, Félix. *Anti-Oedipus: Capitalism and Schizophrenia.* Minneapolis: University of Minnesota Press, 1983.

Eagleton, Terry. *Walter Benjamin or Towards a Revolutionary Criticism.* London: Verso Ed. and NLB, 1981.

Fabian, Johannes. *Time and the Other: How Anthropology Makes its Object.* New York: Columbia University Press, 1983.

Foster, Hal, ed. *Discussions in Contemporary Culture.* No. 1. Dia Art Foundation. Seattle: Bay Press, 1987.

Freedberg, David. *The Power of Images: Studies in the History and Theory of Response.* Chicago: University of Chicago Press, 1989.

Freud, Sigmund. *Civilization and Its Discontents,* translated by James Strachey, ed. Reprint. New York: W. W. Norton and Co. 1961 [1930].

————. *A General Introduction to Psychoanalysis.* Reprint. New York: Washington Square Press, 1965 [1924].

Fustel de Coulanges. *The Ancient City: A Study of the Religious and Civil Institutions of Greece and Rome,* translated by Willard Small. Reprint. Garden City, N.Y.: Doubleday Book Co., 1956 [1864].

Geertz, Clifford. "Thick Description: Toward an Interpretive Theory of Culture." In *The Interpretation of Cultures: Selected Essays by Clifford Geertz.* New York: Basic Books, 1973.

————. *Works and Lives: The Anthropologist as Author*. Stanford, Calif.: Stanford University Press, 1988.

Hartog, François. *The Mirror of Herodotus: The Representation of the Other in the Writing of History*, translated by Janet Lloyd. Berkeley: University of California Press, 1988.

Harari, Josué, ed. *Textual Strategies: Perspectives in Post-Structuralist Criticism*. Ithaca: Cornell University Press, 1979.

Hayun, Andrée. *The Isenheim Altarpiece: God's Medicine and the Painter's Vision*. Princeton, N.J.: Princeton University Press, 1990.

Hegel, G. W. F. *The Philosophy of History*, translated by Sibree. Reprint. New York: Dover, 1956 [1837].

Herskovits, Melville J. *Dahomey: An Ancient West African Kingdom*. 2 vols. Reprint. Evanston: Northwestern University Press, 1967 [1938].

Herskovits, Melville J., and Frances S. *Dahomean Narrative: A Cross-Cultural Analysis*. Evanston: Northwestern University Press, 1958.

Jackson, Michael. *Paths Toward a Clearing: Radical Empiricism and Ethnographical Inquiry*. Bloomington: Indiana University Press, 1989.

Jameson, Fredric. *The Ideologies of Theory. Essays 1971–1986*. Vol. 1 of *Situations of Theory*. Minneapolis: University of Minnesota Press, 1988.

Janson, H. W. *History of Art*. 3d ed. New York. Harry N. Abrams, 1986.

Jewsiewicki, Bogumil. 1988. "Presentation: Le langue politique et les arts plastiques en Afrique." *Canadian Journal of African Studies* 22, no. 1 (1988): 1–10.

Kant, Immanuel. *Observations on the Feeling of the Beautiful and Sublime*, translated by John T. Goldthwait. Berkeley: University of California Press, 1960.

Kasfir, Sidney Littlefield. 1984. "One Tribe, One Style? Paradigms in the Historiography of African Art." *History in Africa* 11 (1984): 163–93.

Kuhn, Thomas S. *The Structure of Scientific Revolutions*. 2d ed. Vol. 2, no. 2 of *Foundations of the Unity of Science*. Chicago: University of Chicago Press, 1970.

Kristeva, Julia. *The Kristeva Reader*. New York: Columbia University Press, 1986.

Kuper, Adam. *The Invention of Primitive Society: Transformations of an Illusion*. London: Routledge, 1988.

Maine, Henry James Sumner. *Ancient Law: Its Connection with the Early History of Society and Its Relation to Modern Ideas*. Boston: Beacon Press, 1963 [1861].

Mair, Lucy. *Witchcraft*. New York: McGraw-Hill Book Company, 1969.

Marcus, George, and Fischer, Michael. *Anthropology as Critical Critique: An Experimental Moment in the Human Sciences*. Chicago: University of Chicago Press, 1986.

Marx, Karl. *Capital*. Vol. 1, translated by Ben Fowkes. Reprint. New York: Random House, 1977 [?].

Maupoil, Bernard. *La géomancie à l'ancienne Côte des Esclaves*. Trauvaux et Memoires de l'Institut d'Ethnologie 42. Paris: Institut d'Ethnologie, 1981.

Mbiti, John S. *African Religions and Philosophy*. Reprint. Garden City, N.Y.: Anchor Books, 1970 [1969].

Merleau-Ponty, Maurice. *The Visible and the Invisible*. Evanston: Northwestern University Press, 1968.

Métraux, Alfred. *Voodoo in Haiti*, translated by Hugo Charteris. New York: Schocken Books, 1972.

Mudimbe, V. Y. *The Invention of Africa: Gnosis, Philosophy, and the Order of Knowledge*. Bloomington: Indiana University Press, 1988.

———. "African Art as a Question Mark." *African Studies Review* 29, no. 1 (1986): 3–4.

Paris, Centre Georges Pompidou. *Magiciens de la Terre*. Paris: Centre Georges Pompidou, 1989.

Pearce, Roy Harvey. *Savagism and Civilization: A Study of the Indian and the American Mind*. Rev. ed. Berkeley: University of California Press, 1988 [1953].

Pietz, William. "The Problem of Fetish, 1." *Res 9* (1985): 5–17.

Price, Sally. *Primitive Art in Civilized Places*. Chicago: University of Chicago Press, 1989.

Riegl, Alois. *Die spätrömische Kunstindustrie*. Vienna: Kaiserlich-königlichen hof—und staatsdruckerei, 1901.

Risatti, Howard, ed. *Postmodern Perspectives: Issues in Contemporary Art*. Englewood Cliffs, N.J.: Prentice-Hall, 1990.

Rubin, William. "Picasso." In Vol. 2 of *Primitivism in 20th Century Art: Affinity of the Tribal and the Modern*, edited by William Rubin. New York: Museum of Modern Art, 1984.

Said, Edward. *Orientalism*. New York: Pantheon Books, 1978.

Silverman, Kaja. *The Subject of Semiotics*. New York: Oxford University Press, 1983.

Stewart, Susan. *On Longing*. Baltimore: Johns Hopkins University Press, 1984.

Stocking, George. *Victorian Anthropology*. New York: Free Press, 1987.

Szombati-Fabian, Ilona, and Fabian, Johannes. "Art, History, and Society: Popular Painting in Shaba, Zaire." *Studies in the Anthropology of Visual Communication* 3, no. 1 (1976): 1–21.

Torgovnick, Marianna. *Gone Primitive: Savage Intellects, Modern Lives*. Chicago: University of Chicago Press, 1990.

Vonnegut, Kurt. *Cat's Cradle*. New York: Dell Books, 1963.

———. *Slaughterhouse 5*. New York: Dell Books, 1970.

White, Hayden. *Tropics of Discourse: Essays in Cultural Criticism*. Baltimore: Johns Hopkins University Press, 1978.

———. "The Forms of Wildness: Archaeology of an Idea." In *The Wildman Within: An Image in Western Thought from the Renaissance to Romanticism*, edited by Edward Dudley and Maximillian E. Novak. Pittsburgh: University of Pittsburgh Press, 1972.

Zerner, Henri. "Editor's Statement: The Crisis in the Discipline." *Art Journal* 42, no. 4 (1982): 279.

6

African Histories and the Dissolution of World History

STEVEN FEIERMAN

ONCE UPON A TIME historians used to know that certain civilizations (Western ones) were their natural subject matter, that some political leaders (Thomas Jefferson, Napoleon, Charlemagne) were worth knowing about, and that particular periods and developments (the Renaissance, the Age of Enlightenment, the rise of the nation-state) were worthy of our attention. Other places, other people, other cultural developments less central to the course of Western civilization did not count. Now all of that has come into question. Historians no longer agree on the subjects about which they ought to write.

Peter Novick, in a book on the evolution of the historical profession in the United States, tells about its current state in the titles of his last two chapters: "The Center Does Not Hold," and "There Was No King in Israel." He describes "the collapse of professional historical study as an even minimally cohesive venture" (1988, p. 579). Theodore Hamerow writes that "historians despair of being able to bring order out of chaos" (Novick 1988, p. 578).

The loss of agreement on history's subject is only one part of the change that provokes scholars to write about fragmentation and chaos. The debate on history's subject emerged at the same time that increasing numbers of historians began to doubt their own methods. Many now find it impossible to sustain the claims they might once have made that their choices of subject and method are based on objective knowledge. These historians have become acutely aware that their own writings, their ways of constructing a narrative, conceal some kinds of historical knowledge even while they reveal others, and that their choice of subject and method is a product of their own time and circumstances, not an inevitable outcome of the impersonal progress of historical science. This change, which has roots within contemporary philosophy, also emerges from the evolution of the historian's craft itself.

It is a profound paradox of history-writing in the most recent era that our faith in objective historical knowledge has been shaken precisely because of the advance of "knowledge" in its objective sense. The authoritative version of historical knowledge has been undermined because historians, in recent decades, have built bodies of knowledge about which their predecessors could only have dreamed. By carrying assumptions about historical knowledge through to their conclusions, historians have discovered some of the limits of those assumptions.

The evolution of African history shows just how dramatic the growth of our understanding has been within the inherited framework of history as positive knowledge. In the mid-1950s graduate students of history at Harvard, Princeton, Chicago, Berkeley, Columbia, and almost all of America's other historically white universities lived in a world where African history did not exist. None of these major postgraduate institutions offered courses in the subject. In 1958–59 the American Historical Association surveyed department chairmen on the major fields of their graduate students. The total number of graduate students was 1,735; the number reported as concentrating in African history was 1.[1]

By the late 1970s there were 600 professional African historians in the United States, and the number has continued to grow (Curtin 1980). Most of these wrote Ph.D. dissertations in African history, and many continue to do research after the doctorate. The growth in numbers has therefore led to an enormous expansion in knowledge. Among the Africanists are scholars who read the European archives in a new light to see what they reveal on African society; or there are those who study sources written in Arabic, whether by Africans or by Muslim visitors from outside the continent; and there are others who read sources in African languages, also collectors and critical analysts of oral traditions, historical linguists, scholars who specialize in African religion, in the history of African agriculture, of disease, of gender, of peasant movements, and of an endless range of other subjects.

One obvious consequence of the expansion of historical research in the years since 1960 has been to show just how limited were our earlier understandings. Much of the new specialized research focuses on people previously excluded from the general history of humanity. The history of Africa is not alone in this respect. Alongside it are new bodies of knowledge on the history of medieval peasants, of barbarians in ancient Europe, of slaves on American plantations, and of women as the previously silent majority (silent, at least, in historians' accounts) in every time and place.

The very substantial dimensions of the gains in our knowledge have led to a sense of doubt rather than triumph. Historians now understand the dubious criteria according to which women and Africans, peasants and slaves were excluded from the histories of earlier generations. They therefore cannot help but wonder which populations, and which domains of human experience, they themselves are excluding today.

The previously excluded histories do not only present new data to be integrated into the larger narrative; they raise questions about the validity of that narrative itself. University historians integrate African history into the history of the eighteenth century, or the nineteenth, and yet many histories written or recited in Africa do not measure historical time in centuries. Academic historians appropriate bits of the African past and place them within a larger framework of historical knowledge which has European roots—the history of commodity exchange, for example. They rarely think of using bits of European history to amplify African narratives, about the succession of Akan shrines or the origin and segmentation of Tiv lineages.

Even before these more difficult issues began to trouble historians, the growth of knowledge about non-European societies began to undermine earlier histories, to bring into question narratives of academic history which, in the 1960s, seemed to be beyond reproach. The new knowledge showed that what was once thought to be universal history was in fact very partial and very selective. The narrative of human history which Western historians held at that time could no longer stand. Its destruction contributed to the sense of fragmentation and lost coherence.

We can trace the process by which history undermined itself from within, by which knowledge grew and brought itself into doubt, by examining a number of books about history on a world scale, all of them published during the years of African history's growth. Some of these cover all the ages of human history, others cover only a brief period, but all of them attempt to integrate the history of every part of the world in a single narrative.

In the early 1960s it was still possible to describe human history in terms of a story with a single narrative thread, from the earliest periods until modern times. Now that possibility is gone. It is difficult for us to remember how profoundly our historical vision has changed unless we return to examine important works of that time. For example, William McNeill's *The Rise of the West,* published in 1963 when African history was just beginning to emerge, presented a unicentric and unidirectional narrative, of a kind that would not be acceptable today.

The Rise of the West divided the ancient world between "civilizations" and the land of "barbarians." The book focused on the diffusion of the techniques of civilization, originally from Mesopotamia, and then within the area McNeill calls the *ecumene,* as opposed to the land of the barbarians. *Oikoumenê* (one of Arnold Toynbee's terms) had been used also by the great anthropologist A. L. Kroeber to mean "the range of man's most developed cultures" and therefore "the millennially interrelated civilizations in the connected main land masses of the Eastern Hemisphere" (1952, p. 379). This was an intercommunicating zone within which the basic techniques of civilization were created, and within which they spread. The zone's boundaries shifted with time, but its early core was in the ancient Near East.

The origin of civilization, in McNeill's narrative, grows out of the introduction of agriculture. On this subject he takes contradictory positions but tries to maintain a single narrative thread. Even though the introduction explains that agriculture was introduced more than once, the book's narrative focuses on the central role of Mesopotamia, making a partial exception only for the introduction of agriculture in China (1963, p. 11). About the Americas, McNeill wrote, "Seeds or cuttings must have been carried across the ocean by human agency at a very early time" (1963, p. 240). Then a bit later he explained that "contacts were far too limited and sporadic to allow the Amerindians to borrow extensively from the more advanced cultures of the Old World. As a result, the Andean and Mexican civilizations developed belatedly and never attained a mastery of their environment that could rival the levels attained by their contemporaries in Eurasia."[2] He saw no possibility that domestication had independent beginnings in Africa and wrote that agriculture came to eastern and southern Africa only within the past five centuries. Until then, "primitive hunters roamed as their forefathers had done for untold millennia" (McNeill 1963, p. 481).

This statement is itself incorrect by millennia. We now know, as scholars of that generation did not, that animal domestication came very early to Africa (possibly earlier than to Southwest Asia), and that there were autonomous centers of crop domestication in Africa south of the Sahara.[3]

Historians of McNeill's generation knew that great empires had grown up in sub-Saharan Africa by the first half of the present millennium—Ghana, Mali, Songhay, and other kingdoms in West Africa, and a great many kingdoms in eastern, central, and southern Africa, of which Zimbabwe was famous because of its great stone ruins. McNeill saw all of these as borrowings. The more advanced of Africa's societies, he wrote, "were never independent of the main civilizations of Eurasia" (1963, p. 252). Islam, in his view, played a central role in bringing Eurasia's civilization to Africa. Even the southward migration of Bantu-speaking agriculturalists "may have been reinforced by the migration of tribes fleeing from Moslem pressures in the northwest" (1963, p. 560).

Recent archaeological research in West Africa has shown that urbanism based on commerce came to West Africa before the birth of Islam. By about A.D. 500, Jenne, on the Niger River, emerged as a town built on local trade in agricultural surpluses drawn from lands flooded by the river. In this case, West Africans built their own town, which then grew further when Islam became important (McIntosh and McIntosh 1988).

In central and southern Africa, also, kingdoms grew out of local roots. Zimbabwe is only one among the region's many stone ruins built in similar styles. These were sited so as to make farming and transhumant cattle-keeping possible as well as long-distance trade. As in West Africa, the evidence points to the growth of locally rooted centers which came ultimately to participate in long-distance trade. History can no longer be written as a single clear narrative of the spread of civilization's arts from the *ecumene,* the historical heartland, to Africa and other parts of the world.[4]

Accounting for the new patterns challenged historians to find new ways of defining the spatial boundaries of important processes in world history. In this, as in so much else, the development of the *Annales* school of history writing in France interacted in creative ways with the development of African history. The creators of *Annales* history had a fresh historical vision; they challenged the orthodoxies of a style of history (associated with the legacy of Leopold von Ranke) that focused on the critical study of archival documents, especially as they related to the minutiae of political events. The early *Annalistes* reacted against the narrowly political definition of the historian's subject matter. Marc Bloch, in his early work, wrote about collectively held understandings of the world, in what seems to us now like an anthropological approach (Bloch 1924, 1925). Bloch, Lucien Febvre, and others were concerned with the history of society more generally, and not only with that narrow stratum to which the main political documents referred.[5]

Fernand Braudel, the great leader of second-generation *Annales* historians, opened up the boundaries of historical space in a way that made it easier for us to understand Africa in world history. Many earlier scholars had limited themselves to national histories, of France, or of Italy, or of Spain. Others moved beyond national boundaries to continental ones. Braudel in his masterpiece saw the Mediterranean, with its palms and olive trees, as a significant historical unit, even though it took in parts of Europe and parts of Africa and Asia. It was tied together by its sea routes, but then extended wherever human communication took it: "We should imagine a hundred frontiers, not one," he wrote, "some political, some economic, and some cultural" (1976, p. 170).

A flexible approach to spatial boundaries gives us a tool with which to break out of narrow definitions of core and periphery in world history. We do not need to see West African Muslims in a narrow framework which casts them only as bearers of culture from the center of civilization to the periphery. We can see them as West Africans, in economy, in language, and in many elements of discursive practice, and yet at the same time Muslims. We do not read from a single historical map that inevitably separates Africans from Middle Easterners. We read many maps side by side, some for language, some for economy, some for religion. Similarly, when we define the boundaries of African healing practices we do not need to stop at the continent's edge; our history can extend to the Americas. If we adopt a flexible and situationally specific understanding of historical space, the plantation complex, which is often seen as narrowly American, as a phenomenon of the Caribbean, Brazil, and the southern United States, can now be understood as extending to the East Coast of Africa and to northern Nigeria (see Cooper 1977; Sheriff 1987; Lovejoy 1979).

Braudel, along with the other *Annales* historians, insisted on asking how representative our historical knowledge is in relation to the totality of the universe that might be described, if only we knew the full story. He saw the economy as studied by economists, for example, as only one small part of a much larger and more shadowy sphere of economic activity. He observed that "The market economy still controls the great mass of transactions *that show up in the statistics*," as a way of arguing that the historian ought to be concerned also with what does not show up in the statistics (1981, p. 24, emphasis in original). A concern with the representativeness of historical knowledge was at the heart of African history's growth, which in this sense can be seen as Braudelian in its inspiration.[6] African historians were saying that even if conventional sources were silent on Africa, this could not be taken as evidence that nothing had happened in Africa. If the contours of world history were determined by the silence of our sources, and not by the shape of history's subject matter, then we needed to find new sources.

Yet Braudel himself could not break out of a unidirectional history of the world with Europe at its center. *Civilisation matérielle, économie et capitalisme,* his three-volume history of the world between the fifteenth and eighteenth centuries, is driven by a tension between Braudel's disciplined attempt to find the correct spatial frame for each phenomenon (to explain the eighteenth-century rise of population on a worldwide basis, for example), and his definition of modern world history as the rise of a dominant Europe.

Civilisation matérielle, as a world history, touches on Africa's place in comparative context. The first volume is concerned with the history of everyday material life: food, clothing, crops, housing, furniture, and so on. Braudel's weakness in understanding sub-Saharan Africa does not undermine his more general analysis, except as it shapes his most general reflections on the full range of human experience.[7] The same is true of the second volume, on the techniques by which people exchanged goods in various parts of the world. In the third volume, however, the question of Africa's place in history (and Latin America's) comes closer to the center of the analysis. This volume, which draws heavily on the thought of Immanuel Wallerstein, asks about the process by which a dominant capitalist world economy emerged, with its core in the West. In 1750, he says, the countries which were later to become industrialized produced 22.5 percent of the world's gross product. In 1976 the same countries produced 75 percent of that product. What were the origins of this movement from the relative economic parity of the world's parts to the dominance of the capitalist core (1984, p. 534; 1982, p. 134)?

Wallerstein, whose analytic framework (of that period) Braudel adopts, began to explore the history of the world economy in order to answer questions which came to him as a specialist in the sociology of Africa. The 1970s were a time when many African nations, born in optimism during the 1960s, were forced to come to terms with the intractable nature of their poverty. Wallerstein reflected on its causes and origins. He borrowed from writings about dependency in Latin America and formulated an interpretive framework describing the whole of the world, in the most recent period, as a capitalist system, irrespective of local forms of labor organization or ownership. The most important inequalities, Wallerstein argued, may be understood in terms of a spatial metaphor. The powerful countries of the capitalist core draw strength from their relationship to the poor countries of the periphery; the semi-periphery plays a mediating role that is important for the political stability of the total system (Wallerstein 1974*a*, Wallerstein 1974*b*, and the forthcoming book by Cooper et al. explore the way in which writing about Africa and Latin America has led to the fragmentation of Wallerstein's world history. See also Stern 1988, DuPlessis 1987, and Jewsiewicki 1987).

Braudel adopted this framework, with its concern for the systematic character of inequality between the people he called "les *have* et les *have not*" (1979, p. 16). He was interested in how the dominance of the capitalist center grew out of developments within Europe, and out of relations among local world-economies. These latter were the spatial units which achieved a certain organic integration because of the density of exchange relations within them. The Mediterranean of the sixteenth century was a world-economy in this sense.

Braudel tried to make a serious assessment of the degree to which wealth drawn from outside Europe contributed to the rise of capitalism, but he treated Africans, and to a lesser extent people of the Americas, as historical actors only to the extent that they met European needs (1984, p. 386):

> While we might have preferred to see this "Non-Europe" on its own terms, it cannot properly be understood, even before the eighteenth century, except in terms of the mighty shadow cast over it by western Europe. . . . It was from all over the world . . . that Europe was now drawing a substantial part of her strength and substance. And it was this extra share which enabled Europeans to reach superhuman heights in tackling the tasks encountered on the path to progress.

This is a rather strange statement, lumping together much of the world simply on the basis that it is not Europe and proposing to ignore non-Europe on its own terms.

Braudel describes African developments, in particular, in terms of racial essences. In his view all civilization originated from the north, radiating southwards. He writes, "I should like now to concentrate on the heartland of Black Africa, leaving aside the countries of the Maghreb—a 'White Africa' contained within the orbit of Islam" (1984, p. 430). Braudel's understanding of historical space is usually a subtle one in which each spatial frame is carefully differentiated. Here, however, he merges several frames in an inflexible and inaccurate way. Firstly, he merges race ("White" or "Black") with religion (Islamic or non-Islamic), even though many of the Muslims were people he would otherwise have described as "Black."

Secondly, he characterizes "Black Africa" as passive and inert. He writes that European ships on the West Coast met "neither resistance nor surveillance" and that the same thing happened on the shores of the desert: "Islam's camel-trains were as free to choose their entry-points as Europe's ships" (1984, p. 434). This is demonstrably incorrect. A very large body of historical literature explores the complex interactions between West African kings or traders and those who came across the desert from the north. The spread of Islam and of the trans-Saharan trade was shaped by initiatives taken on both sides of the desert.[8]

According to Braudel, all movement was in a single direction. "Curiously, no black explorers ever undertook any of the voyages across either the desert or the ocean which lay on their doorstep. . . . To the African, the Atlantic was, like the Sahara, an impenetrable obstacle"

(1984, p. 434). He writes this despite the knowledge (with which he was certainly acquainted) that many Muslims who traded across the desert, or who went on the pilgrimage to Mecca from the West African Sudan, were Africans he would describe as black, carrying the cultural heritage of West Africa with them. Black African rulers are reported as having made the pilgrimage to Mecca as early as the eleventh century (Al-Naqar 1972, p. 27). Mansa Musa of Mali traveled from West Africa to Cairo and then to Mecca in the fourteenth century with a retinue reported to number 60,000 (Hiskett 1984, p. 15; see also pp. 29, 34, and 55). Even though the correct number is likely to be smaller, there is no question that thousands of Africans crossed the desert to visit the world of the Mediterranean and the Red Sea, and others (from the East Coast) crossed the Indian Ocean to reach the Persian Gulf and India.

Finally, it appears to be the case that Braudel's characterization of the difference between "Black Africa" and "White Africa" is based on his understanding of race. In *Grammaire des civilisations* he acknowledges that Ethiopia (in this case Christian) was a civilization, explaining that it "undeniably possesses white ethnic elements, and is founded on a *métisse* population, very different, however, from those of the true Melano-Africans" (1987, p. 152). At times he denies the existence of facts in order to preserve the clear distinction between a Black Africa that is uncivilized and a White Africa that is civilized. In a 1963 book he acknowledges that the region near the Gulf of Guinea was urbanized very early (1987, p. 164; originally published 1963). But then in a later book which argues that towns were one of the distinguishing marks of civilization, he writes that there were no towns on the fringes of the Gulf of Guinea (1981, pp. 292–93).

Because historians have come to a fuller understanding of African urbanization, and of African initiatives in intercontinental exchange, it is now easy to see the weakness of this small part of Braudel's work. A central question remains, however: whether his unidirectional interpretation of Africa is merely an unfortunate idiosyncracy of an otherwise great historian, or whether it is a sign of deeper problems in the way many historians construct their narratives.

In the work of Pierre Chaunu and Bartolome Bennassar, members of the third generation of *Annales* historians, we can see the tension between the new African evidence, showing autonomous processes, and the older vision of world history in which progress radiated from a few historic civilizations. In their history of the world between the fourteenth and sixteenth centuries, the central process is the merging of local historical spaces into a single interconnected worldwide space. Bennassar took care to read the new Africanist work, but then only partially assimilated it. He explains, for example, that many of the Muslim merchants of West Africa were black West Africans, and that Islam played no role in the advanced agriculture and metallurgy of the "Bantu civilization" of the great lakes region of East Africa (Bennassar and Chaunu 1977, pp. 71 and 73). In the same chapter, however, he writes about the great lakes region "from Lake Rudolf to Lake Nyasa, where black states with diversified economies were . . . able to establish themselves insofar as Arab penetration stimulated the commercial function" (Bennassar and Chaunu 1977, p. 72). This view of Arab penetration, for which there is no evidence, appears aimed at fixing the position of Africa clearly within the broader narrative.

The broader narrative in Bennassar and Chaunu's book, in Braudel's work, and in McNeill's, tells about the impact of "civilizations" on the world. Despite the centrality of "civilizations," the term is not always the subject of careful discussion. McNeill, who wrote that "civilized society had much to impart and relatively little to learn from peoples not yet civilized," defined civilization as "a style of human life characterized by a complexity, wealth, and general impressiveness that justify the epithet 'civilized'" (McNeill 1963, pp. 65 and 32).

"Civilization" in its usage over the centuries in the English language has carried connotations of self and other, or of the proper and improper ordering of society. To "civilize," in the *Oxford English Dictionary* (1933), is "to polish what is rude or uncouth . . . to domesticate, tame (wild animals) . . . to make 'civil'" in the sense of "having proper public or social order." "Civilization" is a civilized condition or state in these senses, but then also "a developed or advanced state of human society."

Braudel makes a distinction between "civilizations" and "cultures," with the societies of black Africa counted among the cultures. In *The Structures of Everyday Life* he writes that "a culture is a civilization that has not yet achieved maturity" (1981, p. 101), but then in *Grammaire des civilisations* he borrows from Lévi-Strauss' division of societies between clocks and steam-engines, to argue:

> The societies which correspond to cultures are those . . . which have a tendency to maintain themselves indefinitely in their initial state, which explains furthermore why they appear to us as societies without history and without progress. . . . In brief primitive cultures will be the fruit of egalitarian societies, for whom relations between groups are regulated once and for all and repeat themselves, whereas civilizations are founded on hierarchical societies, with . . . changing tensions, social conflicts, political struggle, and perpetual evolution. [Braudel 1987, p. 48]

African cultures, according to this argument, are egalitarian and static, European civilizations hierarchical and dynamic.

The strongest external sign of civilization, according to Braudel, is the presence of towns (1987, p. 48), but these in turn are indicators of the existence of hierarchic space, divided between rich centers and poor peripheries (Braudel 1979, p. 16). Spatial inequalities emerge where intercommunication and commerce are well developed and where agriculture is productive. The productivity of civilized society is the fruit of farming with a plough; cultures usually rely on the hoe (Braudel 1981, pp. 56–64, 174–82). Chaunu is clear on the reason for the importance of agricultural change: increased productivity leads to rising population densities, which are accompanied in turn by the emergence of hierarchy (Bennassar and Chaunu 1977, pp. 47–51). One of the central elements in the emergence of civilization is the existence of writing. Chaunu writes that he follows Braudel on the importance of writing for civilization: "The arts of memory are situated at the heart of accumulation" and writing is "the most efficacious" of the arts of memory (Bennassar and Chaunu 1977, p. 56, n. 49).

We have here a complex of elements which together form a coherent configuration: political and economic hierarchy, towns, commerce and intercommunication, writing, the plough, high densities of population, and historical dynamism.

The problem with this complex when applied to Africa, in the context of world histories like Braudel's or Bennassar and Chaunu's, is that the interrelations do not hold. In much of sub-Saharan Africa ploughs are not used because they are damaging to tropical soils. Some areas boasted thriving commerce, considerable intercommunication, and high population densities, but without political hierarchy.

The Igbo-speaking areas of southeastern Nigeria, for example, had very high population densities; in recent times some parts of the region have reached 800 per square mile. People cultivated the land with hoes, had a very dense network of periodic markets (in which markets took turns with one another on four- or eight-day cycles to make it easy for merchants to move from one to another), and had a network also of long-distance trade fairs. By late in the first millennium A.D. the region was importing substantial quantities of trade goods overland from the Mediterranean—all this without writing and, in most parts of Igboland, without clear forms of political hierarchy. Egalitarian councils maintained the market peace, and the agents of religious oracles communicated over long distances. Many different kinds of ritual functionaries coexisted in Igboland, each preserving one or another form of knowledge, to be transmitted orally to the next generation. Artisans practiced numerous crafts. The region was an economically dynamic one both internally and in relation to export trade; when demand for palm oil grew in the early nineteenth century, Igboland and the area to the south of it rose to the challenge, and by 1853 were exporting 30,000 tons of palm oil a year, using indigenous forms of organization.[9] It did not by any means belong in the set of societies to which Braudel would assign it—those with a "tendency to maintain themselves indefinitely in their initial state . . . for whom relations between groups are regulated once and for all and repeat themselves."

The point of this is extremely important: the historical experience of southeastern Nigeria followed a pattern for which the historians' category of "civilization" was largely irrelevant. The region had high population densities in the absence of hierarchical states, commerce without literacy, and productive agriculture without ploughs. "Civilization's" characteristics—high population density, commerce, hierarchy, and so on—are meaningful only insofar as the separate elements have relational significance for one another: to the extent that the plough, political hierarchy, and mercantile activity are interrelated, for example. The elements have no explanatory significance if treated simply as a check list. In this part of Nigeria, it is clear, a different set of interrelations was at work. It is no wonder that historians, faced with the obligation to take seriously the history of Igboland, complain of "fragmentation" and "chaos" in historical knowledge. Some of the long-accepted categories of historical understanding are irrelevant.

This is not to say that Braudel, or Bennassar and Chaunu, were uninterested in the principles underlying change in African societies. Bennassar, for example, explored the principles of African social organization in his search for an answer to the central question asked also by Braudel: Why was Africa not the place where economic change took off? Why was it not Africa where the great breakthrough to capitalism occurred? In order to answer this question, Bennassar began from an understanding of the social factors that led to the breakthrough in Europe. The central factor, in his view, was the partial freedom of merchants from political control, and their capacity to accumulate wealth in their own right. He looked for the same factors in Africa, beginning with what seem to him the most advanced of the African kingdoms. In the kingdom of Kongo, he argued, merchants were closely controlled by the king. Land reverted to the king at the owner's death, thus cutting off the possibility of accumulation. The king was the source of poverty and prosperity, merchants lacked autonomy, and economic growth was restricted (Bennassar and Chaunu 1977, pp. 85–87).

The analysis falls down, however, not only because of the wide diversity of state structures in Africa, but also because of the incorrectness of its more basic assumption that autonomous merchants require a state structure in order to carry on their business. John Janzen has written the history of a set of institutions with mercantile functions which cut across regions occupied by states and regions of acephalous political organization. It is an area extending beyond the northern edge of the Kongo kingdom, mostly to the north of the Congo River as it descends to the Atlantic Ocean. This was a region of intense activity among merchants who traded locally and contributed to the export trade. The seventeenth-century ivory trade was fed by an annual kill of 3,000 to 4,000 elephants. Estimates, also in the seventeenth century, had it that the region was capable of exporting up to forty tons of copper a year.[10] Yet a crucial part of the region's economy was outside the borders of any kingdom. It was an area in which a number of important governmental functions were borne by Lemba—a healing association or, in Janzen's (and Victor Turner's) term, "a drum of affliction."

People were initiated into Lemba as a way of treating their illnesses, yet it was also a form of commercial organization. Initiates played an essential role in maintaining free passage across an entire network of four-day markets. Lemba was a form of religious expression, a consecrated medicine, in which the highest levels of initiation were very expensive. The richest merchants were most likely to rise to the top of Lemba, and they used ritual networks to advance their economic interests. It is an example of exactly the sort of mercantile autonomy for which Bennassar was searching. He did not find it (or other similar institutions), however, because the world historian does not normally search for mercantile activity in "'the sacred medicine of governing'; . . . 'the government of multiplication and reproduction . . . and 'sacred medicine integrating people, villages and markets'" (Janzen 1982, p. 4).

The problem here is that the categories of historical analysis are normally drawn from Europe, and therefore the historian looks in Africa for a familiar constellation of king, nobles, church, and merchants. "The sacred medicine of governing" is alien to the analysis. V. Y. Mudimbe has explained that functional analyses depend on a contrast between the normal and the pathological. If what is European is defined as normal, then the non-European appears to be disordered, abnormal, primitive (1988, pp. 27 and 191–92).

How, then, do we construct an account of world history within a single framework, if the principles of social organization of Lemba, or in Igboland, are different from principles in Europe? Eric Wolf tries to do this, to construct a coherent account while giving full weight to non-Europeans, in *Europe and the People without History* (1982). Because he works so hard to reverse the balance of emphasis from Europe to "the people without history," we can see the limits and the difficulties of the enterprise.

The early parts of the book make no attempt to picture a unified process in world history. Wolf orients the early description around three "modes of production." In other hands these might be used to reduce diverse experience to a few simple types within a scheme made in Europe. If this were the case, Wolf would have done violence to locally specific principles of organization, African ones among others. But it is not the case. The "modes" are heuristic categories. These are not types of societies, he writes, but rather "constructs in which to envisage certain strategic relationships."[11] He makes a broad sketch of the world's social geography and political organization in 1400, emphasizing autonomous political forms, especially those which are not purely local, and which make regional integration possible. Wolf then moves on to the career of capitalism, from the time of its early origins.

It is for the capitalist period that Wolf aims to construct a universal history, based on regularities in the historical process and not only in the historian's frame of analysis. The rise of the world market leads to the emergence of money (and of prices) as a universal language. Goods everywhere in the world become commodities, and these "can be compared and exchanged without reference to the social matrix in which they were produced" (1982, p. 310). Each commodity has a quantitative value in relation to all other commodities because of the existence of market institutions.

For the period when a world market exists, the historian can write a universal history of the way commodities are produced and exchanged. This is Wolf's project. He sketches the political and economic consequences of the fur trade for the peoples of North America, and of the slave trade for Africa. Later in the book he tours the world, showing the effects of commodity production—explaining the impact of rubber production, for example, on the Amazon basin and on southern Asia.

Wolf's focus on non-Europeans in world history is especially useful in revealing how difficult it is to construct a single master-narrative, for there must necessarily be levels of experience he does not describe— levels at which people struggle to create new ways of giving cultural form to social action, levels at which local experience escapes from the regularity of "universal" processes.[12]

Recent work by Arjun Appadurai and Igor Kopytoff shows, for example, that objects become commodities in culturally specific ways (Appadurai 1986; Kopytoff 1986; see also Geary 1986; Cassanelli 1986). Objects, in this view, have a life history during which they move into and out of commodity status, as in the case of an heirloom which family members will not sell until a particular point in the family's life cycle when it becomes available for sale. The pattern by which objects move into and out of commodity status varies from one society to another.

Sharon Hutchinson, writing on the Nuer of the southern Sudan, shows that money and commodities are culturally constructed in ways radically different from the expected ones. The culture of commodities is locally constructed, not a universal pattern. Nor can one "predict how money will be conceptualized and incorporated by other cultures" (Hutchinson 1988, p. 179).

Nuer these days work for wages, become active as merchants, and engage in the trade of cattle and other commodities as buyers and sellers. They can therefore be said to have entered the capitalist world of commodity exchange; they speak the universal language of money and price. Nevertheless, cattle are commodities in relatively circumscribed contexts; they are unlike the commodities described by Wolf, or the commodities found in Marx, for whom capitalist exchange breaks down boundaries and opens free movement. Nuer sell cattle for money, but they may not exchange the money thus earned in all the ways they might have exchanged cattle. The crucial difference between money and cattle is that "cattle have blood," which people equate with procreative force; "money has no blood." For this reason money cannot be used in contexts where the blood of cattle is relevant: for bloodwealth, or sacrifice, or (except to a limited extent) for bridewealth. Even when cattle are used in social transactions, distinctions are made between the uses of animals bought with money ("cattle of money") and animals which came as bridewealth ("cattle of girls").

Money itself is not a homogeneous medium of exchange for people in Nuerland. Money earned emptying latrines or doing domestic work is called "money of shit," and it cannot be used to purchase cows. "Cattle bought with the money of shit cannot live" (Hutchinson 1988, p. 152). Other wages are called "money of sweat," and earnings from the sale of livestock are "money of cattle." For the Nuer, money is not universally fluid. There are several kinds of it, with several uses (Hutchinson 1988, pp. 108, 110, 115–16, 148, 149, 152–62, 176, and 179).

Nuer have constructed a new synthesis of market and community, a new set of exchange categories, to meet their own particular needs. It is this sort of creative process which is not accounted for in a narrative of the spread of commodities in world history. To say this is not to deny the existence of commodities, nor of their commensurability on a worldwide basis, nor of the significance of the emergence of a world market. It is simply to say that the history of commodities is not a total history, that there are realms of experience beyond its reach.

Comparative history is still possible for historians who set modest goals. *Cross-Cultural Trade in World History,* by Philip Curtin, explores the form taken by preindustrial trading networks which link people across cultural boundaries. This is a comparative historical sociology focusing on settlements of commercial specialists, removed physically from their home communities and living as strangers among their hosts, linked together with other such settlements in a commercial network, a "trade diaspora." Chinese traders created a trade diaspora in Southeast Asia, as did the Juula in West Africa, and Phoenicians and Greeks in the Mediterranean. The interlinked communities of merchants provided trading services and information to one another across widely dispersed areas. Curtin uses the trade diaspora to explore the definition of intercommunicating zones in world history. This is a return to the issues raised by McNeill (Curtin writes about "regions of ecumenical trade"), but with unidirectional history now dead. "One of the myths of African history," he writes, "is the old view that commerce in Africa was largely pioneered by outsiders. . . . In fact, trade beyond the village level began on African initiative" and moved outward from there (Curtin 1984, pp. 15–16). Curtin rejects the idea that trade diasporas are linked to all-encompassing economic systems, in the style of Wallerstein or Andre Gunder Frank. "They are only one influence on the course of history among many" (Curtin 1984, p. 9).

A reading of McNeill, Braudel, Bennassar and Chaunu, Wolf, Curtin, and others points to a larger and more general development: that the emergence of African history (and of Asian and Latin American history) has changed our understanding of general history, and of Europe's place in the world, in profound ways. It is no longer possible to defend the position that historical processes among non-European peoples can be seen as the consequence of all-encompassing influences emerging from a dominant European center. This shift in our understanding is uncomfortable for those who see history as the spread of civilization from a European center, and it is equally uncomfortable for those who sketch history in terms of an all-determining system of capitalist exploitation.

The shift away from historical narratives that originate in Europe has been both accompanied and enabled by innovations in methods for constructing knowledge about people who had previously been left out of academic histories. These renovated methods, some of which achieved their fullest early development among historians of Africa, include oral history, historical archaeology, and historical linguistics, as well as anthropologically informed historical analysis. The new methods and modes of interpretation made it possible for scholars to approach the history of non-literate people, and in many cases powerless ones, without departing from the accepted critical canons of historical research. Scholars were able to know histories they had never known before. The consequences were, once again, paradoxical. These significant advances in the range and quality of historical knowledge helped to shake historians' faith in the quality of their knowledge. To glimpse whole regions of history previously unknown, to see the dark side of the moon, inevitably shook scholars' faith in their own omniscience.

The methodological advances were not narrowly African ones. They had an impact in a number of historical fields, but many of them emerged with particular clarity and power amongst historians of Africa.[13] The impact of oral history was bound to be great in studies of sub-Saharan Africa, where many societies were ideally suited for this form of research: their people transmitted substantial bodies of knowledge from one generation to the next and sustained complex political and economic hierarchies, all without practicing writing. Oral traditions were still alive (in many cases *are* still alive) when the historians of the 1960s and 1970s went about their work. Unlike Latin America, where the colonial period had begun several centuries earlier, it was only in the late nineteenth century that most of sub-Saharan Africa experienced conquest. Before this Europeans did not, in most cases, intervene directly in the transmission of knowledge.

Jan Vansina's *De la tradition orale* was the first to make a coherent case among Africanists that oral traditions could be usable as historical sources, and it offered basic elements of a method (Vansina 1961, revised in 1985; see also Miller 1980; Cassanelli 1982; Cohen 1985). In many cases the academic historians were Africans who themselves had opportunity to learn bits of orally transmitted history in their own childhoods, and who returned with historians' tools to study some of the same traditions (Kimambo 1969; Ogot 1967; Samatar 1982; Alagoa 1964, 1972, 1980; Were 1967). Historians have come to understand that the narratives themselves, as told within African society, are not socially neutral recitations that serve all equally. They are as much a subject of struggle, located in a web of power relations, as are accounts of the glories of Western civilization or of Afrocentric creativity. The historical interpreter must read traditions (must listen to them and watch them performed) with attention to the forms of domination inscribed in them, and the web of social relations in which they are embedded (see Feierman 1990 and Tonkin 1992).

The sense that there was a world of historical experience in Africa beyond what was described in documents led historians to explore other techniques of historical reconstruction alongside those for studying oral history. Historical archaeology—the archaeology of relatively recent periods (the past 3,000 years)—combining oral traditions, ethnography, and the more usual archaeological techniques, has served historians well in the absence of a rich documentary record (Schmidt 1978, 1983*a*, 1983*b*, 1990; Chittick 1974; Posnansky 1969; McIntosh and McIntosh 1980*a*, 1980*b*, 1984, 1986; Shinnie and Kense 1989). African historians have also made creative use of historical linguistics (Ehret 1968, 1971, 1988; Schoenbrun 1990).

The amplified range of methods employed by African historians has proven useful not only in societies that lack writing, but also for studying the underclasses of societies with a considerable range of literacy. Historians have used these amplified methods to construct rich accounts of the African majority in colonial society and especially to bring us magnificent accounts of peasant resistance to colonial domination.[14]

The best studies of resistance to conquest, the work of Allen Isaacman, for example, explore the central tensions of African society before conquest—the course of resistance to domination by indigenous authorities—so that even the history of colonial rule is divided between histories made in Europe and others which find their sources of coherence within African histories, as rooted in oral traditions (Isaacman 1972, 1976, 1990; Ranger 1985a).

The sense that we can no longer tell history as a single story, from a single consistent point of view or from a unified perspective, strikes deep resonances in recent social and cultural thought. Michel Foucault wrote, in *Language, Countermemory, Practice,* that the idea of the whole of society "arose in the Western world, in this highly individualized historical development that culminates in capitalism. To speak of the 'whole of society' apart from the only form it has ever taken is to transform our past into a dream" (quoted in Jay 1984, p. 521). The very categories by which we understand universal experience originate in the particular experience of the core of the capitalist world.

This is the same lesson taught by an examination of African history: the categories which are ostensibly universal are in fact particular, and they refer to the experience of modern Europe. That we have learned this lesson in two different ways—through philosophically based writings on Europe and through histories of non-Europeans—forces us to ask about the relationship between the two sets of developments. A central question which has not yet been fully addressed is the relationship between the crisis of historical representation that came about when historians began to hear the voices of those who had been voiceless, and the more general epistemological crisis affecting all the social sciences and humanities.

To answer this question one would need to write a general political and intellectual history of the years since World War II. It is only possible, in the scope of a few paragraphs, to make tentative suggestions.

In the decades after 1945, the politics of race turned in a decisively new direction in the European colonial empires and in the United States. The struggles which led to decolonization—wars in Indochina,

Algeria, and Kenya, and less violent independence movements in innumerable other territories—led to a reconsideration among European intellectuals of the qualities and values that had been defined as European. The loss of empire happened at a time when some thinkers were questioning whether historians and others in the human sciences were at all capable of describing the Other, or whether by doing so they were engaging in what Emmanuel Levinas called "ontological imperialism," in which otherness vanishes and becomes part of the same (Young 1990, p. 13).

Some thinkers argued that descriptions of the native, the colonial Other, were embedded in a discourse in which Europeans defined themselves. In Edward Said's words, "The Orient was . . . not Europe's interlocutor, but its silent other" (Said 1985, p. 17).[15] How was it possible to define freedom unless one could contrast it with bondage, autonomy except in contrast to slavery, or civilization (itself at the heart of world history, as we have seen) except in contrast to barbarism? Without the native, without the slave, the bondsman, or the barbarian, the central values of the West are difficult to imagine. The slave and the barbarian were not incidental to civilization, aberrant conditions at the margins; they were constitutive of civilization, a way civilization defined itself. With the civil rights movement in the United States, similar perceptions began to emerge, that slavery and later forms of racial oppression were not errors at the margins of American society; they had, in some fundamental way, defined American society. The relationship between race and America's central egalitarian values was, in Gunnar Myrdal's term, "An American Dilemma."[16]

The decline of the colonial empires and the end of official segregation in the United States brought increasing numbers of nonwhites into the world's historical profession and into the audiences that historians addressed. In the 1960s many newly independent African nations founded their own universities. The Africans who staffed the new history departments had a compelling interest in reconstructing the autonomous history of Africans within the national borders. British, or French, or American historians, who were now looking at the history of nations in a very different way than they had seen the history of colonies, were influenced also by the expanded presence of Africans and African-Americans as colleagues and as students. The result of all these developments was that a growing group of historians began to work seriously in Africa, in Europe, and in North America, to reconstruct and recover the African past.

There were other forces at work in the wider intellectual transformation—the rise of women in academia and of feminism, and radical shifts in the history of science which influenced thinking about history as a science. Nevertheless, two of the most central ones grew out of the racial politics of the postwar decades: a sense of the defining place of the subordinated Other in European discourses, and the opening up of non-Western histories as legitimate subjects of historical research.

The specialist work of historical reconstruction served to take the people about whom anthropologists had always written and to insist that they be placed within the larger historical narrative. The change in context required a change in how historians understood agency. Previously mute people now had to be seen as authors and actors. Exotic cultures were not new to the academic imagination, but the style of description was new. The new knowledge broke with a long intellectual tradition that treated exotic cultures as though they existed at a different time from the rest of humanity—stone age, or bronze age, or iron age peoples, remnants of the past, not living in the same world where historians live, not subject to the same political and economic forces (Fabian 1983).

Once historians of Africa took exotic cultures out of their "culture gardens" and into their own world, that world no longer existed in the same form. Treating Africans and women, peasants and slaves as historical actors presented a fundamental challenge to general historical understanding. It challenged the notion that history told from the point of view of a narrower and less representative population was value-neutral or universal.

The challenge it presents to African history is just as fundamental. The historical experiences of Africans on their own continent must be understood in the terms of the actors themselves, with a culturally specific sense of the actors' language and motivations. What did it mean, for example, when a young dependent man took a "wife" within the Lemba healing association? She was not a wife with whom he expected to build a household, farm together, and procreate; she was a "wife" with whom he established a social tie only in the context of healing. What did a childless Igbo woman see as her alternatives when she came before the Aro oracle to learn the causes of her childlessness? When do Nuer men resort to blood sacrifice? What do they mean to accomplish by it? These are questions that can only be answered by a historian who sinks deep roots in the particular local forms of historical experience.

Having done this, the historian cannot assume that Africans, taking culturally grounded actions, only had the power to shape local events or to take part in local processes. Lemba marriages helped to establish networks of relationship that would enable men to participate in the overseas trade in slaves and ivory, in copper and other goods. In Igboland the Aro oracle ruled in many cases that local offenders should be sent off in the Atlantic slave trade. Nuer men lived under colonial rule, and they needed to adjust their activities within the colonial economy so as to accumulate wealth in forms that made sacrifice possible. In doing so they changed the shape of colonial control.

The Lemba initiate, the Igbo woman, and the Nuer man were all helping to shape historical processes of enormous scope. The problem for the historian, then, is how to capture all different levels at the same time, how to do justice to the local, the regional, and the international in a single description or a single framework of analysis.[17]

It is worth making a brief exploration of the history of the place of Africans in the Atlantic slave trade to understand some of the problems of multilayered interpretation. The slave trade was a set of actions which articulated with one another on an enormous scale, reaching across several continents. Individual slaves might have been torn from their homes hundreds of miles into the interior of Nigeria, or of Angola, or of some other part of the continent. If we can imagine a brother and sister taken together, then perhaps the brother found himself walking to the coast to embark on a ship, while his sister stopped along the way to toil as an unfree worker nearer to home. Once the brother crossed the ocean he would forge bonds with other slaves, perhaps from the Gold Coast or the Guinea Coast. He might well have worked on a sugar plantation owned by a capitalist in the north of England. Defined as a spatial system, in Braudelian terms, a system of slavery extended to the Caribbean, to North, South, and Central America, to Europe, and also to the Indian Ocean.

Within an imagined system, understood in this way, there were many other boundaries: local ones, and the boundaries of subsystems. Each local area had its own patterns of custom and of language, its own characteristic forms of social interaction. People spoke to one another in local languages, became Lemba brides and grooms, or consulted the Aro oracle. Yet they also participated in a coordinated meta-system of meaning and action reaching all the way across from the interior of Africa to the Americas, and to Europe.

Historians have long worked to place the diverse and heterogeneous elements of the slave trade within a clear narrative of the way history unfolded, moving in a single direction to shape the world as we know it. *Capitalism and Slavery,* published by Eric Williams in 1944, opened a continuing debate on the relationship between slavery and the rise of capitalism. According to Williams, slavery in the Caribbean contributed to the formation of capital in Great Britain. The industrialization of Europe, in this view, was built on the backs of slaves in the Americas. Debate over these issues has continued, but historians of a later generation have also extended their reasoning about economic interrelations beyond its original focus in Europe and the Americas; they have moved into Atlantic Africa.

Historians ask why Africans were taken as slaves, and not people from other continents. Patrick Manning (1990) and Stefano Fenoaltea try to answer this question by asking whether African labor was less productive in Africa than it was in the Americas. Could the trade have come about as a way of increasing the productivity of labor? Was this the reason slaves were relatively cheap at most times compared to the amount they could produce in the Americas? Claude Meillassoux (1986) argues that slaves were cheap not because they were unproductive in Africa but because they were taken by theft. The users of slave labor did not need to pay the cost of feeding slave children or caring for slave mothers; they needed only to pay the costs of maintaining armies and other political institutions that made theft possible. Joseph Miller (1988) analyzes the economic logic of the slave trade at each of its stages, beginning with the uses of European capital in transforming African societies from within, so that they come to supply slaves, and then following the capital flows on across the Atlantic. Our base of knowledge on the economics of the slave trade is qualitatively better than it was twenty-five years ago, and that knowledge extends into African societies.

Our understanding of the demographic consequences of the slave trade grew at the same time. Ever since Philip Curtin opened up the field of inquiry with *The Atlantic Slave Trade: A Census* (1969), our knowledge of the places of origin and destination of the slaves has become more substantial. (See Lovejoy 1983, and Inikori 1982.) Ralph Austen (1979) followed up with an important survey of the trans-Saharan trade. Historians went on to study the larger effects of the slave trade on long-term population trends in Africa (Manning 1990). These were influenced by gender differentials in slave use—for example, the Atlantic trade took more men than women, and slave owners within Africa employed more women than men (Robertson and Klein 1983).

The history of the slave trade raises questions of cultural specificity and historical process in extreme form. A man who was sold to traders in Central Africa and who ultimately crossed the Atlantic to work on a plantation in Jamaica was clearly a slave. But it is doubtful that his original owner in Africa knew the English word "slave," and doubtful also that the local term defining the person's form of dependency was the precise equivalent of "slave." The major associations of "slavery" in English are with the plantation slavery of the American south, the Caribbean, and Latin America. Yet historians also use the word for statuses within Africa that seem very much unlike plantation slavery.

In Shambaai, in the mountains of northern Tanzania where I did ethnographic research and collected oral narratives, poor men who could not feed their children during famines relied in precolonial times on the food stores of the chief. A man who could not feed his daughter would leave her at the chief's court where she ate and where she worked. At famine's end the father would come bringing goats to redeem his daughter from the chief's control, and he would take her home. The girl, while at the court, might be called an *mtung'wa*, the same as the word for "slave," and she was also called an *mndee* of the chief—the chief's "girl," an ambiguous term which might at times be translated as "slave." An American would not be likely to think of her as a slave, but if her father did not return to reclaim his daughter, she remained in servitude (Feierman 1990, pp. 53–64).

In the late 1960s, I interviewed a man whose mother, born in a part of East Africa distant from Shambaai, had been a "slave" (*mtung'wa*) at a chief's court. Soon after the German conquest, the chief sold her to a commoner and she became a wife. My informant described his mother as an unhappy woman who had been abused by her co-wife and by her husband because she had no birth-family to insist on her rights. The other woman in the household, the co-wife, had a greater level of protection because her husband had made a bridewealth payment to her male relatives. The woman could therefore ask them for help when she needed it.

In the period when all this was happening, Arab plantation owners on the Tanzania coast, and on the islands of Zanzibar and Pemba just off the coast, employed slave labor to grow cloves, and sugar, and grain. A few years earlier, the woman without a family, my informant's mother, might have been sold as a plantation slave if the chief had chosen to do so. Instead she became a wife without full rights.

The case illustrates that slavery was only one in a range of related statuses. The woman in question was a wife, not a slave, but a wife without full rights. She might easily have become a plantation slave, and she might also have been a wife with full rights if she had been married at home, and if her brothers or father had received a bridewealth payment. An omniscient social observer would be able to place these different statuses within a total range of women's statuses, as a social map. But if the statuses are seen instead from the point of view of the woman at the time, for whom they were possible life choices, it is clear that they presented a challenge: how to negotiate so as to become a wife without rights rather than a slave, or better still to become a wife with full rights.

The woman of the period understood that her life chances were defined by the constellation of relationships of dependency. If her negotiations were unsuccessful, if she was taken in the intercontinental slave trade, she experienced a disastrous simplification of her possibilities. Now only the slave status was relevant. Historians find it difficult to characterize the status of a woman in the process of becoming enslaved. If they treat her as a slave they appear to be denying the importance of locally based forms of dependency; if they treat her status in local terms they are denying the importance of the intercontinental process. An adequate explanation must, I think, do both.

Historians of Africa have tended to make a clear choice for one side or the other, and in doing so have misrepresented social processes within Africa. These issues first came up in the 1960s in a debate between Walter Rodney (1966), the great Guyanese scholar, and John Fage (1969). Fage argued that slavery had existed long before the slave trade, which merely sent slaves further from home than they might have gone, but did not change their status. Rodney said that the institution of slavery was called into existence by the trade. Today, many historians say that Africans practiced kinship slavery in the earlier period, and then shifted to commoditized forms of slavery with the coming of the trade.

Suzanne Miers and Igor Kopytoff, in an important attempt to create a culturally specific interpretation of forms of slavery on the African continent (1977), compared a "slave" (always in single quotes in their essay) to a person going through the liminal stage in a rite of passage. In such a rite the initiate is separated from one social status in the first stage, then undergoes a phase of liminality or transition, and finally is reintegrated into society in a new social status. Miers and Kopytoff picture a social landscape occupied by a number of lineages. At times individuals become detached from all lineages, perhaps as prisoners of war, or as in the case of a child for whom there is not enough food within her own lineage, which then transfers all rights in her to another lineage. These are the "slaves," "strangers in a new setting" (1977, p. 15). Miers and Kopytoff do not picture "slavery" as a permanent status but as a phase along the way to a final stage of reincorporation as full social beings in their new lineages.

According to this interpretation it is a mistake to see "slaves" as chattel or property, except at the extreme end of a continuum of social forms. Not all "slaves" in Africa could be sold. "Slavery," according to Miers and Kopytoff, needs to be understood as one example of a broader system in which lineages transfer rights in persons. The most obvious example of this was in bridewealth, the payment made by the husband's lineage to acquire rights in a woman's labor and in her capacity to bear children.

Kopytoff returned to this subject in an essay on the end of slavery (1988) to argue that when slavery ended, after colonial conquest, slaves did not experience manumission as "freedom." Since slavery was one dependent status on a continuum of dependent statuses, each former slave was interested in achieving a different and better dependent status—not "freedom."

A number of African historians have subjected Miers' and Kopytoff's argument to intense criticism. One major complaint is that it was based on a spatial definition which marked the boundaries of historical institutions as identical to continental boundaries: African "slavery" existed in Africa and American slavery in the Americas. This was not so. Plantation slavery of the American kind came to Africa in the late days of the slave trade. Frederick Cooper (1977) wrote an excellent book about plantation slavery in East Africa, in a setting where the slave masters were Arabs who took Islamic law into account in regulating relations between slaves and masters.[18] Paul Lovejoy (1979) also showed that plantation slavery had become part of the African scene, in this case in Northern Nigeria, with Africans as the slave owners.

For Lovejoy (1983), the kinship slavery described by Miers and Kopytoff was limited not only in space but in time. It was an early and increasingly marginal form of slavery that came to be supplanted within Africa by the chattel slavery of the plantations. The institutions that appeared central to Miers and Kopytoff were insignificant to Lovejoy. Only one kind of slavery was historically important in his view, and this was slavery at the core of a system of production, as in the case of plantations. He placed the greatest emphasis on a limited number of times and places in African history: on the western Sudan, which relied on production by slaves from an early date, on the Sahel in the nineteenth century, when local people were finding uses for slaves who might in an earlier period have been sold in the Atlantic slave trade, and on a limited number of other places.

Meillassoux, in *Anthropologie de l'esclavage* (1986), joins the attack on kinship slavery, but on very different grounds. He argues that slavery cannot be interpreted as one of a range of kinship or descent statuses, as Miers and Kopytoff would have it, because slavery is outside kinship relations; in fact it is "antikinship." All major students of slavery emphasize the status of the slave as an outsider, with no public rights as a person. The slave must be represented in the public world by the master. The slave cannot negotiate a position in the wider kinship system in his or her own right. Orlando Patterson (1982) described this condition as "natal alienation"; Moses Finley (1968) saw it as central to the definition of the slave's status.

These discussions recall the important but unpublished work of Franz Steiner, as reported by Paul Bohannan. According to Bohannan,

A servile relationship can be said to exist when one person . . . has legal rights in another, if these rights are held to the exclusion of other persons and are not derived from either contractual or kinship obligations. The rights of the master in the slave are legal rights, derivable neither from kinship nor from contract, and they exclude all other people from similar rights. [1963, p. 179]

Bohannan accepts the idea that slavery is only one of many ways in which one person can hold rights in another, but he then shows how this way is different from others, on three grounds. Firstly, only a single individual, the master, holds rights in the slave. Within the domain of kinship it is possible for two people to share rights in a single individual, as in the case of a married woman in many African societies, subject to rights held by both her husband and by her father or brother. In the case of a slave, only the master holds rights. Secondly, the person who holds rights does not do so on a contractual basis. When an American sports team holds rights in a player (rights it is able to sell), it does so on a contractual basis. Finally, the rights in a slave are not derived from kinship obligations.

Meillassoux goes further and argues that it is better not to define slavery in terms of legal rights in persons; what is more important is the institutional context of slavery amidst slave markets and wars of capture. Slavery, the market, and violence were necessarily tied to one another in a single nexus. This leads to an understanding of slavery as antikinship in a second sense: slaves were not likely to reproduce. Their labor was cheap on American plantations (or African ones) because the plantation owner did not pay the costs of raising children. A slave labor supply did not reproduce itself; it was acquired ultimately by acts of violence, by theft. The theft-based spatial system included slave-using societies, the organization of trade, and the societies from which slaves were stolen.

Since the cheap and violent production of a labor force counted for everything, the process of reintegrating slaves into kinship relations (a process at the heart of Miers' and Kopytoff's analysis) was not relevant. In saying this, Meillassoux underestimates the importance of slavelike forms of dependency. He does so because he focuses narrowly on violent appropriation; he does not explore the possibility that subtle negotiation could have led to enslavement. In his view, the zones of slave origin did not themselves use slaves in production and, therefore, had no slaves to offer for sale, except for captives taken by brigands who struck at random. Meillassoux does not consider the possibility that slaves within the producing societies were chosen through a complex negotiated process, in which kinship factors played a role.

Some of the most important zones of slave origin are outside the scope of Meillassoux's analysis because they did not themselves use slave labor in a systematic way. Igboland, for example, was a major source of slaves for the Americas, and yet slave labor was unimportant in many parts of the region; earlier forms of organization held (Northrup 1981). Slave-producing regions did not necessarily need to base their own economies on slave labor. These regions were capable of producing slaves for the international trade through a negotiated social process even though most dependents within local societies held social statuses defined in terms of kinship and descent.

To see why this was so, I would like to look briefly at the life of a single "slave," as reported to us in her own words, and as brought to the attention of historians by Marcia Wright (1975, 1984). This is Narwimba, a woman who lived in the region between Lake Tanganyika and Lake Nyasa, near the border between what are now Tanzania and Zambia. The time of Narwimba's story, the 1880s and early 1890s, was a time of great upheaval in the region, a time when slaves were captured and used locally, and when some were sent off to plantations of the East African coast.

This was a period of great difficulty for Narwimba, beginning with her husband's death in about 1880. At one point Narwimba was taken captive by soldiers of a foreign chief and offered for sale to slave traders. She escaped but lived to see her granddaughter taken captive and released on two separate occasions. Narwimba lived through the transition to colonial rule and ultimately came to live with her son, who had been converted by Christian missionaries.

The period was one of intense danger and intense struggle for Narwimba, much of it engendered by the violent theft of people for the slave trade. Narwimba's own strategies all show how important she thought it was to avoid being made marginal in kinship terms, and to retain an attachment to a protective male, preferably in a marriage relationship marked by the payment of bridewealth. We can see this at several important moments. After Narwimba's husband died, one of his relations came to visit and to decide whether to marry her. Narwimba, in her own account, said, "And I, on my part, begged him to take me to wife so that we might be protected" (Wright 1984, p. 2). Lacking his protection, she would become very much more vulnerable. Narwimba's daughter took up residence with a man who paid no bridewealth. It is possible that she felt it necessary to accept this irregular liaison because of the weakness of her mother's position. At any rate, the daughter born to this union belonged to the household of the chief. Her father held no rights in her, because he had paid no bridewealth for her mother. The result of this was that Narwimba's granddaughter Musamarire was a vulnerable member of the chief's household. On one occasion, when diplomacy required the chief to give up a person in order to make peace, he proposed to give up Musamarire. Narwimba fled with her instead. On another occasion the granddaughter was seized again, in a dispute over a debt.

Note the shift here in angle of vision. Miers and Kopytoff cast lineages as actors that reintegrate marginal people. In my own argument, lineages are never actors; people act. The years since Miers' and Kopytoff's book have produced thorough-going critiques of the conception of lineage as an actor (Guyer 1981; Kuper 1982). If scholars treat the lineage as a functioning unit, they direct attention away from differences in the rights and obligations, privileges and duties, of different lineage members. Actions that serve the interests of older men in a lineage might be damaging to the interests of women, or of younger men. Property rights held by the lineage as a group do not necessarily serve men and women, or older and younger women, equally. In the present case the interests of particularly male-based lineages might imaginably have been served by letting Narwimba's granddaughter go. The grandmother had to act in a difficult environment to shape events. Her most important goals were to find a protective male and to rescue those dear to her from enslavement. She was not driven by concerns for lineage integrity but by the need to find a secure position as a wife or (later in the story) as the mother of an adult son.

In Narwimba's time, enslavement as violent theft was taking place. In this regard Meillassoux is correct. But it was taking place within a context where there was room for Narwimba to maneuver. The way she could protect herself over the long term was by negotiating a place for herself within a male-dominated kinship system.

Slavery may have been antikinship, but it existed within a context where the alternatives to enslavement were kinship alternatives, and where the character of slave-capturing and slave-trading was shaped by their relation to networks of kinship. The character of relationships between master and slave, in this case, was shaped by the existence of other forms of dependency alongside slavery. The existence of kinship and gender alternatives to slavery shaped the struggle between Narwimba and the potential slave-masters who would have taken control of her or her granddaughter.[19]

The case of Narwimba shows, in addition, that just as local traditions of dependency had an effect on African plantation slavery, the introduction of slavery had a profound impact on other forms of dependency. Narwimba was clearly willing to accept the possibility of extreme and relatively brutal subordination in marriage because a marriage, even of this kind, was protection against enslavement. A woman's capacity to resist a brutal husband would undoubtedly have been greater in the generation of Narwimba's mother, before the slave trade presented extreme dangers. To understand the slave trade in this particular context, we need to understand local traditions of dependency, their place in shaping the internal dynamics of slavery, and then the place of slavery in shaping local patterns of kinship.

In the 1950s, decades after Narwimba's death, debates opened up in Shambaai (not far from the east African coast) about the meaning of slavery and freedom. Julius Nyerere appeared at local meetings to demand that Tanganyika be given *Uhuru*—"Freedom." This was a word that appeared over and over in Swahili language history texts for colonial schools. The textbooks taught that Africans had practiced slavery and that colonial rule brought *uhuru*. Nyerere reminded local people of this association in order to argue that colonial rule was a new form of slavery, and that *uhuru* was not in any event something people could be given by their rulers. They had to win it for themselves. Peasants who heard this remembered "slavery" in lineage terms, as the condition of marginal people (like Narwimba) who were subject to arbitrary control. Local peasants, men and women, began to argue that "slavery" still survived not only in the control exercised by British over Africans, as Nyerere had said, but also in control by chiefs over subjects, by old men over young men, and by men over women. They demanded that *uhuru*, now understood as "manumission," be instituted in order to overturn all the central forms of social hierarchy (Feierman 1990, pp. 212–14, and 219–20).

Describing Narwimba's struggle as precipitated by the development of the international slave trade but rooted in local social forms, does not entirely break out of the structure of the European master-narrative. The problem, of course, is that in this account the central thrusting forces that shaped Narwimba's life originated on the international scene and with the history of capitalism. This is not at all how Narwimba's contemporaries in Central Africa would have seen things. They would have placed the events of her life within the context of the narratives of individual language groups, or narratives of general distribution among the region's Bantu-speaking peoples. Quite possibly these narratives would not have assigned a major role to international trade or to a Europe-centered economy.

As a child, Narwimba fled with her family from attacks by Ngoni soldiers and found refuge with the Kyungu (the paramount chief) of the Ngonde polity. It was the Kyungu, later on, who instructed a relative of her dead husband to marry her. Ngonde narratives from the Kyungu's land (or Ngoni ones, or others of the region) offer the historian alternatives to the Europe-centered ones, alternatives closer to Narwimba's own life and language.

Ngonde histories would have remained true to their own principles in their construction of Narwimba's story. Their political histories were built on the understanding that the Kyungu's (the chief's) wholeness and social health shaped the basic conditions of health and prosperity for the whole of his land. There was an identity between the Kyungu's physical health and the well-being of his domains. If a drop of his blood fell to the ground it was a sign that the whole land would suffer famine or disease unless he was killed. There was an identity also between the Kyungu's uncontested sexual dominance within his household and his life-giving dominance within the polity. According to some traditions, in early generations, most of the Kyungu's sons were killed because the people of Ngonde "feared that, if the Kyungu had many [living] sons, they might seduce his wives and so bring sickness on himself and on his country" (Wilson 1939, p. 13). In Ngonde, as in other parts of the region, adultery with a chief's wife was an act of war or of treason.[20] At the level of the nobles, also, rank found its expression in marriage practice. A chief paid and received higher bridewealth than a commoner.

A local person, trying to make sense of Narwimba's life, might well have understood it within the context of marriage as a range of forms that express degrees of political dominance. Narwimba and her close relatives would, for much of their lives, have practiced forms of marriage which were very humble when seen within the larger hierarchy. The size of bridewealth payments expressed rank, and Narwimba's daughter married entirely without bridewealth.

Most university historians would focus on an entirely different context for Narwimba's life, as we have seen. They would pay significant attention to the history of trade. From this viewpoint, a major event would be the opening up of Ngonde's trade with the Indian Ocean. This important change came as a result of the reorientation of the Kyungu's ivory trade towards the east (across Lake Malawi). The shift to the east was associated with fundamental change in the constitution of the polity, towards the growth of secular authority. The Ngonde narratives themselves, however, do not assign a central place to the history of trade as university historians do. Godfrey Wilson, who studied these oral traditions in the 1930s, complained that they gave him only glimpses of the important commercial changes (Wilson 1939, p. 18). Instead, the traditions recounted by senior Ngonde men described constitutional changes as precipitated by crucial political marriages (Wilson 1939, pp. 12–18). According to the Kyungu's own narrative, as told to Wilson, the eastward shift in trade took place when an early Kyungu "struck the lake and walked over to Mwela [the land of Mwela boat-men] to marry a woman, Mapunda" (Wilson 1939, p. 18).

Ngonde historians, then, might well have understood Narwimba's story as a very humble and minor part of a much larger story in which rank and political change are marked by marriage. To these historians the Atlantic slave trade would have appeared to be distant, and indeed largely irrelevant. The world historian who chooses to focus on the Atlantic slave trade or the rise of capitalism needs to explain why this context is privileged, why Narwimba's life ought to be explained in this way and not in relation to the personal history of the Kyungus and their marriages.

The European or American historian might well argue that Ngonde history is local and the history of capitalism global—that if we want to understand events on a wide scale, we must stick to the European narrative. In fact, African historical processes are not so narrowly localized. Some interrelations among gender, descent, and rank are broadly distributed, and they can be studied by historians using the tools of historical linguistics and comparative historical ethnography. Some of the events in Narwimba's own life were embedded in historical movements of enormous sweep. At the very beginning of her story, for example, came the Ngoni raid that dispossessed her family. The Ngoni, at this time, were a new presence in central African society. Each Ngoni state was organized by a ruling group which originated in South Africa, over a thousand miles away, in the wars surrounding the creation of the Zulu kingdom. The small bands of armed Ngoni men took wives and children as captives in order to build "snowball" states. They, too, like the Kyungu, were operating within the regional politics of marriage and dependency, which they were using for new forms of state building.[21]

The study of African history presses us to move beyond forms of historical representation in which the energy driving the story originates in Europe, while African history (or Latin American) provides local color, a picturesque setting for the central drama. There is no way to understand Narwimba's story without sinking roots into the longer story of the development of social forms in Africa. What was the range of paths by which people established relations of dependency? How was authority instituted? What were the idioms of power in the regional histories of Africa? Everything we know about the study of history tells us that we cannot understand something as complex as the idioms of power without studying their variation in space and their history in time. African narratives must carry their full weight.

The search for African narratives reveals that they are multiple narratives. It would be a mistake to give a privileged place to Ngoni royal narratives, or to the Kyungu's narrative, or to those of Ngonde nobles. There is no reason these should carry greater weight, or be accorded greater privilege, than Narwimba's own account, no reason the words of the Kyungu's rituals should count more than the words of subject women's rituals.

Each of the many African narratives carries the marks of its own history, including the history of relations with Europe. In Rwanda, for example, Joseph Rwabukumba and Alexis Kagame, Rwandan scholars, have written histories of the kingdom based on extensive collections of local oral traditions. They take varieties of local knowledge that were meant to be separate and secret—*ubwiiru* as a dynastic ritual code, for example—make a written record of them, and compare them with other traditions in order to construct a general narrative. Rwandan oral historians of the nineteenth century had methods for making critical comparisons of traditions, but they were not the same as Kagame's techniques. Nor would the oral histories have found an easy place, as do Kagame's, within a general framework of historical knowledge created among academics outside Rwanda.[22] Kagame and Rwabukumba are Rwandan historians, using Rwandan materials, writing within a genre created in Europe.

The task of finding purely African narratives is no easier if we shift our attention from university scholars to the peasantry. In Rwanda under the Belgians and Tanganyika under the British, the colonial authorities ruled through African chiefs so as to build on what, in the words of one British governor, was the "loyalty and 'free awe'" of subjects for their chiefs. The effect was to cast peasant debates on colonial policy in terms of ancient forms of political discourse. When the oral histories of the dynasties took on marks of colonial domination, dissident oral historians responded by searching out antidynastic histories in their own past and (in the case of Tanganyika) stories of regicide from textbooks of English history (Feierman 1990; Newbury 1988).

We are left, then, with an enormously expanded subject matter, with historical narratives originating in Africa that must be given full weight alongside those originating in Europe. We have seen, however, that this is not a simple process of adding one more body of knowledge to our fund, of increasing the balance in the account. The need for historians to hear African voices originates with the same impulse as the need to hear the voices that had been silent within European history. Since that is so, it hardly feels satisfying to listen to a single authoritative African voice, leaving others silent, or to read African texts without seeing marks of power, or without asking about the authority of the historian (African or American, European or Asian) who presumes to represent history. Historians have no choice but to open up world history to African history, but having done so, they find that the problems have just begun.

NOTES

1. The statement about the lack of African history at Berkeley is based on the *Bulletin: General Catalogue* . . . (see California, University of, 1955). The statement about the University of Chicago is based on the Announcements: Graduate Programs . . . (see Chicago, University of, 1956). The statement about Columbia is based on memories of my search for an African historian in 1960, when I was an undergraduate. The statement about Princeton is based on personal communication from Robert Tignor. The survey of department chairmen is reported in Perkins and Snell 1962, p. 32. It is probable that there were a number of graduate students working on the history of Egypt and of the Maghrib who were not reported at the time as studying African history.

2. McNeill 1963, pp. 242–43. McNeill continued to develop in new directions after *The Rise of the West*. *Plagues and Peoples* (1976) does not reduce all of world history to the fate of a few central civilizations. *The Human Condition* (1980) recapitulates some of the main themes of the 1963 book, but with important shifts of emphasis away from unidirectionality. In *Polyethnicity and National Unity in World History* (1985), McNeill makes it clear that the centers of the great empires drew people from a wide diversity of origins. "The result . . . was ethnic mixture and pluralism on a grand scale" (McNeill 1985, p. 15).

3. New research on early pastoralism is described by Wendorf, Close, and Schild 1987, and Bower 1991, pp. 56–57. On the origins of agriculture, see Harlan, DeWet, and Stemler 1976, and Clark and Brandt 1984.

4. On the indigenous origins of the kingdoms of the East African lakes, see Schmidt 1978; Tantala 1989; Schoenbrun 1990; Berger 1981; Karugire 1971; and Centre de Civilisation Burundaise 1981. Reefe (1981) writes on the Luba empire. On the indigenous origins of Zimbabwe, see Garlake 1973 and 1978. Henrika Kuklick (1991) describes the interaction between racial politics and archaeological research that led to earlier interpretations of Zimbabwe as alien to Africa. Martin Hall (1987) provides a general synthesis of archeological knowledge on the relationship between political organization and the economy for the southern African region. Graham Connah (1987) does the same for the whole of Africa. For a general history, see Curtin, Feierman, Thompson, and Vansina 1978.

5. On *Annales*, see Burke 1990; Stoianovich 1976; Chartier 1988.

6. I am not suggesting that Africanists were all reading Braudel. This influence may have come indirectly, when Africanists read and discussed the work of their Europeanist colleagues.

7. Braudel does not cite many works about Africa written by modern scholars. More than a third of the citations about Africa in this volume refer

to a work of 1728, edited by Father Labat, who himself had never visited the African continent; the descriptions of Africa are those of Andre Brue, who lived in Senegal in the late seventeenth and early eighteenth centuries (*Nouvelle Biographie Générale*, vol. 28 [Paris: Firmin Didot Frères, 1859], pp. 333–35; *Dictionnaire de Biographie Française*, vol. 7 [Paris: Librairie Letouzey, 1956], p. 473).

8. The literature on these subjects includes many hundreds of books and articles. For a discussion of the African roots of notables in a center of Islamic learning, see Saad 1983. For interesting local case studies see Roberts 1987 and Bathily 1989. An interesting regional case study is given by Last 1985. For a general picture of West African economic history, see Hopkins 1973; for later literature on this subject, see Austen 1987. Local economic roots of Islamic forms of action are discussed in Hanson 1990.

9. On the organization and development of precolonial trade, see Northrup 1978, and Ukwu 1967. Northrup is also the source of the figure on population density (1978, p. 13). For a sophisticated interpretation of precolonial Igbo social organization and culture, see Afigbo 1981. The figure on palm oil exports is from Dike 1956. On early long-distance trade, see Shaw 1970 and 1975. The literature on Igboland is enormous; the region is practically a separate subfield of African history. For some important twentieth-century events, see Susan Martin 1988.

10. Janzen 1982, pp. 28 and 32; some of the most important work of reconstructing the history of trade was done by Phyllis Martin 1972.

11. Wolf 1982, p. 100. For an excellent critique of this part of Wolf's work, see Asad 1987.

12. Michael Taussig says something like this in a review essay (1989), but his extravagantly diffuse literary style sometimes makes it difficult to know what he is saying. Taussig himself appears at times to fall into an understanding of capitalist culture in which all local forms are but expressions of universal characteristics. He writes about the "coupling and decoupling of reification with festishization" as "the basis of capitalist culture"—clearly a totalizing statement (1989, p. 9).

13. Oral history, as practiced among Africanists, has had significant influence among historians of Europe (see Stock 1983; Clanchy 1979). It is important to note, however, that the Africanist who has won the greatest influence among them is Jack Goody, who is not a historian, and who has not used oral tradition for purposes of critical historical reconstruction. Non-Africanists read Goody because it is possible to understand his argument without having to master substantive issues of African history.

14. Beinart and Bundy 1987; Berry 1985; Chanock 1985; Cohen and Atieno-Odhiambo 1989; Cooper 1987; Coquery-Vidrovitch 1988; Crummey 1986; Elphick 1977; Hay and Wright 1982; Iliffe 1979; Kanogo 1987; Karp 1978; Kea 1986; Kimambo 1991; Kitching 1980; Lan 1985; Lemarchand 1970; Mandala 1990; Mbembe 1991; McCann 1987; Moore 1986; Newbury 1988; Packard 1989; Prins 1980; Ranger 1985*b*; Robertson 1984; Schmidt

1992; Strobel 1979; Vail 1980; Van Onselen 1982; Vincent 1981; Watts 1983; White 1990.

15. On the relationship between the general intellectual crisis and the end of empire, see Robert Young, *White Mythologies: Writing History and the West* (1990), who argues that the French intellectual crisis was precipitated by the loss of Algeria, and not by the events of 1968. On the place of the Other, see Fabian 1983; Mudimbe 1988; and Said 1979. For some of the discussion on ethnocentrism, history, and intellectual categories, see Lévi-Strauss 1962, pp. 324–60; Derrida 1978, pp. 278–93; Derrida 1974, pp. 244–45. Foucault, of course, found the other within European society, in his study of madness.

16. For an elegant analysis of these issues in the writings of white American novelists, see Morrison 1992.

17. For two out of many possible examples of fine historical works which aim at giving full weight to both the local and the regional, see Harms 1981 and Ewald 1990.

18. A decade later, Abdul Sheriff (1987) placed these plantations more firmly in the history of the region's economy.

19. Glassman (1991, 1988) makes a very similar argument about the plantation sector on the East African coast—the region to which Narwimba might have been taken if she had been sold. He shows that there was not a single category of "slave," but multiple dependent statuses, including urban artisan-slaves and caravan-trading slaves, with varying levels of capacity to engage in social reproduction. Struggle between slaves and masters involved manipulation of the alternative possibilities. Unlike the slavery of the Caribbean, in which slaves did not share a common background with their masters, African forms of slavery arose out of earlier systems of personal dependency. Masters who wished to increase economic production using slave labor tried to reduce the slaves' opportunities for social reproduction; slaves in their turn resisted by manipulating the older ideologies in attempts to win the capacity for social reproduction. The shape of the actual slave system emerged from this struggle.

20. Wilson describes the ranked bridewealth payments (1939, p. 44). On adultery with a chief's wife as an act of war among the Bemba, see Roberts 1973, pp. 41–42, 107n., 122, 140, 143, 167, 237, 250, and 263.

21. On the Ngoni of this region see Barnes 1954; Fraser 1970; Elmslie 1970. Spear 1969 offers a guide to the sources.

22. Kagame 1972, 1975, and 1981; Rwabukumba and Mudandagizi 1974. See also Vansina 1962; Coupez and Kamanzi 1962; and Vansina 1985, pp. 38 and 86.

REFERENCES

Afigbo, Adiele. *Ropes of Sand (Studies in Igbo History and Culture)*. Ibadan, Nigeria: University Press Limited in Association with Oxford University Press, 1981.

Alagoa, Egieberi J. *The Small Brave City-State: A History of Nembe-Brass in Niger Delta*. Ibadan, Nigeria: Ibadan University Press: Madison: University of Wisconsin Press, 1964.

———. *A History of the Niger Delta: An Historical Interpretation of Ijo Oral Tradition*. Ibadan, Nigeria: Ibadan University Press, 1972.

———. *Eminent Nigerians of the Rivers State*. Ibadan, Nigeria: Heinemann Educational Books, 1980.

Al-Naqar, 'Umar. *The Pilgrimage Tradition in West Africa*. Khartoum: Khartoum University Press, 1972.

Appadurai, Arjun. "Introduction: Commodities and the Politics of Value." In *The Social Life of Things: Commodities in Cultural Perspective,* edited by Arjun Appadurai, pp. 3–63. Cambridge: Cambridge University Press, 1986.

Asad, Talal. "Are There Histories of Peoples without Europe? A Review Article." *Comparative Studies in Society and History* 29, no. 3 (1987): 594–607.

Austen, Ralph. "The Trans-Saharan Slave Trade: A Tentative Census." In *The Uncommon Market: Essays in the Economic History of the Atlantic Slave Trade,* edited by H. A. Gemery and J. S. Hogendorn, pp. 23–76. New York: Academic Press, 1979.

———. *African Economic History: Internal Development and External Dependency*. London: James Currey, 1987.

Barnes, J. A. *Politics in a Changing Society: A Political History of the Fort Jameson Ngoni*. London, Cape Town, and New York: Oxford University Press, 1954.

Bathily, Abdoulaye. *Les portes de l'or: Le royaume de Galam (Sénégal) de l'ère musulmane au temps des nègriers (VIIIe–XVIIIe siècle)*. Paris: Editions L'Harmattan, 1989.

Beinart, William, and Bundy, Colin. *Hidden Struggles in Rural South Africa*. London: James Currey; Berkeley and Los Angeles: University of California Press, 1987.

Bennassar, Bartolomé, and Chaunu, Pierre, eds. *L'ouverture du monde, xive–xvie siècles*. Vol 1 of *Histoire économique et sociale du monde*. Pierre Léon, series ed. Paris: Armand Colin, 1977.

Berger, Iris. *Religion and Resistance: East African Kingdoms in the Precolonial Period*. Annales, no. 105. Tervuren: Musée Royal de l'Afrique Centrale, 1981.

Berry, Sara. *Fathers Work for Their Sons*. Berkeley and Los Angeles, and London: University of California Press, 1985.

Bloch, Marc. *Les rois thaumaturges*. Strasbourg: Librairie Istra, 1924.

———. "Mémoire collective." *Revue de Synthèse Historique* 40 (1925): 73–83.

Bohannan, Paul. *Social Anthropology*. New York: Holt Rinehart and Winston, 1963.

Bower, John. "The Pastoral Neolithic of East Africa." *Journal of World Prehistory 5*, no. 1 (1991): 49–82.

Braudel, Fernand. *The Mediterranean and the Mediterranean World in the Age of Philip II*, translated by Siân Reynolds. Vol. 1. New York: Harper and Row, 1976.

———. *Le temps du monde*. Vol. 3 of *Civilisation matérielle, économie et capitalisme, XVe–XVIIIe siècle*. Paris: Armand Colin, 1979.

———. *The Structures of Everyday Life: The Limits of the Possible*. Vol. 1 of *Civilization and Capitalism, 15th–18th Century*, translated by Siân Reynolds. New York: Harper and Row, 1981.

———. *The Wheels of Commerce*. Vol. 2 of *Civilization and Capitalism, 15th–18th Century*, translated by Siân Reynolds. New York: Harper and Row, 1982.

———. *The Perspective of the World*. Vol. 3 of *Civilization and Capitalism, 15th–18th Century*, translated by Siân Reynolds. London: Collins, 1984.

———. *Grammaire des civilisations*. Paris: Arthaud-Flammarion, 1987.

Burke, Peter. *The French Historical Revolution: The* Annales *School, 1929–89*. Cambridge and Oxford: Polity Press, 1990.

California, University of. *Bulletin: General Catalogue, Fall and Spring Semesters, 1955–1956*. Berkeley: University of California, 1955.

Cassanelli, Lee V. *The Shaping of Somali History: Reconstructing the History of a Pastoral People, 1600–1900*. Philadelphia: University of Pennsylvania Press, 1982.

———. "Qat: Changes in the Production and Consumption of a Quasilegal Commodity in Northeast Africa." In Appadurai 1986, pp. 236–57.

Centre de Civilisation Burundaise. *La Civilisation ancienne des peuples des Grands Lacs*. Paris: Karthala, 1981.

Chanock, Martin. *Law, Custom and Social Order: The Colonial Experience in Malawi and Zambia*. Cambridge: Cambridge University Press, 1985.

Chartier, Roger. *Cultural History: Between Practices and Representations*, translated by Lydia G. Cochrane. Cambridge: Polity Press, 1988.

Chicago, University of. *Announcements: Graduate Programs in the Divisions, Sessions of 1957–1958*. Chicago: University of Chicago Press, 1956.

Chittick, Neville H. *Kilwa: An Islamic Trading City on the East Africa Coast*. Nairobi: British Institute in Eastern Africa, 1974.

Clanchy, M. T. *From Memory to Written Record*. Cambridge, Mass.: Harvard University Press, 1979.

Clark, J. Desmond, and Brandt, Steven A. *From Hunters to Farmers: The Causes and Consequences of Food Production in Africa*. Berkeley and Los Angeles, and London: University of California Press, 1984.

Cohen, David William. "Doing Social History from *Pim's* Doorway." In *Reliving the Past: The Worlds of Social History*, edited by Olivier Zunz. Chapel Hill: University of North Carolina Press, 1985.

Cohen, David William, and Atieno-Odhiambo, E. S. *Siaya: The Historical Anthropology of an African Landscape.* London: James Currey, 1989.

Connah, Graham. *African Civilizations—Precolonial Cities and States in Tropical Africa: An Archaeological Perspective.* Cambridge: Cambridge University Press, 1987.

Cooper, Frederick. *Plantation Slavery on the East Coast of Africa.* New Haven and London: Yale University Press, 1977.

———. *On the African Waterfront: Urban Disorder and the Transformation of Work in Colonial Mombasa.* New Haven and London: Yale University Press, 1987.

Cooper, Frederick, et al. *Confronting Historical Paradigms: Peasants, Labor, and the Capitalist World System in Africa and Latin America.* Madison: University of Wisconsin Press, forthcoming.

Coquery-Vidrovitch, C. *Africa: Endurance and Change South of the Sahara.* Berkeley and Los Angeles: University of California Press, 1988.

Coupez, A., and Kamanzi, Th. *Récits historiques Rwanda.* Sciences humaines 43. Tervuren: Musée Royal de l'Afrique Centrale, 1962.

Crummey, Donald, ed. *Banditry, Rebellion and Social Protest in Africa.* London: James Currey, 1986.

Curtin, Philip D. *The Atlantic Slave Trade: A Census.* Madison: University of Wisconsin Press, 1969.

———. "African History." In *The Past before Us: Contemporary Historical Writing in the United States,* edited by Michael Kammen, pp. 113–30. Ithaca and London: Cornell University Press, 1980.

———. *Cross-Cultural Trade in World History.* Cambridge: Cambridge University Press, 1984.

———. *The Rise and Fall of the Plantation Complex: Essays in Atlantic History.* Cambridge: Cambridge University Press, 1990.

Curtin, Philip; Feierman, Steven; Thompson, Leonard; and Jan Vansina. *African History.* London: Longman, 1978.

Derrida, Jacques. *Of Grammatology,* translated by Gayatri Chakravorty Spivak. Baltimore and London: The Johns Hopkins University Press, 1974.

———. *Writing and Difference,* translated by Alan Bass. London and Henley: Routledge and Kegan Paul, 1978.

Dike, K. Onwuka. *Trade and Politics in the Niger Delta, 1830–1865.* Oxford: Clarendon Press, 1956.

DuPlessis, Robert. "The Partial Transition to World-Systems Analysis in Early Modern European History." *Radical History Review* 39 (1987): 11–27.

Ehret, Christopher. "Linguistics as a Tool for Historians." In *Hadith 1,* edited by B. A. Ogot, pp. 119–33. Nairobi: East African Publishing Co., 1968.

———. *Southern Nilotic History: Linguistic Approaches to the Study of the Past.* Evanston, Ill.: Northwestern University Press, 1971.

———. "The East African Interior." In *General History of Africa,* edited by

M. El Fasi, pp. 616–42. Vol. 3. Unesco International Scientific Committee for the Drafting of a General History of Africa. Paris, London, Berkeley: Unesco, Heinemann, California, 1988.

Ehret, Christopher, and Posnansky, Merrick, eds. *The Archaeological and Linguistic Reconstruction of African History*. Berkeley and Los Angeles: University of California Press, 1982.

Elmslie, W. A. *Among the Wild Ngoni*. 3d ed. London: Frank Cass and Co., 1970. [1899].

Elphick, Richard. *Kraal and Castle: Khoikhoi and the Founding of White South Africa*. New Haven: Yale University Press, 1977.

Ewald, Janet. *Soldiers, Traders, and Slaves: State Formation and Economic Transformation in the Greater Nile Valley, 1700–1885*. Madison: University of Wisconsin Press, 1990.

Fabian, Johannes. *Time and the Other: How Anthropology Makes Its Object*. New York: Columbia University Press, 1983.

Fage, J. D. "Slavery and the Slave Trade in the Context of West African History." *Journal of African History* 10, no. 3 (1969): 393–404.

Feierman, Steven. *Peasant Intellectuals: Anthropology and History in Tanzania*. Madison: University of Wisconsin Press, 1990.

Finley, M. I. "Slavery." *International Encyclopedia of the Social Sciences*. Vol. 14, 1968, pp. 307–13.

Fraser, Donald. *Winning a Primitive People*. 1st ed., 1914. Westport, Conn.: Negro Universities Press, 1970.

Garlake, P. S. *Great Zimbabwe*. London: Thames and Hudson, 1973.

———. "Pastoralism and *Zimbabwe*." *Journal of African History* 19, no. 4 (1978): 479–93.

Geary, Patrick. "Sacred Commodities: The Circulation of Medieval Relics." In Appadurai 1986, pp. 169–91.

Glassman, Jonathon. "Social Rebellion and Swahili Culture: The Response to German Conquest of the Northern Mrima, 1888–1890." Ph.D. dissertation, University of Wisconsin, Madison, 1988.

———. "The Bondsman's New Clothes: The Contradictory Consciousness of Slave Resistance on the Swahili Coast." *Journal of African History* 32, no. 2 (1991): 217–312.

Guyer, Jane. "Household and Community in African Studies." *African Studies Review* 24, no. 2/3 (1981): 87–137.

Hall, Martin. *The Changing Past: Farmers, Kings and Traders in Southern Africa, 200–1860*. Cape Town: David Philip, 1987.

Hanson, John. "Generational Conflict in the Umarian Movement after the *Jihad*: Perspectives from the Futanke Grain Trade at Medine." *Journal of African History* 31 (1990): 199–215.

Harlan, Jack R.; DeWet, Jan; and Stemler, Ann. *Origins of African Domestication*. The Hague: Mouton, 1976.

Harms, Robert. *River of Wealth, River of Sorrow: The Central Zaire Basin in the Era of the Slave Trade, 1500–1891.* New Haven, Conn.: Yale University Press, 1981.

Hay, Margaret Jean, and Wright, Marcia, eds. *African Women and the Law: Historical Perspectives.* Papers on Africa, no. 7. Boston: Boston University, 1982.

Hiskett, Mervyn. *The Development of Islam in West Africa.* London and New York: Longman, 1984.

Hopkins, A. G. *An Economic History of West Africa.* London: Longman, 1973.

Hutchinson, Sharon. "The Nuer in Crisis: Coping with Money, War, and the State." Ph.D. dissertation, Department of Anthropology, University of Chicago, 1988.

Iliffe, John. *A Modern History of Tanganyika.* Cambridge: Cambridge University Press, 1979.

Inikori, J. E. *Forced Migration: The Impact of the Export Slave Trade on African Societies.* London: Hutchinson University Library, 1982.

Isaacman, Allen. *Mozambique: The Africanization of a European Institution, The Zambesi Prazos 1750–1902.* Madison: University of Wisconsin Press, 1972.

———. *The Tradition of Resistance in Mozambique: Anti-Colonial Activity in the Zambesi Valley, 1850–1921.* Berkeley and Los Angeles: University of California Press, 1976.

———. "Peasants and Rural Social Protest in Africa." *African Studies Review* 33, no. 2 (1990): 1–120.

Janzen, John M. Lemba, *1650–1930: A Drum of Affliction in Africa and the New World.* New York and London: Garland Publishing, 1982.

Jay, Martin. *Marxism and Totality: The Adventures of a Concept from Lukacs to Habermas.* Berkeley and Los Angeles: University of California Press, 1984.

Jewsiewicki, Bogumil. "The African Prism of Immanuel Wallerstein." *Radical History Review* 39 (1987): 50–68.

Kagame, Alexis. *Un abrégé de l'ethno-histoire du Rwanda precolonial.* Vol. 1. Butare: Editions Universitaires du Rwanda, 1972.

———. *Un abrégé de l'ethno-histoire du Rwanda.* Vol. 2. Butare: Editions Universitaires du Rwanda, 1975.

———. "La documentation du Rwanda sur l'Afrique interlacustre des temps anciens." In *La civilisation ancienne des peuples des Grands Lacs,* edited by Centre de Civilisation Burundaise, pp. 300–330. Paris: Editions Karthala, 1981.

Kanogo, Tabitha. *Squatters and the Roots of Mau Mau.* Athens: Ohio University Press, 1987.

Karp, Ivan. *Fields of Change among the Iteso of Kenya.* London: Routledge and Kegan Paul, 1978.

Karugire, Samwiri. *A History of the Kingdom of Nkore in Western Uganda.* Oxford: Clarendon Press, 1971.

Kea, Ray A. "'I Am Here to Plunder on the General Road': Bandits and Banditry in the Pre-Nineteenth Century Gold Coast." In *Banditry Rebellion and Social Protest in Africa,* edited by Donald Crummey, pp. 109–32. London: James Currey, 1986.

Kimambo, Isaria. *A Political History of the Pare of Tanzania.* Nairobi: East African Publishing House, 1969.

———. *Penetration and Protest in Tanzania: The Impact of the World Economy on the Pare, 1860–1960.* London: James Currey, 1991.

Kitching, Gavin. *Class and Economic Change in Kenya.* New Haven, Conn.: Yale University Press, 1980.

Kopytoff, Igor. "The Cultural Biography of Things: Commoditization as Process." In Appadurai 1986, pp. 64–91.

———. "The Cultural Context of African Abolition." In *The End of Slavery in Africa,* edited by Suzanne Miers and Richard Roberts, pp. 485–503. Madison: University of Wisconsin Press, 1988.

Kroeber, A. L. "The Ancient Oikoumenê as a Historic Culture Aggregate." In *The Nature of Culture,* pp. 379–95. Huxley Memorial Lecture for 1945. Chicago: University of Chicago Press, 1952.

Kuklick, Henrika. "Contested Monuments: The Politics of Archeology in Southern Africa." In *Colonial Situations: Essays on the Contextualization of Ethnographic Knowledge,* edited by George Stocking, pp. 135–69. Madison: University of Wisconsin Press, 1991.

Kuper, Adam. "Lineage Theory: A Critical Retrospect." *Annual Review of Anthropology* 11 (1982): 71–95.

Lan, David. *Guns and Rain: Guerrillas and Spirit Mediums in Zimbabwe.* Berkeley and Los Angeles: University of California Press, 1985.

Last, Murray. "The Early Kingdoms of the Nigerian Savanna." In *History of West Africa,* edited by J. F. A. Ajayi and Michael Crowder, pp. 167–224. Vol. 1. Harlow, Essex: Longman, 1985.

Lemarchand, Rene. *Rwanda and Burundi.* New York: Praeger, 1970.

Lévi-Strauss, Claude. *La pensée sauvage.* Paris: Plon, 1962.

Lovejoy, Paul E. "The Characteristics of Plantations in the Nineteenth-Century Sokoto Caliphate (Islamic West Africa)." *American Historical Review* 84, no. 5 (1979): 1267–92.

———. *Transformations in Slavery: A History of Slavery in Africa.* Cambridge: Cambridge University Press, 1983.

Mandala, Elias. *Work and Control in a Peasant Economy.* Madison: University of Wisconsin Press, 1990.

Manning, Patrick. *Slavery and African Life: Occidental, Oriental, and African Slave Trades.* Cambridge: Cambridge University Press, 1990.

Martin, Phyllis. *The External Trade of the Loango Coast, 1576–1870.* Oxford: Clarendon Press, 1972.

Martin, Susan. *Palm Oil and Protest: An Economic History of the Ngwa Region, South-Eastern Nigeria, 1800–1980*. Cambridge: Cambridge University Press, 1988.

Mbembe, Achille. "Domaines de la nuit et autorité onirique dans les maquis du Sud-Cameroun (1955–1958)." *Journal of African History* 31 (1991): 89–121.

McCann, James. *Famine in Northeast Ethiopia: A Rural History 1900–1935*. Philadelphia: University of Pennsylvania Press, 1987.

McIntosh, Roderick J., and McIntosh, Susan Keech. "Jenne-jeno: An Ancient African City." *Archaeology* 33 (1980*a*): 8–14.

———. *Prehistoric Investigations in the Region of Jenne, Mali*. Cambridge Monographs in African Archaeology 2. Oxford: BAR, 1980*b*.

———. "The Early City in West Africa: Towards an Understanding." *African Archeological Review* 2 (1984): 73–98.

———. "Recent Archaeological Research and Dates from West Africa." *Journal of African History* 27 (1986): 413–42.

———. "From *Siècles Obscurs* to Revolutionary Centuries on the Middle Niger." *World Archaeology* 20, no. 1 (1988): 140–65.

McNeill, William H. *The Rise of the West: A History of the Human Community*. Chicago and London: The University of Chicago Press, 1963.

———. *Plagues and Peoples*. Garden City, N.Y.: Anchor Press/Doubleday, 1976.

———. Contribution to "Beyond Western Civilization: Rebuilding the Survey." *History Teacher* 10 (1977): 509–15.

———. *The Human Condition*. Princeton, N.J.: Princeton University Press, 1980.

———. *Polyethnicity and National Unity in World History*. Toronto: University of Toronto Press, 1985.

Meillassoux, Claude. "Female Slavery." In *Women and Slavery in Africa*, edited by Claire Robertson and Martin Klein, pp. 49–66. Madison: University of Wisconsin Press, 1983.

———. *Anthropologie de l'esclavage: Le ventre de fer et d'argent*. Paris: Presses Universitaires de France, 1986.

Miers, Suzanne, and Kopytoff, Igor. *Slavery in Africa: Historical and Anthropological Perspectives*. Madison: University of Wisconsin Press, 1977.

Miller, Joseph C. *The African Past Speaks*. Folkestone and Hamden: Dawson and Archon, 1980.

———. *Way of Death: Merchant Capitalism and the Angolan Slave Trade, 1730–1830*. Madison: University of Wisconsin Press, 1988.

———. "The World According to Meillassoux: A Challenging but Limited Vision." *IJAHS*, 22, no. 3 (1989): 473–95.

Moore, Sally Falk. *Social Facts and Fabrications: "Customary" Law on Kilimanjaro, 1880–1980*. Cambridge: Cambridge University Press, 1986.

Morrison, Toni. *Playing in the Dark*. Cambridge, Mass.: Harvard University Press, 1992.

Mudimbe, V. Y. *The Invention of Africa: Gnosis, Philosophy, and the Order of Knowledge*. Bloomington and Indianapolis: Indiana University Press, 1988.

Newbury, Catharine. *The Cohesion of Oppression: Clientship and Ethnicity in Rwanda, 1860–1960*. New York: Columbia University Press, 1988.

Northrup, David. *Trade without Rulers: Pre-Colonial Economic Development in South-Eastern Nigeria*. Oxford: Clarendon Press, 1978.

———. "The Ideological Context of Slavery in Southeastern Nigeria in the Nineteenth Century." In *The Ideology of Slavery in Africa*, edited by Paul E. Lovejoy, pp. 101–22. Beverly Hills and London: Sage Publications, 1981.

Novick, Peter. *That Noble Dream: The "Objectivity Question" and the American Historical Profession*. Cambridge: Cambridge University Press, 1988.

Ogot, B. A. *History of the Southern Luo*. Vol. 1. Nairobi: East African Publishing House, 1967.

Packard, Randall. *White Plague, Black Labor: Tuberculosis and the Political Economy of Health and Disease in South Africa*. Berkeley and Los Angeles: University of California Press, 1989.

Patterson, Orlando. *Slavery and Social Death: A Comparative Study*. Cambridge, Mass., and London: Harvard University Press, 1982.

Peel, J. *Ijeshas and Nigerians: The Incorporation of a Yoruba Kingdom, 1890s–1970s*. Cambridge: Cambridge University Press, 1983.

Perkins, Dexter, and Snell, John. *The Education of Historians in the United States*. New York: McGraw Hill, 1962.

Posnansky, Merrick. "Bigo Bya Mugenyi." *Uganda Journal* 33, no. 2 (1969): 125–50.

Prins, Gwyn. *The Hidden Hippopotamus. Reappraisal in African History: The Early Colonial Experience in Western Zambia*. Cambridge: Cambridge University Press, 1980.

Ranger, T. O. "African Initiatives and Resistance in the Face of Partition and Conquest." In *General History of Africa*, edited by A. Adu Boahen, pp. 45–62. Vol. 7. UNESCO. Berkeley and Los Angeles: University of California Press, 1985a.

———. *Peasant Consciousness and Guerrilla War in Zimbabwe: A Comparative Study*. London: James Currey, 1985b.

———. "Resistance in Africa: From Nationalist Revolt to Agrarian Protest." In *In Resistance: Studies in African, Caribbean, and Afro-American History*, edited by Gary Y. Okihiro, pp. 35–52. Amherst: University of Massachusetts Press, 1986.

Reefe, T. *The Rainbow and the Kings: A History of the Luba Empire to 1891*. Berkeley and Los Angeles: University of California Press, 1981.

Roberts, Andrew. *A History of the Bemba.* Madison: University of Wisconsin Press, 1973.

Roberts, Richard. *Warriors, Merchants, and Slaves: The State and the Economy in the Middle Niger Valley, 1700–1914.* Stanford, Calif.: Stanford University Press, 1987.

Robertson, Claire C. *Sharing the Same Bowl: A Socioeconomic History of Women and Class in Accra, Ghana.* Bloomington: Indiana University Press, 1984.

Robertson, Claire C., and Klein, Martin A., eds. *Women and Slavery in Africa.* Madison: University of Wisconsin Press, 1983.

Rodney, Walter. "African Slavery and Other Forms of Social Oppression on the Upper Guinea Coast in the Context of the Atlantic Slave-Trade." *Journal of African History* 7, no. 3 (1966): 431–43.

Rwabukumba, Joseph, and Mundandagizi, Vincent. "Les formes historiques de la dependance personelle dans l'état rwandais." *Cahiers d'Etudes Africaines* 14, no. 1 (1974).

Saad, Elias. *Social History of Timbuktu: The Role of Muslim Scholars and Notables, 1400–1900.* Cambridge: Cambridge University Press, 1983.

Said, Edward. *Orientalism.* New York: Vintage Books, 1979.

————. "Orientalism Reconsidered." In *Europe and Its Others,* edited by Francis Barker, Peter Hulme, Margaret Iversen, and Diana Loxley, pp. 14–27. Vol. 1. Colchester: University of Essex, 1985.

Samatar, Said. *Oral Poetry and Somali Nationalism: The Case of Sayyid Mahammad "Abdille Hasan."* Cambridge and New York: Cambridge University Press, 1982.

Schmidt, Elizabeth. *Peasants, Traders and Wives: Shona Women in the History of Zimbabwe, 1870–1939.* London: James Currey, 1992.

Schmidt, Peter. *Historical Archaeology: A Structural Approach in an African Culture.* Westport, Conn.: Greenwood Press, 1978.

————. "Cultural Meaning and History in African Myth." *International Journal of Oral History* 4 (1983a): 167–83.

————. "An Alternative to a Strictly Materialist Perspective: A Review of Historical Archaeology, Ethnoarchaeology, and Symbolic Approaches in African Archaeology." *American Antiquity* 48, no. 1 (1983b): 62–79.

————. "Oral Traditions, Archaeology and History: A Short Reflective History." In *A History of African Archaeology,* edited by Peter Robertshaw, pp. 252–70. London: James Currey, 1990.

Schoenbrun, David. "Early History in Eastern Africa's Great Lakes Region: Linguistic, Ecological, and Archaeological Approaches, ca. 500 B.C. to ca. A.D. 1000." Ph.D. dissertation, Department of History, UCLA, 1990.

Shaw, Thurstan. *Igbo-Ukwu.* 2 vols. London: Faber and Faber, 1970.

————. "Those Igbo-Ukwu Dates: Facts, Fictions and Probabilities." *Journal of African History* 11 (1975): 515–33.

Sheriff, Abdul. *Slaves, Spices and Ivory in Zanzibar: Integration of an East*

African Commercial Empire into the World Economy 1770–1873. London: James Currey; Athens: Ohio University Press, 1987.

Shinnie, P. L., and Kense, F. J. *Archaeology of Gonja, Ghana: Excavations at Daboya.* Calgary: University of Calgary Press, 1989.

Spear, Thomas T. "Zwangendaba's Ngoni 1821–1890: A Political and Social History of a Migration." Master's thesis, University of Wisconsin, Madison, 1969.

Stern, Steve. "Feudalism, Capitalism, and the World-System in the Perspective of Latin America and the Caribbean." *American Historical Review* 93, no. 4 (1988): 829–72.

Stock, Brian. *The Implications of Literacy.* Princeton, N.J.: Princeton University Press, 1983.

Stoianovich, Traian. *French Historical Method: The* Annales *Paradigm.* Ithaca and London: Cornell University Press, 1976.

Strobel, Margaret. *Muslim Women in Mombasa 1890–1975.* New Haven, Conn.: Yale University Press, 1979.

Tantala, Renee Louise. "The Early History of Kitara in Western Uganda: Process Models of Religious and Political Change." Ph.D. dissertation, Department of History, University of Wisconsin, Madison, 1989.

Taussig, Michael. "History as Commodity in Some Recent American (Anthropological) Literature." *Critique of Anthropology* 9, no. 1 (1989): 7–23.

Tonkin, Elizabeth. *Narrating Our Pasts: The Social Construction of Oral History.* Cambridge: Cambridge University Press, 1992.

Ukwu, Ukwu I. "The Development of Trade and Marketing in Iboland." *Journal of the Historical Society of Nigeria* 3 (1967): 647–62.

Vail, Leroy. *Capitalism and Colonialism in Mozambique.* Minneapolis: University of Minnesota Press, 1980.

Van Onselen, Charles. *Studies in the Social and Economic History of the Witwatersrand, 1886–1913.* 2 vols. Harlow: Longmans, 1982.

Vansina, Jan. *De la tradition orale: Essai de méthode historique.* Annales, Sciences Humaines, no. 36. Tervuren: MRAC, 1961.

———. *L'évolution du royaume rwanda des origines à 1900.* Brussels: ARSOM, 1962.

———. "Western Bantu Expansion." *Journal of African History* 25, no. 2 (1984): 129–45.

———. *Oral Tradition as History.* Madison: University of Wisconsin Press, 1985.

Vincent, Joan. *Teso in Transformation.* Berkeley and Los Angeles: University of California Press, 1981.

Wallerstein, Immanuel. *The Modern World-System: Capitalist Agriculture and the Origins of the European World-Economy in the Sixteenth Century.* New York, San Francisco, and London: Academic Press, 1974*a*.

———. "The Rise and Future Demise of the World Capitalist System: Concepts for Comparative Analysis." *Comparative Studies in Society and History* 16, no. 4 (1974b): 387–415.

———. *The Modern World-System II: Mercantilism and the Consolidation of the European World-Economy, 1600–1750.* New York: Academic Press, 1980.

———. *The Modern World-System III: The Second Era of Great Expansion of the Capitalist World-Economy, 1730–1840s.* New York: Academic Press, 1989.

Watts, Michael. *Silent Violence: Food, Famine and Peasantry in Northern Nigeria.* Los Angeles and Berkeley: University of California Press, 1983.

Wendorf, F.; Close, A. E.; and Schild, R. "Early Domestic Cattle in the Eastern Sahara." *Palaeoecology of Africa and the Surrounding Islands* 18 (1987): 441–48.

Were, Gideon. *A History of the Abaluyia of Western Kenya.* Nairobi: East African Publishing House, 1967.

White, Luise. *The Comforts of Home: Prostitution in Colonial Nairobi.* Chicago: University of Chicago Press, 1990.

Williams, Eric E. *Capitalism and Slavery.* Chapel Hill: University of North Carolina Press, 1944.

Wilson, Godfrey. *The Constitution of Ngonde.* The Rhodes-Livingstone Papers, no. 3. Livingstone, Northern Rhodesia: Rhodes-Livingstone Institute, 1939.

7

Literary Studies and African Literature: The Challenge of Intercultural Literacy

CHRISTOPHER L. MILLER

I HAVE RESPONDED TO THE CHALLENGE posed by the editors of this volume in a way that may appear to be indirect. The most obvious approach to the question of African literature within United States universities would consist of cataloguing all the wealth of thematic knowledge and cultural insight that African writers have to offer. This wealth is vast, and students in American institutions are already learning important lessons in perspective by reading African texts. However, in earlier discussions and battles over curriculum, proponents of African literature were challenged to demonstrate the value of their subject, to prove that there was any wealth of knowledge at all to be found in African texts. Responses to such challenges were inevitably defensive and apologetic. Twenty years after those first debates, there have been considerable but not sufficient changes in this situation. Greater numbers of non-Africanist academics now recognize the unique perspective offered by African writers and welcome their contributions to the curriculum. But my thesis in this essay will be that a more subtle and more fundamental set of obstacles continues to impede the potential impact of African literature here, and that an analysis of those obstacles is more to the point than any *apologia* for African literature as a whole. Therefore I will not attempt to provide an introduction to the field. (Excellent introductions are widely available [see Irele 1981 and Ngate 1988].) Rather, I will try to situate the place of African literature within recent debates on culture and the curriculum.

AMERICAN UNIVERSITIES ARE CURRENTLY being pulled in opposite directions. On the one hand, there is a burgeoning of programs that invite students into less-explored corners of the globe and to make their inquiries across rather than within disciplinary boundaries. Beginning with the emergence of African-American Studies programs in the late 1960s and continuing with the broad institutionalization of women's studies, ethnic studies, and other programs, this movement has encouaged attention to neglected sources and suppressed voices. Hearing what these voices have to say about, for example, the history of colonialism and slavery has not always been easy; but as Jean-Paul Sartre asked in 1949: What else could we expect to hear, once colonized peoples began to talk back (Sartre 1949, p. ix)? By widening the scope of legitimate research, this movement has taken the university several steps closer to realizing the grand design implicit in its name.

On the other hand, in the last few years, powerful voices have begun sounding an alarm. Claiming that the movement toward diversity has gone too far and resulted in fragmentation, conservatives have appealed for a return to Western culture as the solid foundation, the "core" of studies. Allan Bloom's bestseller *The Closing of the American Mind,* Lynne V. Cheney's report on *Humanities in America,* Roger Kimball's jeremiad *Tenured Radicals,* and Dinesh D'Souza's *Illiberal Education* all have contributed to a wave of reaction against changes that have taken place in the humanities since the 1960s. They are particularly concerned about literature: what texts are taught and how they are taught. The academic year 1990–91 was marked by an explosion of antiacademic backlash in the upper-middle-brow press, reflecting a dim understanding of "political" changes in the humanities and a popular distaste for the decentering of the West.

In an address to the newly arrived class of 1994 (later reprinted as an opinion piece in the *New York Times*), Dean Donald Kagan of Yale College joined the fray, and posed the problem in the following manner:

> The study of Western civilization in our schools and colleges is under heavy attack. We are told that we should not give a privileged place in the curriculum to the great works of its history and literature. . . . These attacks are unsound. It is both right and necessary to place Western civilization and the culture to which it has given rise at the center of our studies, and we fail to do so at the peril of our students, our country, and of the hopes for a democratic, liberal society emerging throughout the world today. [Kagan 1990]

Kagan's apocalyptic and bellicose language disguises one basic fact: that non-Western studies have already been widely institutionalized and rendered unexceptionable to a wide community of scholars. Furthermore, his sentiments were expressed within the context of a university where new initiatives in the study of non-Western cultures are actively being pursued. Throughout academia, "diversity" is institutionalizing itself, while conservatives struggle against it; both ends are pulling against the middle. Bemused bystanders might conclude that this quarrel pits radical revolutionaries against radical reactionaries, and that the only choice is between a purely "political" anti-Western stance and a baldly Eurocentric, chauvinistic ideology. Are these the only options open to those making decisions about curriculum, hiring, and tenure?

Within this debate, E. D. Hirsch's highly influential bestseller *Cultural Literacy* provides a more rational exposition of the basic issues than most of the other conservative publications. Hirsch begins by taking Jean-Jacques Rousseau and John Dewey to task for their "content-neutral" conception of education (Hirsch 1988, p. xv); he seeks to redeem cumulative information (as opposed to general skills) as an important goal of education. Hirsch's theory is based on "the anthropological observation that all human communities are founded upon specific shared information" (p. xv). While this idea embraces only the more traditional forms of anthropology, it nonetheless reveals a common denominator between Hirsch and many African and African-American studies scholars: on both sides there is attention to culture as system, and devotion to literature as a building-block of identity. (For reasons that I will review presently, this position is more controversial than it may appear.) For Hirsch, the question then becomes, Which cultures—or "accumulations of shared symbols"—should we study? His answer is similar to Kagan's, although his vision is somewhat less apocalyptic. Hirsch places all his faith in a notion of *national* culture that assumes the integrity and unity of the nation (in fact, his intervention can be construed as an effort to "save" the nation; the missionary zeal is even more evident in Kagan). Again, there is common ground with African and African-American studies: black nationalism and national culture were fundamental notions in the struggle for independence in Africa and civil liberation in the United States. But Hirsch differentiates between nations to a radical extent and insists that "multicultural education" must not be allowed to "supplant or interfere with *our* schools' responsibility to ensure *our* children's mastery of American literate culture" (p. 18; emphasis mine). But who are "we"? A repressive moment is necessary within Hirsch's proposal; whatever is marginal must not interfere, and any American who does not identify with his first-person pronoun is simply left out.

While Hirsch's notion of a quasi-monolithic national culture—and a uniform, fact-based "cultural literacy"—invites skepticism, his emphasis on the primacy of "one's own" culture also covers over certain complexities. Cultures are constantly being negotiated and renegotiated within national communities, and in this, the United States is no exception. Hirsch assumes that whatever is taught in schools will be the national culture and that it will inevitably reflect the composition of the populace. Thus a single cultural literacy seems a legitimate goal to him. But those who do not see themselves in Hirsch's (or Kagan's) portrait of Western culture, and those who wish to take a broader view of culture, may be less than satisfied.[1]

The point that Kagan, Hirsch, and others leave out of their thinking is that cultures, nations, and spheres like "the West" do not exist in isolation. The histories of Africa, Asia, and Europe have been intertwined for millennia. Since the dawn of "Western" literature in Homer, the act of imagining Africa has helped various Western cultures to define themselves (see Miller 1985, pp. 3–65). Within Europe, cultures continually refer to their neighbors as examples of what they are not. The history of the United States cannot be accurately studied if no consideration is given to the presence of Hispanic culture and the role of Mexico in defining United States nationalism. Examples of the interdependence of nations are obviously infinite, but attention to these issues tends to be minimal within traditional curricula, which are nationalistic in their organization and motivation.

"Multiculturalism," on the other hand, is all too often conceived as the mere multiplication of discrete cultural or national units; in other words, it adheres to Hirsch's model of culture while expanding the number of cultures about which students should be "literate." Multiculturalism is plural nationalism. While this may be preferable for many scholars in non-Western fields, its intellectual basis may be questioned on both theoretical and practical grounds. Is it theoretically sound merely to reproduce Hirsch's model by multiplying it in application to non-Western cultures? Will this advance the understanding of culture as a process or will it simply reinforce boundaries and further balkanize the curriculum? These questions are of substantial importance. On the practical level, "multiculturalism" faces questions of feasibility: how do we decide what to include? How do we justify the necessary exclusions when inclusion is our only goal? Is the curriculum to be decided by "quota, not quality"? These questions arise because multiculturalism is an inadequate formula, an expedient, incapable of handling the challenges of international and intercultural reality.

I do not propose that either Hirsch's model of culture or "multiculturalism" be utterly rejected. The nationalist attitude that underlies both approaches is too powerful to be simply dismissed; as a matter of practical pedagogy and theoretical realism, nationalism must be given its due. Rather I would suggest that these points of view be *supplemented* in undergraduate and graduate education with a more challenging and, I believe, more accurate model of cultural knowledge based on intercultural comparison. The goal is to make students consider not just the "accumulations of symbols" of their own culture but the different inflections given to these symbols by subgroups and the relation of their symbols to alien ones. If, therefore, Western values and canons must be "protected" within modern American universities, such a project can only claim intellectual validity within a framework where serious if not equal attention is also given to the issues and challenges of non-Western cultures.[2] Otherwise, we lapse into narcissism.[3]

Instead of Hirsch's nationalist cultural literacy, I would therefore propose intercultural literacy as a more ambitious and a worthier goal for advanced undergraduate and graduate education. (I leave aside the question of any relevance this might have for elementary through early college education.) Intercultural literacy would consist of a mode of inquiry that respects the accumulation of shared symbols (thus the term "literacy") but also invites research into the processes by which cultures are formed and particularly encourages analysis of how cultures constitute themselves by reference to each other. Intercultural literacy is to be distinguished, on the one hand, from Hirsch's cultural literacy, and on the other, from what Hirsch calls "biliteracy," which is knowledge of two discrete cultures (p. 93)—and thus the rudiment of "multiculturalism." I will argue that the study of Africa is particularly well suited to an agenda of intercultural literacy and in fact makes it necessary.

WHAT DOES THE STUDY of African literature bring to the field of literary studies? Does it provide anything more than a vast new supply of raw materials (texts) to which Western methodologies can now be applied? Or does African literature pose more profound challenges? I would submit that the study of Africa demands nothing less than a reconsideration of all the terms of literary analysis, starting with the word "literature" itself, and that such a reconsideration is the best thing that can happen to the field. In order to elaborate on this rather sweeping statement, I will need to begin with a brief review of literary studies in American universities and of the place of African literature in the curriculum.

It is well known that a "revolution" took place in literary criticism in the 1970s, a reorientation toward more theoretical and philosophical issues. Coinciding with a new increase in professionalism and specialization among scholars, this revolution represented both an expansion of claims and an increase in obscurity. The questions addressed by critics no longer ended at disciplinary boundaries; a new metalanguage allowed them to break down old barriers. Critics (such as Paul de Man), who had previously focused on strictly literary subjects, turned more and more to philosophical issues. French philosopher Jacques Derrida was a leader of this movement, which became associated with the word "deconstruction." Derrida's critique of Claude Lévi-Strauss is a classic example of the increasing power of theory, and the example is relevant to the cultural issues I have been discussing here. Derrida "deconstructed" (that is, he revealed the internal contradictions within) Lévi-Strauss' interpretation of writing in a South American Indian culture merely by reading it (Derrida 1967, pp. 149–202). Derrida did not need to train himself as an anthropologist or travel to South America; by reading and thinking theoretically about the nature of writing, he was able to "invalidate" Lévi-Strauss' claims about the difference between writing and speaking. "Writing," as Derrida redefines it, is the outermost envelope of representation, an inescapable agent of difference. For a whole school and a new generation of literary critics working under the influence of Derrida, "writing" is everywhere: in anthropology, history, the social sciences in general, and, of course, literature. The new theoretical criticism was thus emboldened to make incursions anywhere texts were to be found, which is to say everywhere (for a powerful defense of this approach, see J. Hillis Miller 1987, pp. 1–11). The implications and consequences of this revolution have been far-reaching, and I will only attempt to explain what it has meant for African studies.

On one side, much has been gained. Derrida's critique of Lévi-Strauss was emblematic of a general attack on all forms of deluded authenticity-seeking: the processes by which the West has constructed and controlled non-Western identities, seeking in Africa answers to Western preoccupations. The 1960s and 70s marked the beginning of a reappraisal. The overlapping between anthropology and colonialism could no longer be ignored; new notions of African identity would have to come from Africa itself, or at least in genuine dialogue with African voices. So, in a very broad sense, Derrida and the general critique of "Western metaphysics" in the new literary theory were part of the decolonization movement. Deconstruction provided tools with which anthropologists would rework notions of African identity (see, for example, Amselle and M'Bokolo 1985). The association of "deconstructionism" with pure "meaninglessness" is merely a hostile caricature drawn by ideological foes.

But back in certain literary circles, the theoretical revolution became an end in itself. Derrida's critique of "Western metaphysics" led some of his disciples into more critiques of "Western metaphysics" rather than beyond. Although theory and difference were synonymous, theory only allowed for a kind of difference that was purely theoretical.[4] The consideration of cultures as aggregate wholes, à la Hirsch, had been discredited as a form of self-delusion, notably in Derrida's treatment of Lévi-Strauss, and was therefore considered suspect. This made the consideration of African literature rather problematic, if only to the extent that most of this literature has been concerned with some degree of cultural representation, of speaking for a racial or national group. This is the block to seeing culture as system that I referred to earlier.

Furthermore, the entire edifice of theory constructed by De Man, Derrida, J. Hillis Miller, and others was based on a reading of Western texts only. While remaining ignorant of non-Western traditions, deconstructive theory people nonetheless felt empowered to comment on "the West" (without any outside comparison) and on "writing" wherever it occurred (which was everywhere). The complexities of culture and history were all absorbed into the same abstraction. Clearly, this did not establish an auspicious intellectual climate for readers of African literature.

But the theoretical revolution had spawned numerous reactions. After history and culture were "repressed" by deconstruction, a "new historicism" and a new kind of cultural studies were invented. The theoretical revolution having changed the general approach to reading, history and culture could no longer be taken for granted; they would now be analyzed as ever-changing constellations of discourse. Marxism and feminism, two schools of thought that, like deconstructive theory, had been marked by their European origins,[5] contributed to a new pluralism in literary studies, a climate that developed in the 1980s. A new confluence of literary studies and anthropology produced exciting new perspectives within both fields (see, for example, Clifford 1988). This set up a positive intellectual atmosphere for the teaching of African literature, an atmosphere conducive to multicultural inquiry and intercultural literacy. But what was the actual condition of African studies throughout this period?

Before the 1960s, Africa had been almost exclusively the province of anthropologists. Africans were seen more as cultural objects than as producers of cultural interpretations; cultures were studied as systems, but African depictions of African cultures in literature were rarely given attention. Then, in the late 1960s, the demand for black studies programs in American universities provided the first impetus for institutionalizing African literature within the curriculum. The rehabilitation of the image of Africa was a central concern in the minds of those organizing black studies; it was part of a project of "scholarly correction of historical and cultural myths" (Reid 1970, p. 11).[6] Literature was one of the best means to this end, and African literature was seen by some to hold a lesson for African-Americans, to exemplify an ethic of community solidarity (Mutiso in Richards 1971, pp. 159–70). Black studies thus brought African texts into the American curriculum to serve African-American needs. As these programs matured, more attention was eventually given to the divergence between African cultures and African-American cultures within the world of the black diaspora, and specificity would become a watchword. There are now as many ways of institutionalizing the relationship between African Studies and African-American Studies as there are colleges and universities that support them, ranging from total separation to total integration.

In the 1980s, with increasing political pressure on universities to diversify both curriculum and human resources, the study of Africa seemed assured of a bright future. But what has been the real position of Africanists within this framework? In order to gain legitimacy and achieve tenure, Africanists have had to respond to the requirements of their departments—usually English or French departments—whose very raison d'être has, of course, been Western literary canons and national literatures. Literary Africanists—often self-taught in African literature, usually required to teach Western materials, except on occasion—have tended to be marginal figures.

I would like to illustrate this condition of marginality with a story that reveals the current structure of things. A large English department is seeking an assistant professor in the field of African or African-Caribbean literature. The candidates, in their written work and in their interviews, feel compelled to provide cultural, geographical, and historical information that helps to explain the context of the literary works in question. One younger tenured professor, who works on European texts only, observes in response that the field seems to be plagued by "journalism." The candidates have been attempting to fill an information deficit, so that their readers might understand something outside the Western canon; they are caught in a double bind of having to provide "mere information" yet being condemned as "journalists" for doing so.

For the purposes of my argument, I would like to retain this figure of the marginalized Africanist: it is largely true to life. My contention is that Africa has been allowed to contribute almost nothing to the Western academy up to the present moment, and that everything remains to be done. As a subject matter and as a source of cultural interpretation, Africa has been let in only within a rigidly hierarchized structure of center and margin that automatically devalues the margins. What is considered "literature" is still the European canon, with minor adjustments having been made to accommodate certain women and certain ethnic groups; non-Western writers and Africans in particular, even as they use European languages, have had little or no impact on "literature" as a whole. My bleak assessment is supported by Abiola Irele, a

Nigerian critic working in the United States, in an essay on the condition of African scholarship in the broadest sense. Irele asserts that "African scholarship is at best marginal, and at worst nonexistent in the total economy of intellectual endeavor in the world today" (Irele 1991, p. 63). His conclusion is that "the opportunity is still open to us . . . of making an appreciable impact upon scholarship, and indeed upon the world system of knowledge" (p. 69), and it is in this spirit of potential influence that I would like to pursue my argument here.

What, then, could everyone interested in literature gain from the study of Africa? Why does the study of Africa, as I have suggested, throw everything into question?

BEGINNING WITH THE TERM "literature" itself, the study of Africa upsets received ideas and forces one to think. In its etymology, the Latin word for letter, "literature," implies writing, and in literary studies it is taken for granted that the object in question will be written. This is largely true for Africa as well, with one important difference: the long shadow cast by oral traditions. It is impossible to consider African "literature" in any broad sense without taking orality into account. The majority of African cultural traditions were preserved and adapted over long periods by oral traditions, which have had a great influence on the written literatures (often beginning, we should note, with transcriptions into Arabic, an important source of writing in parts of West and East Africa). But Western academies have had some difficulty adjusting their terms to fit this object: how can there be such a thing as "oral literature"? Uncomfortable with this oxymoron, some Africanists have resorted to the neologism "orature." The relation of the new European-language literatures to prior or parallel oral traditions is one of the predominant problems in the field. Many early texts consisted merely of transcriptions and translations of oral epics or poetry. Many novelists have attempted to recreate the rhythms and patterns of orality in their writing.

The border between the oral and the written is, of course, a subject of considerable curiosity and speculation within Western academies. It coincides with distinctions that have been fundamental in organizing disciplines: the difference between "primitive" and "modern," between the object of anthropology and that of sociology, and also between anthropology and literature. Philosophical attempts to account for the difference between orality and literacy have been far-reaching and inconclusive; a review of the literature on this subject helps students to reconsider a number of their basic assumptions about culture and representation.[7]

What is "literature" in Africa thus cannot be taken for granted. The first question it poses is that of orality; the second is that of the history and politics of literacy. If Africans are writing in European languages, why are they doing so and what is the significance of this act? Courses on African literature must begin by addressing these questions, and they often end by discussing them as well. The question of literacy turns into a consideration of colonialism, for, with few exceptions, literacy arrived in Africa with the missionaries and the colonizers. Present-day African intellectuals, reviewing the history of their cultures, now see literacy as something of a Trojan Horse; a text from the Francophone tradition illustrates this.

The first fictional text written in French by an African was called *Les trois volontés de Malic* (Malic's three wishes), by Ahmadou Mapaté Diagne, published in 1920. Having acquired French-language literacy himself only a few years before, Diagne wrote this text as both a "reader" for students learning French and a piece of propaganda for the French colonial enterprise. The text is in easy French, but its ideological lessons are more complex. Set in a Wolof village in Senegal, the story opens with the arrival of a French commandant, "followed by guards and by a man in civilian clothes," the teacher (Diagne 1920, p. 4). The commandant introduces the teacher and proclaims the values of Francophone literacy:

> We bring you a man of your own race to teach your young children. He will teach them to read, write, and speak French. The children who go through school will turn into hard-working, honest, righteous men. They won't need an interpreter to speak with whites; they won't be fooled by dishonest merchants. At school, your children will develop their habits of politeness and respect. [P. 6])

The hero Malic, a young boy in the village, learns French and amazes the village elders with his ability to "distinguish the little marks which resemble the feet of flies" (p. 16). This astonishment is rather implausible, in a context where Islam had introduced Arabic literacy long before; the omission is significant. French-language literacy is the principal tool of the revolution that is proposed in the text, a turning away from "origin and caste," toward "work, intelligence and virtues" (p. 27), in other words, collaboration with the colonial "mission to civilize." [8]

Les trois volontés de Malic thus supports the idea that literacy is not a neutral "technology of reason" but rather a vehicle loaded with ideology. In the case of colonial Africa at least, this is certainly true. The first "writers" were not novelists and poets but secretaries, scribes, and interpreters employed by the colonizers. Exposure to this history is often discomfiting for students who expect their African literature to be purely and simply liberationist; there are lessons to be learned here not only about the nature of literacy but about the impact of European colonialism. The history of the Francophone literary tradition has been one of continually seeking to overcome this initial condition of dependence, through a variety of strategies and tactics. Why, then, do Africans still write in French or English?

American students almost unanimously assume a certain theory about literary traditions: that one should write in "one's own" language. In the United States, where foreign languages are more foreign—more removed from the everyday life of the dominant culture—than they are in many other societies, the idea of an entire literature being written in a "foreign" language appears bizarre and unnatural. Hirsch supports this theory and justifies it in the following manner:

> *In the modern world* we therefore find linguistic diversity among the nations but, with a few exceptions, linguistic uniformity inside the nations. This pattern did not arise by chance; it is a self-conscious political and educational arrangement. . . . It is contrary to the purpose and essence of a national language, whether English or German or Spanish or French, that a *modern* nation should deliberately encourage more than one to flourish within its borders. [Pp. 71 and 93; emphasis mine]

Hirsch chooses easy examples: the border ("a line painted across the road") between Menton, France and Ventimiglia, Italy shows total national integrity and distinctiveness (p. 92). But if he had considered the border between France and Spain in the Basque country, or in the Cerdanya valley of the Catalan area, would the line painted across the road have the same function and power? Peter Sahlins' fascinating study of a Catalan enclave spanning the French/Spanish border shows this supposedly "dead" boundary to be the locus of "intersecting relations among ethnicity, topography, and politics" (Sahlins 1989, p. 21). So even inside Europe, national distinctions are not as neat as Hirsch wants them to be. He ignores both the ragged edges of European nationalism (which have become all the more evident since the collapse of the Eastern bloc) and the violence of the historical processes that brought borders into existence.[9]

Furthermore, one must assume that Hirsch's "modern world" is meant to exclude Africa; what would happen to his model if it did not? First and most significantly, the whole notion of what is "one's own" would become problematic. Most Africans speak two African languages before they learn a European one; only a small percentage of each nation's population acquires European-language literacy. The concept and structure of the nation, whose integrity is fundamental to

Hirsch's model, came to Africa as a result of colonialism. Borders were determined with some arbitrariness at conference tables in Europe; certain cultures were divided while others were thrust together; and national unity has consequently been the single most difficult issue in postcolonial Africa. The issue of what is "one's own" and what is someone else's thus feeds into cultural and political questions of enormous complexity. The Irish playwright Samuel Beckett made a decision to write in French; his works are considered part of French literature. Beckett's self-exile and adoption of a foreign language was individual and idiosyncratic: How do we come to terms with a continent that seems to have collectively abandoned its native languages in favor of European ones for literary purposes?

This question suggests several others: To whom do the languages of the former colonizers belong? Must we interpret the use of European languages as a sign of unending dependence and alienation? Is it possible for Africans to *appropriate* these languages, lend them an African inflection in literature, and thereby escape the cycle of dependence? These questions are currently very much open to debate in Africa, but they are set against a backdrop in which European-language literatures dominate. There are many obstacles slowing the development of African-language literatures, obstacles rooted in the policies of the various colonizers. France in particular established its languages as the royal road to "civilization"; English as well was advertised as "the bearer of all knowledge in the arts and sciences" (Ngũgĩ 1990, p. 286). This attitude allowed for precious little investment in the task of reducing African languages to writing. Postcolonial governments have been attempting to remedy this, with mixed results: in Tanzania, ninety percent of the population is said to be literate in Swahili; in Senegal, officials are still deciding how to write Wolof and teach it in schools. Generally in Africa, literacy is European-language literacy. The publishing industry reflects and perpetuates the centrality of European languages: to this day, the production of African literature, especially in French, remains largely a European enterprise.

There is, however, great support for the idea of appropriation and Africanization of European languages. Novels such as Amos Tutuola's *The Palm Wine Drinkard* (1952) and Ahmadou Kourouma's *Les soleils de indépendances* (*The Suns of Independence,* 1968) support this theory through a conscious practice of deviance from European standards and a recourse to African speech patterns and vocabulary. But, according to Kenyan novelist Ngũgĩ wa Thiong'o, the most powerful opponent of this idea, appropriation is an illusion; Africanization merely enriches the languages of the colonizers while doing nothing for African cultural independence (Ngũgĩ 1981, pp. 4–33). Ngũgĩ states categorically that European-language literatures are "not African" (p. 26), and he advocates that they be abandoned. His position is righteous and compelling, particularly for those Americans who find the One Language/One Culture theory, à la Hirsch, to be the only natural one.

But African literature in European languages, while perhaps evolving towards its own dissolution like Latin literature in the European Middle Ages, is firmly entrenched for the moment. Americans may find Ngũgĩ's position attractive because of its appeal to authenticity and resistance, but more surprising lessons are to be learned from another school of African thought. A group of Francophone philosophers who could be called radical realists advocates abandonment of the past and acceptance of the postcolonial world as it is. Notions of authenticity, ethnicity, and Africanity are for these thinkers a "ghetto" (Hountondji 1977, p. 49). In order to gain equality and power, they posit an absolute necessity to surrender difference and identity: "We must revolutionize our own spirit completely; in so doing we will assuredly become the same as the European" (Towa 1971, p. 48). There is thus an acceptance of and even a "praise of alienation" (Irele 1982) within this current, a recognition of the impact of colonialism, and a refusal to look backwards. The implications of this position for the language issue are clear: there is no point in returning to African languages, which have been thoroughly disturbed by European vocabulary anyway; you can't go home again.

The notion of what is "one's own" is made quite problematic by these assertions and, I would maintain, by any consideration of Africa. Whether or not the African intellectual actually embraces alienation, colonial and post (or neo-) colonial history has made the influence of Europe impossible to ignore. Even Ngũgĩ's model does not really correspond to Hirsch's; Ngũgĩ's practice of writing in his own language, Gikuyu, and his advocacy of Swahili as "the language for the world" (Ngũgĩ 1990, p. 293) banish European languages but leave in place the question of difference between "one's own" African language and the new world language. The incongruity between nations, languages, and cultures in Africa is the most basic fact of intellectual and political life; it demands a more complex model than Hirsch's.

There are in fact numerous models to choose from, and this is not the space in which to rehearse them all. Answers come from anthropologists, political scientists, and literary critics. The process of describing their hypotheses and of deriving Africa-based models of what is "one's own" is the greatest challenge in an African studies course. In literature, discussions often begin from and return to the language question, in terms that I have described here: the material condition of literacy and its political ramifications are never far from sight. Possible trajectories beyond this include competing models of literary identity such as "national literature" versus "cultural spheres of influence"; literature of ethnicity versus literature of liberation; and positive versus deconstructive models of identity.[10] All of these considerations flow from an initial attempt to define in context the word "literature." As no doubt it has been evident, any such attempt is of necessity interdisciplinary.

I hope it has also been clear from this discussion what an American student (or even an African student who has been subjected to a Eurocentric curriculum) has to gain from taking Africa into account. The discombobulation of Hirsch's model is emblematic of what happens time after time in African literature classes: the theoretical model or unspoken assumption derives from the Euro-American context and proves inadequate when simply applied to Africa. The pedagogical challenge is to lead students beyond the mere surprise and confusion that results, into a positive reconsideration of literature and culture in general. Advanced undergraduate and graduate students are often enamored of theories and eager to "apply" them; the study of Africa provides, in addition to simple cultural pluralism, a vital and necessary stumbling block. The risk in confining oneself to the study of "one's own" culture is that theory and reading will operate in a closed circuit, smoothly confirming each other and leaving an appearance of universal validity—for what is "universal" has until recently been the West's decision. Any number of intellectual topoi could be cited as examples: feminism and silence; the Oedipus complex; Marxist realism; the demarcation of literary genres; and so forth. But, having looked into Africa, and having found an incongruity between the supposedly universal theory and the text in question, the student will ideally be forced to reconsider his or her initial assumptions. Thus, having looked at African cultural and political constructions, the reader of Hirsch's *Cultural Literacy* is less likely to take his notion of absolute borders at face value and more likely to think of the Catalan example. I would even venture to say that a new approach to reading can result from this (I have seen it happen): the student learns to stop treating the theory or the model as holy writ and to work towards a more dialogical model of the relationship between theory and "primary text." For students innocent of the theoretical urge, a similar process takes place in regard to very basic assumptions about "novel," "poetry," and "literature" itself.

AT THIS POINT I WOULD like to move from a consideration of what students can learn by reading African texts to an analysis of the world system within which they do it. While this may go beyond what can be taught in a literature class, it must be taken into account by scholars and administrators.

It is no surprise that an African voice expresses reservations about what "theory" has been until now and how it has been organized as a system. Paulin Hountondji, one of the "radical realists" in Francophone philosophy, has written a critique of the market dynamics that control the relation between Western academies and the African world. Africa provides raw materials—like palm oil or cultural artifacts— which European institutes process into finished commodities—like Palmolive soap or theories of culture. Economics and intellectual institutions are both caught up in a large centripetal movement: by this movement, "the brains of the Third World, all the intellectually and scientifically competent, are rigorously carried by the whole flow of worldwide scientific activity toward the center of the system," that is, toward Europe and the United States (Hountondji 1992, p. 245).[11] Hountondji's analysis raises several issues.

First, his explicit analogy suggests that intellectual constructs behave like soap and other commodities and are subject to the same laws. This requires a mode of thinking that momentarily ignores content in order to study the workings of the "market." This is just the kind of approach that is deplored by American conservatives, who, of course, sit at the top of the world system as Hountondji describes it. Those on the bottom or in the margins find it necessary to consider not just ideas themselves but also their provenance and their consequences. This is not "affirmative action for ideas" or blind "political correctness"; it is analytical thinking about the production of knowledge.

Hountondji's analysis further suggests the troubling possibility that America's gain is Africa's loss. As prominent African intellectuals— often exiled from their home countries—respond to the market demand for multiculturalism in the United States by accepting university positions, a brain drain results in Africa. While the extent of this problem is difficult to appraise, I would like to suggest how we in the United States should approach it. It should most definitely not serve as a pretext for *not* hiring Africans; this would be totally wrong. In some cases, suitable positions are not available anywhere but in this country. What the problem should encourage us to do is to work toward a responsible posture and an awareness of our impact. If more African professors are going to teach in American universities, then more African students— particularly graduate students—should be educated here. This is the only way that we can replenish the intellectual resources that otherwise we would be merely consuming. New initiatives in African studies, such as the African Humanities Institute at Northwestern University, are being designed to work along these lines.

THERE SHOULD BE, THEREFORE, a positive role for American universities to play, on the one hand in enriching American students' intercultural literacy through exposure to African studies, and on the other in developing a fair relationship with the continent in question. Africa is peculiarly well suited to serve as the essential intellectual stumbling block I have described here. The study of Africa has a vital role to play in the broadening of our students' intellectual horizons; studying Africa will make them aware of how those horizons came to exist and what they mean.

Africanist faculty must be given the freedom they need in order to realize the potential of their materials: they must be valued and evacuated in terms of the unique contribution they have to make. If there is one idea that stands between literary Africanists and their colleagues in French and English departments, it is the pernicious notion that the Euro-American canon is the "bread and butter" and that the rest is interesting but secondary, a mere "frill" in the curriculum. This is a backward idea. It ignores, first of all, the impact of decolonization on Britain and France, the emergence of strong literary voices, and the avalanche of new texts from former colonies and immigrants (such as Salman Rushdie in Great Britain and Tahar Ben Jelloun in France). Merely as a question of production, the postcolonial literatures are growing prodigiously; the increased need to research and understand them will have to be met. The "bread-and-butter" approach also ignores a shift in cultural allegiance and interest among many American students, who are now less convinced by history "as told by the winners." Recent Modern Language Association joblists have shown a considerable rise in demand for scholars of African literature, reflecting a growing demand for real experts in the area.

The challenge represented by African literature is thus greater than it might appear at first. The present system of including it but marginalizing it, as I hope to have shown, is inadequate, unjust, and intellectually unsound. At the root of the problem is the current nationalist basis of literary curricula. If the object of the curriculum (or at least the highest level of achievement within it) were intercultural analysis rather than a contest to see who has the highest pile of information, much would be gained. In a well-designed program of intercultural literacy, students would have the opportunity to think for themselves about what is bread and butter—and why.

NOTES

1. Among the most powerful critiques of Hirsch are Guillory, Smith, and Sledd and Sledd.

2. A Yale undergraduate, responding to Kagan's speech, comments: "Previous to coming to Yale, I spent 18 years of life and 12 years of high school [*sic*] with Western Civilization as the foundation of my learning. I do not need a college course on Western Civilization to have a working understanding of the culture which everyday surrounds me" (Austin, p. 2). In fact, he does need courses to help him go beyond a mere "working understanding," but those courses should not teach the West in isolation or to the exclusion of other areas.

3. In an article that largely favors the West-first view in the debate—while seeking a more positively programmatic agenda for it—the philosopher John Searle (1990, p. 42) makes a point similar to mine: "You do not understand your own tradition if you do not see it in relation to others. . . . The claims of the various minorities should have their place. . . . You can never understand one language until you understand at least two." But Searle's "place" for minorities is clearly secondary, subordinated to a unified "dominant tradition . . . the European tradition. The United States is, after all, a product of the European Enlightenment." This it may largely be, but Searle misses two points: first, demographics show that in the future, "minorities," especially in college and university populations, may be the majority; and second, the ideas that built America may have been European, but in many cases the labor was not, and this has consequences we are beginning to see now.

4. Here I am repeating an argument I have advanced in a more detailed fashion in my book (Miller 1990, pp. 7–10; see also 109n).

5. On the problem of Eurocentrism in Marxism, see Dieng 1978, pp. 9–41; on similar problems in feminism, see Miller 1990, pp. 255–56.

6. Cf. C. Vann Woodward (in Kilson 1969, p. 23): "The traditional indifference or repugnance for things African, the shame and abhorrence of association with Africa, gave way to fascinated interest, pride, and a sense of identification. . . . We are destined to hear a lot more about Africa from Afro-Americans as time goes on." See also Henderson in Richards 1971, p. 21, and Huggins 1985.

7. See, for example, Goody and Watt 1968; Street 1984. This subject—the theoretical significance of the distinction between the oral and the written—was precisely the one addressed in Derrida's attack on Lévi-Strauss, discussed above.

8. Parts of this analysis are taken from my "Unfinished Business," forthcoming.

9. For another perspective, on the emergence of the French nation through the suppression of difference, see Weber's *Peasants into Frenchmen*.

10. On national literatures see Huannou 1989; on cultural spheres see Kane 1982; on models of identity in anthropology, see Clifford 1988, and Amselle and M'Bokolo 1985.

11. Portions of this paragraph are taken from Miller 1990, pp. 2–3. In a similar analysis, Michael Crowder (1987) described "the creation of two separate and compartmentalised worlds of Africanists: African and non-African" (p. 109). Crowder did not anticipate the growing African presence in Ameri-

can institutions, which is both a solution to the problem he describes, in that it employs African scholars, and an aggravation of the problem, in that it further depletes the intellectual resources on the African continent itself.

REFERENCES

Amselle, Jean-Loup, and M'Bokolo, Elikia, eds. *Au Coeur de l'ethnie: Ethnies, tribalisme et état en Afrique.* Paris: La Découverte, 1985.

Austin, Roy, Jr. "Is Yale as Integrated as It Claims to Be?" *Yale Daily News,* 13 November 1990.

Bloom, Allan. *The Closing of the American Mind.* New York: Touchstone Books, 1988.

Cheney, Lynn. *Humanities in America: A Report to the President, the Congress, and the American People.* Washington, D.C.: National Endowment for the Humanities, 1988.

Clifford, James. *The Predicament of Culture: Twentieth-Century Ethnography, Literature, and Art.* Cambridge, Mass.: Harvard University Press, 1988.

Crowder, Michael. "'Us' and 'Them': The International African Institute and the Current Crisis of Identity in African Studies." *Africa* 57, no. 1 (1987): 109–22.

Derrida, Jacques. *De la grammatologie.* Paris: Minuit, 1967.

Diagne, Ahmadou Mapaté. *Les trois volontés de Malic.* Nendeln: Kraus Reprint, 1973 [1920].

Dieng, Amady Ali. *Hegel, Marx, Engels, et les problèmes de l'Afrique noire.* Dakar: Sankoré, 1978.

D'Souza, Dinesh. *Illiberal Education.* New York: Free Press, 1991.

Goody, Jack, and Watt, Ian. "The Consequences of Literacy." In *Literacy in Traditional Societies,* edited by Jack Goody. Cambridge: Cambridge University Press, 1968.

Guillory, John. "Canon, Syllabus, List: A Note on the Pedagogic Imaginary." *Transition* 52 (1991): 36–54.

Hirsch, E. D., Jr. *Cultural Literacy: What Every American Needs to Know.* New York: Vintage Books, 1988.

Hountondji, Paulin. *Sur la "philosophie africaine."* Paris: Maspero, 1977.

———. "Recapturing." In *The Surreptitious Speech: "Présence Africaine" and the Politics of Otherness,* edited by V. Y. Mudimbe. Chicago: University of Chicago Press, 1992.

Huannou, Adrien. *La question des littératures nationales en Afrique noire.* Abidjan: CEDA, 1989.

———. *Afro-American Studies: A Report to the Ford Foundation.* New York: Ford Foundation, 1985.

Irele, Abiola. *The African Experience in Literature and Ideology.* London: Heinemann, 1981.

———. "In Praise of Alienation." Inaugural Lecture, University of Ibadan. 22 November 1982.

———. "The African Scholar." *Transition* 51 (1991): 56–69.

Kagan, Donald. "E Pluribus Unum: All Roads Lead to Rome." *Yale Daily News,* 6 September 1990. Reprinted in the *New York Times,* 4 May 1991.

Kane, Mohamadou. *Roman africain et tradition.* Dakar: Les Nouvelles Editions Africaines, 1982.

Kilson, Martin, et al. *Black Studies: Myths and Realities.* New York: A. Philip Randolph Educational Fund, 1969.

Miller, Christopher L. *Blank Darkness: Africanist Discourse in French.* Chicago: University of Chicago Press, 1985.

———. *Theories of Africans: Francophone Literature and Anthropology in Africa.* Chicago: University of Chicago Press, 1990.

———. "Unfinished Business: Colonialism in Sub-Saharan Africa and the Ideals of the French Revolution." Forthcoming.

Miller, J. Hillis. *The Ethics of Reading.* New York: Columbia University Press, 1987.

Ngate, Jonathan. *Francophone African Fiction: Reading a Literary Tradition.* Trenton, N.J.: Africa World Press, 1988.

Ngũgĩ wa Thiong'o. *Decolonising the Mind: The Politics of Language in African Literature.* London: James Currey, 1981.

———. "English: A Language for the World?" *Yale Journal of Criticism* 4, no. 1 (1990): 283–93.

Reid, Inez Smith. "An Analysis of Black Studies Programs." *Afro-American Studies* 1 (1970): 11–21.

Richards, Henry J. *Topics in Afro-American Studies.* Buffalo, N.Y.: Black Academy Press, 1971.

Sahlins, Peter. *Boundaries: The Making of France and Spain in the Pyrenes.* Berkeley: University of California Press, 1989.

Sartre, Jean-Paul. "Orphée noir." In *Anthologie de la nouvelle poésie nègre et malgache de langue française,* edited by Léopold Sédar Senghor. Paris: Presses Universitaires de France, 1949.

Searle, John. "The Storm over the University." *New York Review of Books.* 6 December 1990, pp. 34–42.

Sledd, Andrew, and Sledd, James. "Hirsch's Use of His Sources in *Cultural Literacy:* A Critique." *Profession 88.* New York: Modern Language Association, 1988.

Smith, Barbara Herrnstein. "Cult-Lit: Hirsch, Literacy, and the 'National Culture.'" *South Atlantic Quarterly* 89, no. 1 (Winter 1990): 69–88.

Street, Brian V. *Literacy in Theory and Practice.* Cambridge: Cambridge University Press, 1984.

Towa, Marcien. *Essai sur la problématique philosophique dans l'Afrique actuelle.* Yaoundé: CLE, 1971.

Weber, Eugen. *Peasants into Frenchmen: The Modernization of Rural France 1870–1914.* Stanford: Stanford University Press, 1976.

CONTRIBUTORS

Kwame Anthony Appiah is Professor of Afro-American Studies at Harvard and the author of *In My Father's House: Africa in the Philosophy of Culture* (Oxford University Press, 1992); *Necessary Questions: An Introduction to Philosophy* (Prentice-Hall, 1989); and *For Truth in Semantics* (Blackwells, 1986). He is currently chair of the Joint Committee on African Studies of the Social Science Research Council and the American Council of Learned Societies, President of the Society for African Philosophy in North America, and an editor of *Transition;* and he is also editing the *Oxford Book of African Literature.* Professor Appiah's main interests are epistemology, philosophy of language, African philosophy, Afro-American and African literature, and literary theory.

Robert H. Bates is Henry R. Luce Professor of Politics and Economics and Director of the Program in Political Economy at Duke University. His interests center on the political economy of development, with a special emphasis on agriculture. His books include *Markets and States in Tropical Africa* (University of California Press, 1981); *Essays on the Political Economy of Rural Africa* (University of California Press, 1987); and *Beyond the Miracle of the Market: The Political Economy of Agrarian Development in Kenya* (Cambridge University Press, 1993).

Suzanne Preston Blier is Professor of Art History and Archaeology at Columbia University. Formerly a fellow at the Institute for Advanced Study in Princeton, New Jersey, and the Getty Center for the History of Art, Santa Monica, California, she has received awards from the Guggenheim Foundation, A.C.L.S., Fulbright, and Social Science Research Council. Her recent book, *The Anatomy of Architecture: Ontology and Metaphor in Batammaliba Architectural Expression* (Cambridge University Press, 1987), was a recipient of the Arnold Rubin Outstanding Publication Award. Another book on psychology and art in Dahomey is nearing completion.

Paul Collier is currently a Visiting Professor at the Kennedy School of Government, Harvard University. At Oxford University, he is Director of the Centre for the Study of African Economies, Professor in Economics, and a Fellow of St. Anthony's College. He is a Professor Associate at CERDI, Universite d'Auvergne, and a Managing Editor of the *Journal of African Economies*. His work on African economies has ranged over labor markets, agriculture, industrialization, macro-economic policy, and political economy. He is a winner of the Edgar Graham Prize.

Steven Feierman is Professor of History at the University of Florida. His research has focused on the social and intellectual history of rural Africans over the past two centuries, and especially on peasant discourses concerning health, politics, and the body. His books include *The Shambaa Kingdom* (University of Wisconsin Press, 1974); *Peasant Intellectuals: Anthropology and History in Tanzania* (University of Wisconsin Press, 1990); and *The Social Basis of Health and Healing in Africa*, edited with John Janzen (University of California Press, 1992).

Christopher L. Miller is Professor of French and African and African-American Studies at Yale University. He is author of *Blank Darkness: Africanist Discourse in French* (University of Chicago Press, 1985) and *Theories of Africans: Francophone Literature and Anthropology in Africa* (University of Chicago Press, 1990).

Sally Falk Moore is Professor of Anthropology at Harvard University, Curator of African Ethnology in the Peabody Museum at Harvard, and Fellow of the American Academy of Arts and Sciences. A specialist in legal and political anthropology who has done fieldwork in East Africa, she came to Harvard in 1981, where she teaches in the Faculty of Arts and Sciences and in the Law School. Formerly Dean of the Graduate School of Arts and Sciences, her books include *Power and Property in Inca Peru* (Columbia University Press, 1958); *Law as Process* (Routledge and Kegan Paul, 1978); and *Social Facts and Fabrications, "Customary" Law on Kilimanjaro, 1880–1980* (Cambridge University Press, 1986).

V. Y. Mudimbe is the Ruth F. DeVarney Professor of Romance Studies, Professor of Comparative Literature, and Professor of Cultural Anthropology at Duke University. Among his publications in English are *The Invention of Africa* (Indiana University Press, 1988); *Parables and Fables* (University of Wisconsin Press, 1991); and *The Surreptitious Speech* (University of Chicago Press, 1992).

Jean O'Barr is Director of Women's Studies and Adjunct Professor of Political Science at Duke University and the former editor of *Signs: Journal of Women in Culture and Society*. At Northwestern University, she conducted research among the Pare of Tanzania and has written a number of articles and edited several collections on African women. Her most recent books are *Engaging Feminism: Students Speak Up and Out,* edited with Mary Wyer (University Press of Virginia, 1992); and a collection of essays, *Ideas Into Actions: Feminist Institution Building through Women's Studies* (University of Wisconsin Press, forthcoming 1993).

Richard L. Sklar was educated at the University of Utah and Princeton University. He has taught political science in the United States at Brandeis University, the State University of New York at Stony Brook, and the University of California, Los Angeles, where he is a Professor of Political Science. In Africa, he has been a member of the academic staff at the University of Ibadan and the University of Zambia, a visiting lecturer at Makerere University College, and a Fulbright Professor at the University of Zimbabwe. His publications include *Nigerian Political Parties* (Princeton University Press, 1963), *Corporate Power in an African State* (University of California Press, 1975); and *African Politics and Problems in Development* (coauthored with C. S. Whitaker) (Lynne Rienner, 1991). He is a past president of the African Studies Association and has lectured in several African countries under the auspices of the United States Information Agency.

INDEX

Abiola, Irele, 220–21

Africa: African diaspora, xii, xiii, 220; African Socialism, 102; agriculture, 69, 72–73, 170, 177, 188, 189, 191; American and French anthropologists, 7–8; and anthropology, xiv–xv, 3–57; art, xix, 145, 146–47, 149, 152, 155; and art history, xix, 139–66; Black Africa, 174–75; bridewealth, 181, 189, 190, 193, 196; colonialism, xiv, 8–10, 18–32, 105, 184–85, 222–23; culture areas of, 5; defenses for the study of, xii–xiv; and disciplines, xi–xii; dual authority in, 87–98, 101, 104; Eastern Europe compared to, 63, 64, 70, 76; and economics, xv, 58–82; education, 66–67; famine, 71; food shortages, 26, 71; franc zone, 67–68; and gender, 24, 72, 73; Hegel on, 161 n.20; and history, xviii, 167–212; and the humanities, xviii–xx, 111–229; human rights, 105–6; Indirect Rule, 8–9; kinship, 23–24, 190, 194; land tenure, 26, 69; language, 100–101, 223–25; law, 30, 40 n.39, 104–6; literacy, 132–33, 184, 215–16, 222–23, 224; and literary studies, xx, 213–231; literature, xx, 213–31; magic, 123–26, 140, 147–52, 160 n.15; marginality of, 84–85; markets, 64–71, 177, 180; migration, 65–67; mixed government, 86–98, 104, 105; modernization, 83; monetary union, 67–68, 77; and philosophy, xix–xx, 113–38; policy diversity in, 67; and political science, xv–xvi, 83–110; politics, 28–32, 96; poverty, 72, 173; religion, 26–28, 92–93, 124, 125–31, 134 n.5, 148, 170–71, 174; rural-urban dichotomy in, 97; slavery, 185, 187–97, 200 n.19; and the social sciences, xiv–xviii, 1–110; the state in, xvi, 74, 83, 86–98, 104, 105; trade, 24, 60–61, 177, 181–82; traditional authority, 87–98; tribes, 8, 14–15, 19, 25, 155; unemployment, 65, 66; wages, 65, 66, 181; White Africa, 174–75; women 24, 72, 105–6, 149–50, 188. *See also* countries, regions, and peoples by name

African-American studies (black studies), 214, 219–20

African diaspora: and African literature, 220; and multiculturalism, xii; participation in the modern university, xii

African National Congress (ANC), 97–98

African Political Systems (Fortes and Evans-Pritchard), 12

African Socialism, 102

African Studies Association, 7

Afrocentricity (Africacentricity), xii, 98–102

Agriculture: and civilization, 170, 177; cooperative agriculture, 69; innovations, 72–73; palm oil, 177; plantation slavery, 188, 189, 191; sharecropping, 69

Alexandre, Pierre, 100